Michèle Roberts is the author (
Mistressclass and *Daughters of the H...,
Man Booker prize and was winner of the WHSmith Literary Award.
She has also published short stories, most recently collected in
Playing Sardines, and poetry. Her work has been translated into
twelve languages. Half English and half French, she lives in London
and in the Mayenne, France. She is Professor Emeritus of Creative
Writing at the University of East Anglia.

Praise for *Paper Houses*

'Roberts's sensuous, uninhibited, often beautiful writing is filled with
lush and lavish descriptions of food and places and people and love
affairs.'
Jessica Mann, *Literary Review*

'The twelve novels she has produced . . . are remarkable imaginings of
houses and landscapes and the desire for acquisition. This beguiling
memoir travels the rootlessness that inspired them.'
Penny Perrick, *Sunday Times*

'Radical politics, feminist theatre troupes, demos, communes, all
while smoking and drinking her head off. *Paper Houses* is an honest,
moving account of a talented woman fighting to prioritise her life-
goals and roles'
Metro

PAPER HOUSES

a memoir of the '70s and beyond

MICHÈLE ROBERTS

virago

VIRAGO

First published in Great Britain in 2007 by Virago Press
This paperback edition published in 2008 by Virago Press

Copyright © Michèle Roberts 2007

Photographs of Sara LeFanu on p171 © Patrick Reade

The moral right of the author has been asserted.

A CIP catalogue record for this book
is available from the British Library

ISBN 978-1-84408-408-1

Typeset in Garamond by M Rules
Printed and bound in Great Britain by
Clays Ltd, St Ives plc

Virago Press
An imprint of
Little, Brown Book Group
100 Victoria Embankment
London EC4Y 0DY

An Hachette Livre UK Company
www.hachettelivre.co.uk

www.virago.co.uk

for all the young ones

CONTENTS

ACKNOWLEDGEMENTS

Thanks to Lennie Goodings at Little, Brown/Virago, who first suggested I should write a memoir and saw this one through with calm and generosity. Thanks too to Vanessa Neuling for her patience and efficiency, to Sue Phillpott for her scrupulous copy-editing, and to all their colleagues in editorial, production, design, publicity and marketing. Thanks to Gillon Aitken, Clare Alexander and Sally Riley at Gillon Aitken Associates, and special thanks to Ayesha Karim for her hard work, reliability and professionalism. Thanks to Sarah LeFanu, Jenny Newman and Helen Walton, who read all or most of the first draft and offered helpful criticism, editorial suggestions and information. Thanks to all my friends and comrades on the left and in the women's liberation movement, far too many to mention by individual name, for all the inspiration they have given me.

INTRODUCTION

My student card for Library School

As a child, I liked exploring the interiors of houses and also I liked running away and racing around the streets. When I left home in 1967, aged eighteen, to go to university in Oxford, I continued zigzagging between inside and outside, loving combing the city's back alleys and outlying districts, walking along the river to waterside pubs such as the Trout at Godstow, bicycling out from town into the surrounding countryside and villages to find second-hand bookshops, then coming back indoors to read, huddled over the gas fire in my college room.

This memoir begins at the point when I left university and came to London, and tells of my adventures there, in a wide range of districts and streets and a succession of flats and houses.

My parents met in Dolgelley, Wales, during the Second World War, and got married in the Catholic church in Leicester Square. They started off living with my English grandparents, in Edgware, a north-west London suburb at the end of the Northern Line. I slept in a cot placed across the bath.

Mum and Dad then moved, first to a council house on the local estate and next to a newly built detached house up the road. They transferred to a village near Bristol when my father's firm moved its factory and he had to move too. At the same time I left home and went up to Somerville.

Dad, who was English, worked as a sales manager for the Tan-Sad Chair Company and Mum, who was French, worked as a French teacher, and sometimes a Latin teacher, in Catholic secondary schools. They had five children: Andrew, who died aged three days, Jacqueline, who died aged forty-three, my twin sister Marguerite and myself, and my younger brother, also named Andrew.

As a child I lived much of the time in my imagination and in books. Partly this came from spending long daytime hours alone, in bed with tonsillitis. In our front room, my mother's tall pedimented wooden bookcase, which she had had as a student, looked like a miniature palace rearing up, with glass doors revealing hardback books lined up two deep. I worked my way through most of them. The public library was also my place, and the local church.

I shared a bedroom with my two sisters. Three doors led off it: one to my grandmother's room in the extension my parents had had built (Nana, as we called her, came to live with us after Grandpa died, when I was ten); one to my brother's room; one to the landing. My bed was close to Nana's and my brother's doors. Each night, Nana would pass through apologetically, en route to her bedroom, as we three sisters lay in bed reading. She'd say: oh, it's not right I should come through your room. I felt astonished that an adult would apologise to children. Years later, someone commiserated with me on not having had a room of my own. That surprised me; I accepted what I had. Heroes in fairytales were often faced with a test of three doors. Three possible solutions. They had to make the correct choice; just one; but I could open any of the three doors any time. It seemed normal to be communal and interconnected. At the same time, I dived into private hidey-holes: the cupboard under the stairs, where the Hoover and Singer sewing-machine lived, was a favourite. My doll lived all by herself in her bedsit inside the curved cupboard of my bedside table. I liked outdoor shelters best: the den in the long grass fringing the allotments in the park; the tree-house my French grandfather built us in the apple tree in his garden; the crack in the brick wall in which my doll hid treasures; the caves, sea-washed at high tide, in the cliffs at Etretat in Normandy.

At Oxford, I had a room of my own with just one door (terrifying and lonely at first). I had a whole city to roam through; libraries I could not exhaust. At primary school I had galloped through all the books on the shelves. The teachers put me on to the Bible, to slow me down. I left for secondary school before I'd finished the Old Testament. A revelation, that Book, particularly Psalms, the Song of Songs, Job and Isaiah, bits of which, of course, I knew from hearing them read out (in Latin) at Sunday Mass. At my first convent school, in Mill Hill, run by Franciscans, an old-fashioned place, we were encouraged to read lives of the saints, and the New Testament, not the Old. At my second convent school, in North Finchley, run by a progressive Dutch order, whither I moved for two years to study for A and S levels, I was encouraged to read anything and everything, and to apply for Oxford. I got in. Those were good strong nuns.

All through childhood and adolescence I was intensely religious. I believed I had a vocation to join the Carmelites. It seemed sensible to taste the pleasures of the world first, however, in order all the more grandly to renounce them later. Thus counselled Sister Bonaventure, librarian at St Mary's Abbey (my first convent school), who spent her spare time pasting slips of white paper, like tiny underpants, over the genitals of nudes in the art books. At St Michael's (my second convent school) my adored mentor, Sister Aquinas, said much the same. I returned from my interview at Somerville to find that she had left the convent. She had not been allowed to warn us of her impending departure, nor to say goodbye. Mother Clare Dominic, the headmistress, patiently listened to my blurted-out upset. Soon afterwards she left the convent too. Turbulent times were beginning. Women were thinking of new possible ways to live their lives.

This memoir explores those times, the 1970s and '80s, refracting them through my own story. My narrative in one sense goes in a straight line, chronologically, charting my rake's progress, but in another sense is a *flâneur*. It circles around recurrent images and themes, runs back and forth between inner and outer worlds, loops between sketches of thinking, dreaming and writing and sketches of the culture that made those activities possible, invents its own pattern and rhythm of walking, its own grammar of search and find.

Writing this memoir feels like beginning a stroll through a fantastical city. The desire to take part in things, the desire to let things happen, tugs me out. I am a witness, and I am an actor too. Writing this memoir joins up all the scattered bits of me, makes them continuous, gives me a conscious self existing in history, a self able to make decisions and carry out ambitions, and that feels like a surprise. Often at the time I didn't realise how strong and capable I actually was, in the sense of carrying on writing however hard or difficult life felt.

Writing entails being active, but it also simultaneously involves abandoning oneself, being open, receptive. Life hurls itself in. Out of what often felt at the time like muddle and mess I subsequently make this memoir, this story. I learned how to tell stories first of all through writing fiction; it feels strange to do that in autobiography. Life has so often felt chaotic and I have often not felt in charge of it. Not that I have minded too much. Thinking I ought to be in control of my life all the time feels like shutting out possibility: no thanks. The *flâneur* enjoys being enticed down side streets. She doesn't particularly want to direct the traffic when she's out for a wander. She follows her nose. She follows her desire. When you write you're in charge, in one sense, and not at all in another. Language grips you and you grip it back. You wrestle it into shape, lovingly. You become part of a flow and dance of words. You forget yourself and just get on with writing, just as, walking in the city, you can dissolve into the crowd, simply float, listen, look.

This memoir draws on the diaries I kept, on those written records scrawled in notebooks specially bought for the purpose, each notebook different and distinctive. When I spread them out on the floor of the room where I write they look like the multicoloured pavement of a piazza. This memoir is like fiction, in as much as I have shaped and edited it, but it is as truthful as I can make it, honouring both facts and the way I saw them at the time. On the other hand I know that memory, under pressure from the unconscious mind, is unreliable; and I have forgotten a lot. Out of consideration for others' privacy, I've been obliged to censor some episodes. I have left out some characters, some lovers and love affairs, and I have changed some names. I don't want to bore you, and I don't want to hurt people, either. I have tried to be honest.

Chapter One

REGENT'S PARK

Street-theatre group on Women's
Liberation demonstration in London, March 1971

I prepared for my new life, post university, in London, by buying a new notebook, a midi-skirt (after years of minis it felt daring to conceal one's legs) and a fake-snakeskin nightdress, and by borrowing from the library a clutch of books chosen 'for the first time in ages purely for pleasure' as I noted in my diary, novels by Mauriac, Gide, Sartre and Lawrence. Having chosen the medieval option for my degree, I had stopped at Shakespeare. I had some catching up to do but could do it at my own pace, my own speed. Bliss.

I also took out M.R. James's *The Apocryphal New Testament*. I liked its smell of heresy, of banned stories. For one of my Finals papers I'd studied the medieval English mystics, such as Richard Rolle, Margery Kempe and Julian of Norwich, and their Continental counterparts translated into Middle English, such as Mechtild of Magdeburg. Women writers who believed in direct access to God without the aid of priests had had to negotiate their way through accusations of heresy. Reading these visionary works I don't think I was consciously discovering a tradition of women writers which would nourish my own struggles to write, but I did know how much I was enjoying myself.

I lost my religious vocation easily, in my first term at Somerville, standing on the staircase outside the college library cradling copies of *Paradise Lost* and *Beowulf*, looking out of the tall window on to a crisp, blue and golden October morning and feeling possessed by joy. I realised that nuns were not allowed to stay up all night reading. Very well, then. Don't be a nun. That was that. Whew. I got on with reading voraciously and enjoying myself. I graduated with a Second (unclassified in those days). A very nice degree, Miss Roberts, said my tutor Rosemary Woolf, offering me dry sherry and an untipped Woodbine. She praised my 'outstanding enthusiasm' for medieval literature and suggested we pass over in silence my appalling marks in Middle English philology.

On Sunday 13 September, 1970, I moved into my attic bedsit in a house on the northern edge of Regent's Park, a classy, genteel district just east of Lord's Cricket Ground and just south of St John's Wood, the latter synonymous with discreetly shaded villas in which Victorian gents, in Victorian novels at least, kept their mistresses. The week before I had had lunch with Ernestine, my prospective landlady, whom I had met through her godson Joss, one of my Oxford acquaintances. I had first seen the house, all understated Regency elegance, the previous February, when Ernestine threw a party for Joss's twenty-first. 'A tall thin slice of wedding-cake' I called it in my diary: 'on different tiers one drank champagne, ate salmon, danced, and right at the top, talked to a sexy 60-year-old Frenchman who eventually introduced me to his wife and sat and laughed as we talked about Simone de Beauvoir.'

I felt so nervous at parties, particularly posh ones, that I often drank too much. I smoked Gauloises, as well, in an effort to appear cool. On this occasion, after fending off a rugger player who pawed my bosom and suggested that we retire to Ernestine's bedroom, I must have made a not too tipsy impression on Ernestine, because when I rang her up in September she asked me to lunch and, over it, invited me to look at a room at the top of the house.

Four floors up she took me, above the Regency luxe, pale green fitted carpets all the way, to a tiny room with a sink and Baby Belling cooker crammed into a cupboard. Bathroom, phone and fridge were on the landing outside. I peeped out of the window at the tops of trees fronting Regent's Park and heard a lion roar. The Zoo, Ernestine said. She asked for a rent of five and a half guineas a week; almost double what I'd paid for my Oxford flat. It's not a letting neighbourhood, she explained, and the other people resident (she didn't call them tenants) are the nicest sort.

A guinea, originally a gold coin, was worth one pound and one shilling. I felt abashed by Ernestine asking for guineas (not coined since 1813): they proved how upper-class she was, with a mind above ordinary vulgar pounds, shillings and pence. Middle-class, I both loathed and envied the upper classes. At thirteen, I had devoured Georgette Heyer's romances, fantasising living in a Georgian manor house with a perfect hero. At fifteen I longed to live in Paris, take opium and drink absinthe, write poetry, and outdo Baudelaire in perversity. Oxford had shaken me into questioning these romantic desires. Now, I was moving into what seemed an upper-class house yet knew only too well that, coming from Edgware, I was an impostor. A rent paid in guineas, a sort of fake currency, delicately underlined this. Ernestine was indicating she wasn't just any common land-lady but a gracious chatelaine and hostess.

Finding somewhere to live had turned out to be very easy, though the place felt rather too respectable to fit my dreams of *la vie de Bohème*. Afterwards I fretted to myself that I should have gone somewhere 'cheap and busy-shabby like Camden Town instead of a good address with cleanliness added to the godliness. I would prefer to live over a restaurant in Charlotte Street or catch a glimpse of Bloomsbury Square.' These fantasies had to be put on hold. I told myself I didn't feel able to refuse Ernestine's offer, because kind Joss had been preparing the ground for weeks. And I wanted to hear that lion roar again.

On the Sunday night I moved in. I sat on the single bed under the dormer window and scribbled in my notebook as I had nothing to read but the *A–Z*. All my books were still in boxes at my parents' house. I put money in the slot and got myself light and a bath. I gazed hungrily at the tin of chicken, my mother's parting gift, for which I had no tin-opener.

For the first time in my life I was on my own. At Somerville I had lived, for the first two years, in college, with friends all along the corridor, and, for my third year, in a flat in Leckford Road in north Oxford, near Jericho and Port Meadow, shared with my friend Sian. Here in the bedsit I floated above the tall trees like a balloon, only lightly tethered by Ernestine's hand. I was free. Almost.

Who was that 'I', that young woman of twenty-one? I reconstruct her. I invent a new 'me' composed of the girl I was, according to my diaries, my memories (and the gaps between them), and the self remembering her. She stands in between the two. A third term. She's a character in my story and she tells it too. She's like a daughter. Looking back at her, thinking about her, I mother myself. I listen hard to her silences, the gaps between her words, the cries battened down underneath the surface of her sentences. I sympathise with her ardour, her desperation to read, to learn how to think, to contribute something to the world. How tender, amused and exasperated I feel towards her snobbery, shyness, self-consciousness, priggishness, guilt. She writes her diary so self-critically, suffers so much, berates herself so harshly for suffering and then for writing about it. When she's not rhapsodising about books and nature she's fierce, intolerant of adults' intolerance of youth, enraged when she feels patronised. She wants adventures. She has come to London, in the time-honoured way, to have them. Not to make her fortune, though. She scorns that. She intends to become a writer, is determined to publish a novel before she is thirty, and she expects to be poor.

Yes, I was unrealistic in my would-be bohemianism, she says to me: but at least I had ideals. And in my own muddled way I did get involved in radical politics. It's all right, I shout back at her: I'm not here to judge you.

May '68 had erupted for me at Oxford like a spectacle, a carnival of self-expression. Balliol's wall fronting the Broad became a broadsheet for chalk-scrawled graffiti: 'deanz meanz finez'; 'beautify your city – eat a pigeon'. Michael Rosen declaimed outside the Bodleian Library to passing women: how can you understand Donne's poetry if you've never had sex? Christopher Hitchens made long speeches. Far-left groups picketed and leafleted, agitated at the Cowley Motor Works. Revolutionary committees formed ad hoc to challenge university rules and methods of teaching. Some of my friends, such as Sian and her boyfriend Rod, were far more committed than I was, going off to demonstrations and getting involved in direct action, for example sitting down outside the hairdresser's in north Oxford which refused to serve black clients. I did join in the demo protesting against Enoch ('rivers of blood') Powell speaking at the Town Hall. As the crowd of students surged against the lines of police tiny Sian tumbled off-balance in the urgent pushing and I held her up. She lost her shoes.

I didn't have a gut understanding of socialism. At home the Tory party ruled. My father was from a London working-class background, my mother from a Norman bourgeois one. Both were ardent Conservatives very active in the local branch. They believed in serving the community and giving to charity. Dad, an Anglican, was a mason, a member of the local tennis club, and sang in his church choir. Mum was involved with the Girl Guides, the Women's Institute, the flower rota at her church, the school bazaar, and lots of other things. Both of them expressed horror at the idea of women going shouting about the streets.

I did have an instinctive-feeling need – fuelled by the authoritarian and misogynistic Catholicism, Pope-led, of my religious upbringing in my first convent school, and by my loathing, as a child, of our bullying parish priest – to revolt against those in power over me. The huge injustice that directly affected Oxford undergraduates was of course the gender divisions of the single-sex colleges: only five for women. The student leaders, all male, did not address this. Matters specifically affecting women were dismissed: not important; bourgeois. When directly challenged, they backed the idea of mixed-sex colleges in the interests of free sex for men rather than fairer numbers. None of them ever proposed fewer places for men in order to create more places for women.

I had enjoyed attending a women's college. I liked being part of a community of women who took each other seriously as equals. Women formed the centre of this world. Our Somerville dons had all been tough-minded and amiable; committed and scrupulous scholars; often pleasingly eccentric. As our moral tutors they were sympathetic, in their bracingly cool way, about pregnancies, abortions, depression, freak-outs, anxiety-induced overeating, admissions to Warneford (the local mental hospital). Nobody thought of these as feminist subjects because we hadn't begun using those words. We had problems which we felt were personal and that was that. We were not obviously repressed: we had a college doctor willing to prescribe the Pill, and we signed for gate keys so that we could come in late, and, though men weren't supposed to spend the night in college, they often did. The bedders (the college servants who cleaned our rooms) turned a blind eye.

Nobody was agitating to improve the bedders' pay and conditions, as I remember.

What oppressed me personally, hurt me continually, was the privately educated male undergraduates' crass attitude towards intelligent women: they feared us, and mocked us as ugly sexless spinsters. You bumped into these men everywhere; their views dominated. There weren't enough women to go round, and we were a waste, sexually, in their eyes, because we were not solely decorative: we liked reading, thinking and talking as well as dancing and drinking, and didn't always fall easily into their beds. Women meant notches on men's bedposts. They laid bets about who'd fuck us first, called us frigid, fucked-up and lesbian if we declined. They went out with girls from the secretarial colleges whom they could then despise as stupid because pretty. (If the boys from public school were braying and gross, some of the upper-class women I encountered could act pretty repulsively too.)

Though I wrote and dreamed about sex, I couldn't imagine actually going to bed with anyone, and was very impressed when my friends did. It hurt, Sian reported after her first time. I remained sternly virginal, armoured in the Catholicism I thought I'd discarded. I fell in love with remote, unattainable gods, and chose men friends who'd been to state schools, or were alternative in some way, or gay. Jamie, who boiled suet puddings over the fire in his rooms. Derek, who taught me to cook Viennese food. Tony, who declaimed poems to me in graveyards and longed to live on the Rive Gauche, specifically on the Boul' Mich. Pete, who played me the Doors and said sweetly: don't it make y'go all funny inside?

Groping my way towards feminism, I hovered on the edges of organised leftist politics. I observed from a distance. On the night of Joss's party I had stayed, with several other Somervillians, at the house in Stoke Newington, north London, of our friend Elana, the daughter of Tony Cliff who ran the International Socialists. We got to bed at 3 a.m. on top of scattered heaps of leaflets and posters advertising meetings, demos, discussions. Next morning comrades rang up continually. Elana's little brother and sister rushed around screaming: don't give them any information, they're spies. Then they demonstrated their skill on the trampoline in their bedroom. We sat in the kitchen for hours, getting through bacon and eggs, the two children reciting their favourite dirty jokes, Elana's dad reading the paper, Sian cleaning the gas stove, Elana putting on makeup in front of the only mirror in the house. How chaotic and untidy these busy ultra-leftists were. Just like a student household. Sian and I had taken over our Oxford flat from some upper-class Somervillians who'd thought it amusing to test whether spaghetti was cooked by throwing it at the walls, where it stuck. When we moved in we hacked off their spaghetti fresco, cleaned and whitewashed (though we could do nothing about the mould growths and running damp). They thought us hopelessly petit-bourgeois.

I think the mess and turbulence of the Cliffs' house scared me. Deep down inside me boiled mess and turbulence that I didn't want to face. No wonder I opted for going to live with a landlady with an impeccable house: elegant furniture gleaming with polish, carpets regularly hoovered. Mrs Cliff had sat in her wildly untidy kitchen, the sink piled high with crockery, and talked enthusiastically about women's liberation. First adult woman I'd met who was explicitly for it. But you couldn't see Tony Cliff deciding to tackle the washing-up.

My early writing experiments contained many caricatures. Mocking a left-wing family let me stay away from involvement. Yet that overnight stay in Stoke Newington, after Joss's party, had given me rapturous glimpses of a London I did not yet know and longed to explore. I sketched it in my diary: 'We went to the Rodin exhibition at the Hayward. Driving through London on Sunday morning – empty streets, an old man comes out of a corner shop with a bottle of Corona, a line of hoardings gives way to a fence made of brightly painted blue wooden doors, mountains of earth have been dumped until Monday, drizzle over the Thames from the top of all the concrete at the Festival Hall. Beautiful place in this weather: lucky people who can wander there in the empty silence every Sunday, pass across the far horizon in Hyde Park, look at paintings as far as Notting Hill, walk round the deserted City, find a café for lunch.'

Now I was about to begin doing just that. The day after moving into my bedsit chez Ernestine I took up my post as Library Scholar in the Department of Printed Books at the British Museum, and discovered the bliss of walking across Regent's Park every morning before plunging into Bloomsbury.

I had decided on a two-year postgraduate librarianship training in order to have a day job and finance myself while I got going as a writer. What would that entail? I had no idea.

I had written all my life: stories and poems at primary school, a diary since the age of nine, secret poems about sex, in adolescence, pastiches of eighteenth-century verse to amuse my girlfriends at secondary school. In the sixth form I'd co-founded a literary society and magazine. I wrote my first real poem, that's to say first honest and passionate poem, at the age of sixteen when I fell in love with James, a sweet Irish boy from the council estate beyond the newly built Catholic church in our suburb. I fancied him so much I was terrified. When he asked me to dance, at a youth-club hop, I turned my back on him, unable to believe I could actually dance with a boy I liked. Back home, I sat on the lav to have some privacy, wrote ten lines in free verse about erotic yearning. At Oxford I'd joined the Poetry Society and felt patronised by the other poets, all male. To convince Rosemary Woolf that I was capable of doing the medieval option for my degree, I'd translated *The Tale of Mr Jeremy Fisher* into Old English. I'd worked on *Isis* (the student magazine owned by Robert Maxwell whose mansion at the top of Headington Hill featured drinks cabinets hidden behind fake bookshelves apparently laden with antiquarian books) and written bits of journalism. I remember one piece: sourly angry, would-be amusing portraits of types of Oxford males (who could avoid mocking Gyles Brandreth, pixie-like in his duffel coat, walking into the river spouting Zuleika Dobson and appearing in a TV film as the new Kenneth Tynan?). I'd won a prize, in the poetry competition run by *Honey* (the groovy glossy magazine for 1960s chicks), for a satirical female-student version of 'Come Live with Me and Be My Love', and been contacted, on the strength of it, by a literary agent at Peters, Fraser & Dunlop in John Islip Street (he advised me to stick to comedy as it sold well). I realised that all this might constitute the start of an apprenticeship but didn't know how to continue. In any case, writing felt secret, still. A secret activity. A safe house of art in which my illegal emotions might hide. I did think that becoming a librarian, temporarily, would enable me to go on reading. Books mattered more than anything. I'd applied for the Library Scholarship at the British Museum and won it. Next year I would go on to Library School.

On the evening of Monday 14 September I wrote notes about my first day as Library Scholar. Regent's Park with its low-bending foliage had seemed exotic, and full of noises even at 8 a.m.: those lions; ducks; dogs being walked. Squirrels and pigeons rippled and swayed just in front of me. I went down the Broad Walk, a little way along the Euston Road, down

Gower Street. I arrived at the British Museum, found the Reading Room, at the back of the vast entrance hall, got past the warders and entered an astonishing new country. Oxford had boasted fine libraries, but this one seemed somehow more serious. More urban. More worldly. Certainly more democratic: anyone, not just members of a university, could apply for a reader's ticket. And indeed Karl Marx had done so.

A spinning-top of reading whirled me up into itself. A vast, circular space surrounded by bookshelves twirled under Panozzi's high dome. Nothing but books in every direction.

I was assigned to join the team at the Enquiry Desk, to help answer the queries that came in by letter. This way I'd find my feet. I was relieved not to have to deal directly with the forbidding-looking scholars hunched at their desks, heads down over heaped volumes. I had time to consider in which reference book to look up which bibliography. The Reading Room was walled with these. One long shelf bore the red volumes of the Subject Index. Nothing was computerised at that point. Other libraries had raced ahead in this respect. The following year, at Library School, I delightedly learned computer-applicable theories of classification; they seemed like poetry or algebra. I learned that library could communicate with library by machine. Amazing. Here, in the Department of Printed Books, we used paper, ink and pens, and, sometimes, the telephone.

Far below the high point of the domed ceiling coiled the Catalogue. Placed precisely at the centre of the Reading Room, it formed the latter's heart. Concentric open shelves, laden with cloth-bound folio volumes arranged A–Z by author, enticed you into their little labyrinth. The letters of the alphabet no longer marched in a line but danced in a circle. You walked around the relevant curve of the ring, peering at the spines of the clumped volumes embodying each letter, pulled out, with both hands, the particular heavy volume you wanted, placed it on the desk-like top of the shelf, manoeuvred it open. Entries, printed, and sometimes hand-corrected, were pasted in on paper slips. Each entry represented a particular state of a book; a particular issue of a particular edition. Books were not merely containers of words; they were created objects, each with a distinct provenance and history, a precise personality, that could be pinned down and expressed; described by the cataloguer in exact, scholarly terms. Searching for what you thought you wanted could take some time: you weren't hunting down just any old edition of a text. Spreading my hands over the thick paper of the pages, I knew that knowledge was physical. To gloss really did mean to stroke. Books were material; like beloved bodies; provided not only intellectual but also sensual delight. I could touch them, open them, caress them, feed from them. Books were mothers and lovers who would give me as much as I wanted, whenever I wanted. All I had to do was ask. Paradise regained.

We, as librarians, had privileged access to the books and the bookstacks. Rules and regulations existed, of course, for the ordinary readers. Not quite as draconian as at the Bodleian, where you had to swear not to bring in swords or pistols, not to make smoke or fire. You couldn't order up too many books at once. You had to re-deposit them at the end of the day, indicating which ones you wished to retain for consultation on the morrow. You wouldn't dream of bringing in bottled water and taking regular sips. Mobile phones, of course, did not exist. Above all, you had to keep quiet. Not disturb the thick hush.

The Catalogue shelves housed a resident deity. At the centre of the web of bibliographical knowledge woven by the Catalogue, in a glass-walled box, sat the Superintendent, a large black figure, like a benevolent but strict spider. A tall, burly man, Mr Bancroft always wore a dark suit, white shirt, and a tie. As his title indicated, he kept an eye on the goings-on all around him (plenty of flirting and propositioning). When, standing leaning against the Catalogue shelf, turning over the pages of your selected volume, you decided you wanted to order up a book, you wrote out your order slip and dropped it into a wooden tray under the Superintendent's nose. Porters scuttled off to fetch books from the distant bookstacks, out of sight in the shell of the dome, and delivered them, an hour or so later, to the place where you sat.

Readers had their own allotted space: they occupied the long desks which radiated out like the spokes of a wheel from the circular shelves of the Catalogue. The desks, covered in blue leather, came furnished with pen-rests and blotting paper. If not the ardours of scholarship, then the comfortable blue leather chairs, with padded wooden arms, induced somnolence. On winter afternoons, the weak light and the muggy, airless atmosphere sent people off to sleep. Scholars slumped face-down over their books and snored quietly.

I remember four immediate colleagues. Mavis and Jenny, two librarians in their late twenties, ran the Enquiry Desk itself, which held prime position near the Library entrance. Oval-shaped, accessed via a couple of steps, it reared up like a turret from which Mavis and Jenny peered down, preparing to repel the enemy with scornful glances. It seemed to me that they had not been given lessons in kindness to readers (they certainly did not see them as clients or customers). They guarded the Desk as a castle under siege by barbarian invaders. They despised the enquirers who trotted up so innocently, unaware of the boiling oil of sarcasm about to be poured over their heads, fired off cutting remarks about their stupidity, gave as little help as possible. Dragons protecting treasures, they preferred the readers not to get their hands on the books.

An older woman, Mary Pearce, also took her turn. She was kind to me, invited me out to her cottage at Iver and gave me lunch. We were supervised by Terry, a pleasant-looking, tweed-jacketed Londoner of about fifty; charming and very knowledgeable. He did believe in talking to people. He was from a working-class background and did not act aloof. He got me my big bunch of keys, so that I could move freely about the Department, through all its locked doors, explained how the Library worked, gave me a desk near his own to work at, a pile of enquiries to answer. The first came from a woman asking us to identify the particular Bible translation whence this Numbers quotation came: 'and God descended in a cloud of od'. She added: 'this seems so much nearer the truth than any of our versions.' She apologised for the fact that despite being a disciple of Extra Sensory Perception she had to conduct her researches by post.

The Reading Room, and the North Library just beyond it, in which you consulted early printed books and early news-papers, formed the visible part of the Library. Invisible, behind them, curving around them, clustered the layered bookstacks, separated by lace-like ironwork floors, connected by similarly see-through iron staircases. In the absence of electricity the day-light could filter down from the aperture at the top of the domed roof. Plunging into these dark tunnels of books, via invisible doors, I felt enchanted. Opening a section of bookcase with my key, stepping through it and swinging it shut behind me, I was Alice passing into another, magical world.

Scholars dwelt in their own hidey-holes. George Painter, the biographer of Gide and Proust, worked above the North Library. Mr Nixon, the world-renowned Renaissance bindings expert, had a secret cubby-hole behind the public gallery and its glass cases. They concealed themselves behind the walls of

ordinary activities. They led a secret life in the Library's unconscious mind. They loved the darkness and hiddenness. I could
walk through the walls and join them. They seemed benevolent
gnomes, hammering away, like goldsmiths, digging out jewels
from the depths of the mountain of books, and teaching me
their skills. Bookbindings were indeed golden treasures;
stamped with gold leaf. Later that year, when I worked with
him, kindly, courteous Mr Nixon taught me how to date bindings, to understand how they were made. I pored over his
collections of journals, including the *Proceedings of the Society of
Lady Book-Binders* from the 1890s. I read everything I could
about the history of printing.

One colleague, a short, plump woman with a plain face and
beautiful legs, who wore chic black frocks, told me about her
sex life. She recounted, in her matter-of-fact way, that she could
come five or six times before her lover did. Another colleague,
over beer in the Museum Tavern, confided that going rowing
every weekend made her all the keener for sex afterwards. I
drank in this information. I'd had sex for the first time the previous summer, with an underground playwright whom I'd met
at an Oxford party, in his flat on the Cromwell Road, but,
anaesthetised by Catholicism, hadn't felt any pleasure. The
playwright had been writing me love letters for weeks.
Accordingly, when I decided (spurred on by my cousin getting
married) that the moment had come, I turned up *chez lui*,
marched into his room, took off my sprigged Laura Ashley
frock, lay down on his bed. When I'd danced at the party I'd
been flowing and supple. Now I waited, still and stiff. The poor
playwright, noting my immobility, said incredulously: do you
mean to say you've never done this before? I nodded. Gamely
he got on with the job. In the morning he pecked me on the
cheek and packed me off, making it clear that I was not to seek

him out again. I felt snubbed but relieved: at least I'd got rid of my virginity. Colette, in *Le Blé en Herbe*, describes two adolescents making love for the first time. In the morning the girl whistles as she waters her geraniums, apparently quite unconcerned about the momentous event of the night before, and the boy, watching her, is shocked. I felt like that girl did.

Terry also contributed to my *éducation sentimentale*: he took me to visit the room of a Keeper called Mr Wood, to look up some pornography. This was kept in a secret section called the Private Case. Permission had to be sought to unlock it. I noted in my diary that most of what we looked at was 'soi-disant memoirs from the eighteenth century, with indicative titles, e.g. *Lèvres de Velours*, par la Comtesse de Lesbos'. Terry lent me *The Other Victorians* so that I could read extracts from *My Secret Life*: 'all the bits you suddenly realise are there, ambiguously described, in Dickens, told with immediacy and interest and little of usual male self-glorification. Prick is a good word.' I read *Fanny Hill*: a turn-on until about halfway through, when I grew bored. I read *The Story of O*. Again, I was hooked for a while, then bored. Pornography was repetitive; that was its point; but I wanted stories too. So alongside the porn I read Nabokov's *Ada*: 'mighty, tender, passionate, original work; one long glorious sexual pun'.

Just as interesting to me was the 1813 copy of the *Morning Chronicle* a reader sent in to the Enquiry Desk. After a gossip column about Prinny's levee being cut scandalously short, came a news item: 'on Monday morning, a young woman . . . about twenty-two years of age called a coach from the stand in Bloomsbury square and ordered the coachman to drive to Sloane Street, Chelsea. On arriving at Hyde Park corner, the coachman stopped the horses, and the turnpike-keeper going to the coach to demand the toll, discovered the young woman weltering in her blood. She was immediately conveyed to St George's Hospital, quite dead.'

Perhaps she had had a bungled abortion. Later that year, when I was set to cataloguing seventeenth- and eighteenth-century material, I came across ballad sheets, decorated with coloured woodcuts, commemorating young women hanged on the gallows. My supervisor, Julian Roberts, the Keeper of Printed Books, explained that these were desperate mothers who had killed their illegitimate babies and were then themselves killed by the state. I never forgot his compassion for these unfortunates. He was the first man I'd met who expressed explicit political sympathy for women.

I celebrated my first day at work by going out to supper with Somervillian friends now living in Stoke Newington. Dope, food and wine, chat. Safe and familiar. On the tube back from the Angel I noticed two advertisements. One said: 'unwind on a Sunday', and suggested a day's retreat in a convent. The other, immediately next to it, was an advert for Smirnoff vodka, and showed a naked man and woman thigh-deep in a reedy lake, above the legend: 'We never used to know what to do on Sundays . . .' The two adverts indicated the contradictions of my life, perhaps. On the tube platform at King's Cross a small Frenchman, a Parisian journalist, tried to pick me up, asking me to suggest a cheap hotel. His name was Hafid. I declined to accompany him. We chatted. He gave me a box of matches, with a woman in Provençal costume on the cover, as a parting present.

If you walked around London alone, as I did all the time, presumably looking rather naïve and wide-eyed at the splendour of it all, men accosted you frequently. They assumed you were lonely, all by yourself, and in need of their company. They were certainly in need of sex. They were starving: you were supposed to feel compassionate and give them what they wanted. Some of them were irritating, padding after you going on and on about your breasts, or grabbing you, pinning you against walls and trying to kiss you. Then you had to shove and run. The older men who approached me in cafés or pubs or in the street were practised and polite and could be shrugged off. When they asked you how much you charged, or cried: hey, why don't you show me London? you could get rid of them fairly quickly. Some of the younger ones were quite sweet. One, called John, driving a Mini-Moke (a souped-up Mini), screeched to a halt beside me in Theobald's Road one Saturday afternoon, and suggested a cup of tea. I liked the look of him, so off we went. We sat on a sooty rooftop above Portobello Road, having climbed out of his flat window, and smoked dope. I saw him once more, when we drove over to Hackney to return some borrowed stereo equipment, on the way passing a procession of elephants from the local circus. With a Norwegian student, I remember, I scrambled over the fence into Regent's Park late one night and surveyed the sleeping ducks. One small South African pursued me around Soho, finally cornered me, offered me two bananas, lunged at me, and then, when I ducked, exclaimed: English girls are so sensitive! These casually met strangers tended to drift off once they realised I wasn't going to fuck them. The same thing used to happen all the time in Oxford. I had liked to wander alone in the nearby countryside, to sit alone in meadows reading. Not for long. Men would dart out from clumps of trees, from behind bushes, and start bothering me. I gave up, with inner rage, walking alone in the countryside, but I did not give up walking alone in the city. I refused.

When the men left me alone I could become simply an observer; the one who gazed. One Friday afternoon, for example, after leaving the Museum at five or so, I sat in St Giles's churchyard, on the patch of grass under the sycamore trees, pretending to read R.D. Laing's work of radical psychiatry, *The Politics of Experience*, in order to watch a group of Italian children playing on the swings there. Railed flowerbeds had yellow-painted litter-bins at the corners. The Italian mothers sat on benches in groups, talking. They wore blue and grey cotton dresses, thin black jackets, scarlet mules. Then three boys came in, carrying guitars, and perched in the alcoves of the churchyard wall, and strummed gently. A girl wandered up and started singing with them. Afterwards I walked down Drury Lane, got into St Martin's Lane, met Sian in the Salisbury for a drink and went to the theatre.

As often as I could afford it, I went to the cinema, plays, concerts, exhibitions, poetry readings. Godard films, black farces by Joe Orton, lots of Bach. Sometimes Joss dropped by chez Ernestine, in his Lotus, and roared me off to the Haverstock Arms in Hampstead where we drank beer and listened to poems read by candlelight. I remember a small Israeli poet passionately declaiming a poem about male circumcision. Brave man. A taboo subject in those times. I spent all my spare money on books. Clothes had to be cheap. On Saturdays, after paying the rent, rejoicing in the crisp, smoky autumn weather, I walked over to Church Street market in Paddington, appreciated the stall called 'Doreens Veg's', dived down into the cellars serving as second-hand clothes shops, and bought treats: a black lace evening dress, a black, bias-cut tea-gown with flowered crêpe sleeves, a Victorian brocade dressing-gown I wore as a coat, a red 1940s frock with red-embroidered yoke and elbow-length sleeves. For special occasions I put on my prized Biba outfit: black tunic with tight, long, buttoned sleeves, black trousers with buttoned fly. The buttons were big and cloth-covered. My one pair of shoes had holes in the soles from all the walking I did, but of course I didn't care. Winter had not yet arrived.

I went out a lot with my women friends: Sian, and others. Various men drifted in and out of my life, occasionally making passes. I still yearned for the underground playwright, but he had got together with a new woman, apparently, a tall, thin beauty who was the live-in hostess for a businessman based in Mayfair. I'd lost him. I knew, crossly, I was far too gauche to be able to compete with such sophistication. With one friend, Desmond, who was still trying, despite the head-shakings of his bishop, to become a clergyman, I went to the Zoo, where he pranced camply in front of the gnus: oh, look at their sweet little nipples! With Graham, the boy-next-door from my parents' village, who'd been impressed by my scones one vacation teatime and pursued me to London as wife material, I sat in the French pub in Dean Street and listened to his views on women: say what you like about careers but you were made to have babies. I took him to see a sad Polish film called *Wanda*, which I thought superb. Graham's opinion: well, let's face it, a bit of self-respect and she'd have been able to pull herself out of it. We walked along Old Compton Street to Benoît's Bistro. Those men are looking at me very oddly, Graham said. Afterwards we tried to have sex but it didn't work. Home he drove in his newly purchased Austin. With Harold, a leering acquaintance from Oxford to whom I did not know how to say no, I unwillingly had cups of tea. He liked to wear a First World War flying-cap with fur ear-flaps, and lived in a bedsit in Finsbury Park whither he wished to lure me. He gave me his diary to read, but his sexual fantasies (Somervillians gasping: oh my God) failed to turn me on, and he concluded that I was still frigid as well as too plump (I had comfort-eaten to dull my anxiety over Finals and had become curvaceous). He poked my hips: when are you

30

going to get rid of all this? One Museum colleague, Ron, pursued me determinedly. His technique was to try and make me feel so bad about being frigid and repressed that I'd go to bed with him to prove I wasn't. Over tea in the smoke-filled Museum canteen he lectured me on how much I needed him. Again, I did not know how to say no. I had been brought up by the nuns to be very polite. I ended up in bed with Ron a couple of times. I'm afraid I've got an enormous penis, he said: I hope I won't hurt you.

Increasingly I began going around with Terry, who was good to talk to, well read, funny and kind. Divorced, with two teenage children who visited him at weekends, he represented both a friend and a father figure. Like Dad, he was from a very respectable working-class background. He had a degree, unlike my father, who'd had to leave school at sixteen without being allowed to try for the School Certificate (Dad had been so often ill, as a boy, with bronchitis, that Nana and Grandpa thought he'd never pass). Dad had educated himself, reading voraciously, and wanting to give his children the education he hadn't had himself. He was disappointed, though, when he visited Somerville and the college refectory failed to live up to that celebrated in *Mr Verdant Green: Adventures of an Oxford Freshman*, one of his favourite (Victorian) novels. Prosaically we munched fish and chips; had no wine; no sconcing.

Terry and I went to openings (he liked contemporary prints), exhibitions at the V and A, and lectures on printing (at which Terry always fell asleep), and for walks. He loved the London streets, and knew their history. In the lunch hour he showed me Finsbury, Holborn, Clerkenwell. We dawdled among the second-hand bookstalls on Farringdon Road, where you could scoop up battered armfuls of eighteenth-century literature for practically nothing. Intoxicated by typefaces, by foxed and spotted paper, by crumbling calf spines, I bought sets of the *Spectator*, job lots of sermons, Pope's translations of the *Iliad* and the *Odyssey*. We ate out in cheap bistros. Londoners had just discovered dishes such as moussaka, stuffed peppers, taramasalata. The décor was fake rustic. Pink lampshades dangled empty snail shells. Candles burned in Chianti bottles. Stripped-pine chairs, and tables topped with red-checked cloths, were de rigueur. How worldly I felt. How nice Terry was to me. After these suppers we would go to pubs in the City, or wander down by the river. I took Terry to alternative, underground theatre; to poetry readings. Eventually we spent the night together in my narrow bed. In the morning, in the Reading Room, Jenny and Mavis exclaimed to Terry: where were you last night? You haven't shaved.

We became a couple, though in the name of sexual freedom I did not want to admit this. I admitted it only to my mother, wanting to be honest with her about what I was doing but also wanting, I imagine, to confront her notions of morality. She assumed the relationship must be sordid and exploitative. My cousin's new husband, when he met Terry, took a more lenient view: he's a nice chap but shoes with gold bars are too young for him.

I liked tumbling about with Terry on his sitting-room carpet in front of the gas fire, or upstairs in his bedroom with its wallpaper patterned with Greek urns, but I didn't come. I didn't know how to. Puzzled, he would say to me: but my wife used to come so easily, what's wrong with you? Oh dear. Yet another man telling me I was frigid. Coming didn't seem to be for me but for the man, to reassure him he was a great lover. I could see why women were tempted to fake it, to heave and thrash and moan like the girls in Terry's antique porn or Harold's diaries.

You got out of being reproached and feeling guilty. Perhaps Terry's wife faked it. Why had she left him, after all?

I'm frigid, I confided, months later, to my new acquaintance Alison Fell. She recommended me to read *The Kinsey Report* (on contemporary American sexual practices). It made me feel worse than ever.

Soon, however, I would learn that orgasms were part of politics, however much male comrades jeered. I began to read Mary McCarthy's *The Tyranny of the Orgasm* and learned that the clitoris was supreme. You could have an orgasm on your own or with another woman. Terry did not understand lesbianism. In his beloved porn women made love to each other just to turn on male voyeurs: the penis was what mattered. How could two women enjoy sex together? Men approaching Sian and me in pubs spoke similarly: all on your own, girls? No, we would shout: we've got each other.

I carried on reading. Revolution! You did not need penetration!

Wryly I look back at myself, earnestly studying sex through books. How else was I to study it? I didn't know.

I met Alison, my sexual mentor, at the second Women's Liberation Conference at Ruskin, Oxford, on 9 January 1971. Sian took me to the conference. I realised I'd been a feminist ever since I was ten years old and began resenting my brother for doing no housework or chores at home, resenting horrible Father O'Dwyer ranting on against the permissive society. I'd like to join women's liberation, I said to Sian: where do I sign on? To whom do I make my sub payable? Idiot, she said: it's not about Them, it's about Us.

After a morning of workshops on different topics, over lunch we talked collectively, vociferously, about our demands for equal pay and opportunities and good childcare. I wondered about the women canteen workers: serving us, they were not able to take part in the conference. I wrote in my diary that I found all the women there that day 'lively and attractive', except for 'four grim Maoists, so narrow and ultra-serious and closed-off they made one despair'. We had discussed the forth-coming first-ever women's liberation demonstration; its form, its tactics. The Maoists rejected 'street theatre, which a demon-stration is, in favour of old-style marching and angry fist-shaking'. The fierce foursome constituted the Hemel Hempstead Revolutionary Marxist Group and could always be counted on to turn up at demos, with their enormous banner, whatever the weather. I was entranced by the idea of their fomenting, if miniature, presence in genteel Hemel Hempstead. Thirty-three years later I celebrated their persist-ence by giving them cameo roles in a novel.

Alison, an exquisitely pretty, slender blonde with a soft Scottish accent, was an ex-art student (a sculptor turned writer) who had worked with the radical theatre group Welfare State. She had now co-founded, with Buzz Goodbody (of the RSC) and Sue Todd, the gloriously named Women's Liberation Street Theatre Group. She spoke about women's theatre as women's revolution. I experienced a conversion moment, to which I capitulated with all the ardour of my ex-Catholic soul. Alison was a beautiful, fierce archangel showing me my way into pol-itics, setting me on the pilgrim's path. Henceforth my life would be Different.

I continued to hang out with all my old friends, going to the pub with them, playing bar billiards, listening to local rock bands, dancing, smoking dope. I held dinner parties in my weeny bedsit, cooking up elaborate French meals on the Baby Belling one-ring cooker in stacked pots (a method recom-mended by Katharine Whitehorn in her splendid *Cooking in a*

Bedsitter). I continued my affair with Terry, and went on relishing my encounters with original, eccentric scholars and free-thinkers at the Museum. On 20 January, with Audrey, a Somervillian of forty years back, I watched the striking Post Office workers march past en route to Hyde Park. Audrey suggested blowing kisses to them, then reminisced about demos in the 1930s, in the streets behind the Museum, backing the revolutionary cause in Spain. She was a firm believer in women's rights, and gave me a lot of encouragement. How kind she was to me. How much, now, I wish I'd got to know her better.

By now I was working upstairs, at a desk in the cataloguing room, learning from Julian Roberts how to catalogue early-eighteenth-century books, how to distinguish between a reissue and a new edition; how to record this on the blue slips provided. Punctuation was crucial for making distinctions. All my life as a writer I have loved the semicolon. That love, sparked off by reading the King James version of the Psalms, which deploys semicolons as musical notation, took root there, upstairs in the Department of Printed Books, on those long winter afternoons I passed thinking about printing, about whether to express a decision through a colon or a semicolon. Often I fell asleep over my work, because of too much sex and too little sleep the night before.

Falling in love with feminism, I was falling out of love with the Library. Gossip now circulated in the Museum about my affair with Terry. Julian felt obliged to make discreet enquiries about my mental state and whether I worked enough hours. One Assistant Keeper, Cynthia, who worked on the Catalogue of Early Printed Books, attacked me constantly over my feminism and then as an inarticulate little fool who couldn't even defend her own views. Julian, despite my narcoleptic slowness as a cataloguer, went on being kind to me. He told me to ignore

Cynthia, and invited me to Sunday lunch at his house. His wife impressed me by bearing in a leek tart (a *flamiche*?) and announcing: oh, I'm so sick of quiche, when quiche had only been fashionable for a year or two. After lunch we played games. We had to think up amusing captions for reproductions of Alma Tadema paintings. I suppose Julian felt he had to keep an eye on me. He'd awarded me the Library Scholarship after all. But now I was beginning to let him down.

I began to wonder whether I really wanted to go to Library School and become a librarian at all. I did still enjoy attending meetings of the London Bibliographical Society, just as at Oxford I'd been a member of the Bibliophiles Society, the only woman among aged male dons in rusty black overcoats. Terms ended with Bibliophilic dinners at All Souls hosted by our president John Sparrow; the passing around of ephemera with the port; lots of discreet scholarly competitiveness, Sparrow always trumping everyone by providing something rarer. Lots of absurdity. What had this to do with changing the world? But I did so love books. One day the London Bibliographers went out to look at Graham Pollard's private collection at his house in Blackheath; we were given an excellent tea with three sorts of jam. On another occasion a large amiable bearded Swede talked about Gustaf of Sweden's collection and showed us slides. He kept slipping in prints of luscious nymphs to rest our eyes from all the heavy baroque bindings.

I relished all these pleasures while berating myself for wasting my time, for not reading enough, not being independent enough. I didn't think much of myself at all as a revolutionary. I couldn't connect politics to my continuing intoxication with London; I saw them as strictly separate. I roamed the streets deep in drifts of crackly golden leaves. I wrote about my joy travelling on the top of a bus shooting at fifty m.p.h. over

Waterloo Bridge under a red sunset. I recorded the smell of fruity dustbins in Great Ormond Street, the sight and sound of three beautiful Pakistani girls eating fish and chips on the tube, dipping exquisitely into cones of newspaper and giggling, a man in a park contemplatively rocking a baby and shouting knickers! every time it said waaa.

I attended my first meeting of the street theatre group, in Dinah Brooke's flat in Great Portland Street. I walked up and down looking for the number. Each time I passed the bus-stop the two youths lounging there hissed: I like your nipples. I no longer wore a bra. (NB bras were never ever burned; this is a myth of journalists fond of alliteration; though during one famous demo in the States bras were indeed thrown into trashcans.) Dinah was an excellent novelist. When she became a devotee of the sexual-liberty-preaching guru Bhagwan and went off, orange-robed, to his ashram in Poona, she stopped writing novels. For her leaving party her friends had a cake made for her by Pâtisserie Valerie in Old Compton Street: choux buns, stuck together with caramel, moulded into a tall stupa. Dinah was tall, thin, blonde and beautiful. I felt in awe of her intelligence, posh accent, experience. I felt in awe of everybody in the group: all so bright, so committed, so attractive and confident.

So I thought. Years later Buzz, the brilliant young director, killed herself. Painful conflicts to do with life, family, love, work eventually surfaced for everybody in the group and certainly for me. Nowadays I see that as normal, part of growing up, and certainly as the meat of feminism, but back then I wanted to avoid personal suffering, which I feared meant inadequacy if not madness, by thinking only of other women's struggles; I wanted to wear feminism as a big, shiny shield. That evening, in Great Portland Street, we practised tap-dancing for our routines for the forthcoming demonstration. When we reached

Hyde Park, the plan was to perform a short cartoon-like play, a satire on marriage. 'It's going to be really good, obscene and funny,' I wrote later. I came home to my bedsit delighted.

I went back less frequently now to visit my old friends in Oxford. Some of them, I thought smugly, seemed stuck in ruts. Sian and I remained close but, busy with her B.Phil., she was distracted and on edge. I devoted myself to rehearsals with the street theatre group.

The first London demonstration for women's liberation took place on Saturday 6 March, 1971, to coincide with International Women's Day. About two thousand women, children and supporting men turned up and turned the day into carnival. The street theatre group had a woman perched on top of a car, a Mother Hubbard figure giving birth to long strings of babies; we had an amplifier in a pram; we had a dance troupe doing formation high kicks, singing and miming to 'Keep Young and Beautiful' as we swayed along with huge stick-on red smiles pasted on to our faces. There we are on the TV news, looking impossibly fresh-faced and young. Next day the papers jeered: we'd tried to start too early; we'd gone in the wrong direction; we'd gathered under a phallic symbol (Nelson's Column), silly girls. Our play, disowned by the main organisers of the march and therefore unreported, went off well, people cheering and laughing.

Next day I went to see the *Art in Revolution* exhibition at the Hayward. One wall bore Mayakovsky's slogan: 'the streets our brushes, the squares our palettes'. Now, I knew what that meant. This squared oddly with accompanying my parents, the following weekend, to my father's firm's Ladies' Night dinner dance at the Criterion in Piccadilly. I wore a hideous beaded tube of salmon crêpe, squirmed as Ladies were toasted for charm and sweetness and applauded for escaping for just one night from 'those dreary chores', listened to my mother give the speech on behalf of the Ladies, deprecating 'women libs', won a Biro and a packet of notelets in the raffle, and argued with Dad: darling, you're much too nice a girl to go in for all that anti-men nonsense. On the way back in the car, we were flagged down by medics collecting for Rag Week. One of them, 'mashed as a monkey' (that must have been Dad's phrase), poked his head through the open window. I gave him my bouquet and he planted me a rubbery kiss.

How could I be a librarian, a revolutionary feminist, a would-be novelist, a nice girl who loved her parents, a street theatre actor, a bibliophile, all at the same time? Surely I was a hypocrite? Weren't you supposed to be just One Thing? Either married or single. Either a mother or a career woman. Either sane or mad. Either radical or straight.

I decided to run, and to begin again. The only solution to conflict was to ignore it. I would make a commitment to a very particular form of life and concentrate on that.

I moved out of chez Ernestine, leaving her outraged (according to Joss) at my filthy kitchenette, which I thought I had cleaned rather thoroughly, and went to live with Alison in her communal household off the Holloway Road.

Chapter Two

HOLLOWAY

*Sisterhood is powerful at the Women's
Liberation conference at Skegness, 1971*

Holloway (Hollow Way) Road was formerly one of the thoroughfares from the villages north of London, down which drovers herded their sheep to the market in Islington (Green Lanes was another). The high hedgerow banks were long gone but their memory haunted me, as though a city landscape could be a palimpsest in reverse. You scratched off the top layer of architecture/writing and the one just underneath revealed itself. The city was like one of the manuscripts I studied at the British Museum. Layer upon layer of history lay quietly underneath the current written surface; not gone but just forgotten; biding its time. The city held memory in its very stones and bricks. I knew this not from mystical insight but from my reading. I knew, for example, that just to the north-east of Holloway lay Stoke Newington, former home of Daniel Defoe and Mary Wollstonecraft. This quarter of London had sheltered dissidents and rebels – writers who were critical and passionate. Keats might have walked up this way, I thought, coming from Guy's Hospital in Borough, making towards Hampstead. Elizabeth Gaskell had thought nothing of an evening's stroll from the West End to Highgate. Perhaps she too had walked here. The streets tingled and fizzed with memory and imagination and ghosts. I felt in good company.

Holloway Road in the early 1970s no longer connected city and countryside but had been swallowed up by the metropolis, transformed into a wind-tunnel, noisy with traffic hurtling down from Highgate into the City, which whirled with litter. Redbrick Victorian parades of buildings, with pleasing gables and façades, were disfigured by cheap, ugly plastic shopfronts. Less smart than Regent's Park, more varied, the district charmed me because of its difference from normal high streets. It provided not only pubs, a supermarket, a chemist's, a barber's and so on, but quirky, individual shops: the fetishists' emporium, window filled with spike-heeled boots and black leather bustiers; the weights and measures shop; the headstones shop; the Humanist Association's headquarters, its window filled with curled, yellowing pamphlets. No restaurants that I can remember. We had a couple of burger bars, chippies, and greasy spoons, run by Italians, serving fried breakfasts all day long.

Fairmead Road ran off to the west, at right angles to the main thoroughfare noisy with traffic. Number 42 formed part of a late-Victorian terrace lining one side of the shabby little street and facing one equally unremarkable. Alison and her husband Peter, an artist now teaching at St Martin's School of Art, occupied the back room on the ground floor; close by them, their three-year-old son, Ivan, slept in a cubby-hole under the stairs. Tenants filled all available spaces. A dark, taciturn man called Ed, whom I never got to know, rented the attic flat. A young couple called Jo and Kevin shared a room just below the first landing. Peggy, a friend of mine from convent school, came to live in the room next door to mine and joined the street theatre group. Barbara, also a member of the group, ended up living in a room at the front on the ground floor after she split up with her boyfriend and decided she didn't want to be in a couple any more. Yolanda, another group member, moved in and out according to whim and need. A small, slender person with huge dark eyes, Yolanda seemed very vulnerable, very sweet.

We were a communal household, in that we shared bills and household tasks, but Peter, a tall, burly man with a bellow of a laugh, was indisputably our head, dominating us by his energy, his whoops of delight, his shouts of annoyance, his enthusiasm for the next project. He loved loud rock music and installed speakers throughout so that he could listen to The Band and Bob Dylan wherever he was. Alison, passionate and creative in the street theatre group, was quieter at home. Sometimes worried. She was skint, and Peter was extravagant. When she reproached him for encouraging the rest of us to finish off the Camembert that was supposed to last several days, he roared at her: Scottish puritan! I remember one lunch she cooked for Ivan and herself: two tiny chops lost in a big oven tray.

I rented a good-sized first-floor room, looking out over the front garden. I painted the walls bright yellow above the dado and dark red beneath it, installed a double mattress on the floor, hung my clothes on the back of the door, stacked my boxes of books in a corner. Pete showed me how to build bookshelves resting on wooden battens; to use a spirit level and electric drill; how to get Rawlplugs into the plaster. Thanks to my inaccurate measuring and sawing, my shelves did not fit exactly and snugly into their alcove; they wobbled an inch short. I painted them white, finishing the task in darkness because Pete, whistling and drilling somewhere downstairs, accidentally fused all the lights.

What with my continuing job at the Museum, my relationship with Terry, and my new street theatre activities, I had less time than formerly for introspection, for solitary writing. Moreover, now that I had joined a dynamic, extrovert group household, diary-keeping began to seem too self-conscious. For a while I chose only to make brief entries. I hadn't the words to express all that was going on: the radical politics, the change in lifestyle, the avalanche of new ideas. Perhaps I did not want to recognise the gap that might open up between all the positive commitment I wished to feel towards my new life and activities and the complexities of what these might actually mean to me.

I signalled that gap through denial: white spaces; silences that shouted out. I kept merely a sporadic record. I let a stern self speak, the self I came to label in later years as the nun in my head, the Mother Superior, she of the harsh conscience and puritanical views. When I scribbled an entry describing the street theatre group's Easter Sunday foray to the CND festival at Alexandra Park near the Ally Pally (Londoners' fond term for the Alexandra Palace), I remarked disparagingly on the 'middle-aged liberal crowd strolling in the sun'. Then I went off to Terry's for the weekend and helped him wallpaper his kitchen before sunbathing with him in his garden. Terry, however loving and sweet, was a middle-aged liberal all right. Part of me enjoyed the safety he offered; part of me rebelled against it. The solution was to try and keep my weekend life with him strictly separate, boxed up in his little house in Barking. Part of me wanted just to plunge into radical politics and forget myself in group activity. Part of me wanted to step back and analyse. I wanted to become a writer yet had doubts. Bourgeois individualism was a sin, wasn't it?

We believed in collective action and struggle. Our kind of socialism and feminism was idealistic and libertarian. We worked outside the Labour Party, to its left. People on the ground could take power to change their own lives. The pronoun mattered: we had the power to change our own lives; we did not hang around waiting for leaders to turn up. Parliamentary democracy seemed the business of men in suits at Westminster. The struggle required commitment, time, effort. Hiding in your room, solo, furtively making art all by yourself, you were not contributing to the collective impulse. Art was very important to the cause – dreaming up new forms for the future to take – but it was by the people for the people. Of course it was exhilarating to become part of a group, a movement, to flout convention and experience new freedoms. Politics combined with pleasure. Living collectively meant creating a different sort of family, with no authoritarian parents, no rigid gender divisions, no isolation, no desperate need to consume gadgets and products. The hippy ethos hovered alongside, though as feminists we scorned it. We did not intend to drift about in long cheesecloth skirts, barefoot and pregnant in the kitchen, while our blokes smoked dope and pontificated about peace and love. We felt tougher and more adventurous than that.

For the CND festival we hired a flat-back lorry, parked it in the street outside the house, and began to transform it into a carnival float. We smothered it in white and pink tissue-paper roses. A young woman carrying a baby wandered out from a house a few doors down and asked us what we were doing. Marie was young, dark-haired and very pretty. Shut up at home all day long with the baby in a small flat, she felt isolated and lonely. She watched our preparations and chatted to us. Soon afterwards she joined the street theatre group. Baby Zoë came along to rehearsals or was left with her father. The amiable Steve now arrived home from work to discover, somewhat bemusedly, that he was expected occasionally to look after his child.

We had created a boudoir on wheels so that we could satirise the absurdities of femininity that the magazines pushed relentlessly: the need to achieve and maintain a high-gloss appearance, to please men at all costs. Being a Real Woman was achieved by laborious art; a sort of transvestism. We defined femininity as a performance and dramatised it in the street. We demonstrated and mocked what were in those days women's secret rituals: shaving our armpits, plucking hairs from our legs and top lips, applying mud packs, rolling on girdles, doing slimming exercises. Dressed in my low-cut black lace evening frock from Chapel Street market, elegantly maquillaged, with bouffant hair, I enacted scenes from *The Sensuous Woman*, the bestselling book by 'J'. Less sexual self-knowledge than sex tips on how to keep a man entranced, not let him grow bored and stray. Vigorously I twirled my feather boa and mimed practising with a vibrator how to achieve the multiple orgasms necessary to flatter chaps in bed. Ping! My padded black bra snapped. Out sprang my bosom. Ping! The photographer from the *Sunday Times* captured the moment.

Next day's caption ran: 'woman wants to be liberated but is everywhere in chains.' The chains referred to our piece of situation-theatre satirising left-wing sexism: Pete, bearing a banner saying 'Down with Capitalist Oppression', dragged behind him Dinah and three children, she acting tremendously worn and harassed. He would chain her to the railings outside pubs while he went inside for a quick one with some of the local politicos ogling our lorry, while we graciously shouted down to Dinah about keeping your man happy by not letting yourself go. All good simplistic fun, which nonetheless did provoke people to ask what was going on.

Feminism could be carnivalesque and amusing. It could also disturb. Consciousness-raising, for example, let women meet together in small groups to talk confidentially about any subject we chose. During those hours our allegiance was to each other as women, not to our husbands and lovers. Pamphlets and articles written at this time describe how we put hitherto unexpressed feelings into words. Within the safety of the group we told each other our secrets. We trusted each other not to report back to our men. This meant you could take the lid off your life and have a good look at it. You could try to, anyway. But how did you find the words to express your searches and your discoveries? They did not yet exist. That realisation pushed me towards writing, because the private act of writing allowed me to take all the time I needed to discover what I really thought. Other women, speaking at meetings, often seemed so much more articulate than I. Then later I would discover that they felt exactly the same: that I was very articulate in public. It's true. I was. But my articulateness sometimes felt like glibness to me: opinions rather than true explorations. I could tell my truth in poems, through metaphor. That was true speech; the truest speech, involving doubleness; this is that. But I couldn't speak in poems at meetings.

When we in the street theatre group started a consciousness-raising group in the house, inviting local women to attend our meetings, a couple of husbands stalked in and yanked their wives away. Women talking openly to other women threatened male authority. Women were supposed to relate only to men; not to each other; and certainly not to each other in avowedly political groups that saw women's talk as important, not to be dismissed as gossip or girly chat.

What was a girl, anyway? What was a woman? Two American lesbians, Rachel and Edith, joined our discussion group for a bit. When we discovered that Edith was in fact a chap, penis hidden under his long Indian paisley skirt, we debated earnestly whether or not he had to be banned. Edith *en travestie* was rather nice, I think now. A new sort of woman. An honorary one.

Heady, astonishing, exuberant times: discovering that personal life, domestic life, formed part of politics. This had to be argued for, of course; fought for. For example, most straight men (ordinary men) didn't dream of doing housework because it was women's work; lowly work. They had far more important tasks: earning money. Similarly, many revolutionary men refused even to discuss housework because, yes, it was women's work; lowly work. They had far more important tasks: running a revolution, or, at least, trying to start one. They would quote Mao on the necessity for intellectuals to do physical work alongside the peasants but they wouldn't clean their own lavatories. They called housework shitwork. (Did Peter take his turn at cleaning the lavatory in Fairmead Road? I don't remember.)

People these days assume that feminists despised domestic work, despised housework. We didn't. We didn't want to be defined as the doers of housework, that was all. Our point was that men should do their share. Nowadays that argument has slipped from view. Well-off young capitalists simply buy in help, male or female, and inequalities continue to be perpetuated. Another current myth about the seventies is that feminists despised mothers and motherhood. Wrong. Women's liberation was started by young mothers. How to care for children was crucial to the women's revolution.

The street theatre took these questions and conflicts outside the individual home and displayed them in the street. They were no longer private and silent; they were not petty issues but part of power relationships. Images of what had been traditionally 'inside' now existed outside. Making our theatre in the street, we were ripping off the fronts of houses and showing what went on inside, what had been hidden: women's anger and unhappiness. We were supposed to be dolls to console men. Here were the crazy doll's-houses; we swung open their doors. Our methods may have been raw and crude but our scenes smacked home. Dinah and I did an event at an arts festival in Bath, walking the streets dragging strings of babies (those same well-worn babes we'd stitched for our first play in Trafalgar Square), enquiring of passers-by for launderettes with

50

friendly atmospheres, then washing the babies therein. Shamelessly, I got my mother to drive us over to Bath from Bristol. When she discovered what we were up to, she was outraged. Then she drove us back again. She still feels outraged about this: how dared you use me like that! To her, women making passionate political demands in public was akin to rioting, to mob rule; a loss of control that could easily lead to madness. Her argument: I don't need to be a feminist so you shouldn't need to be, either. No need for collective action: everything could be sorted out inside a marriage. That was that.

At Clapham Junction and Brixton markets we performed our play, in rhyming couplets, using slapstick techniques, about the effects of the Budget on the ordinary housewife. When the Wimpy chain of hamburger bars banned solo women after midnight, apparently, it seemed to us, for fear they were prostitutes who would harass male customers, we acted in support of solo women, whether or not they were hungry prostitutes in need of a quick bite. We paraded outside with sandwich boards in the shape of Wimpys, painted with slogans: 'Make Love Not Wimpys'; 'It's a Wimpy's World'; 'Wimpys of the World Unite'. It was impossible for me to picket deadly seriously: who wanted to eat Wimpys, anyway?

Our next sortie felt tougher. When, dressed as nuns, as babies, as men, we did a sit-in at the Wimpy bar at Earls Court, the police were called. They charged in and threw us out, picking us up and dumping us on the pavement. It had taken some courage to stage this event, but of course the press wasn't interested in the point we were trying to make. They just wanted to mock. I was interviewed by the *Daily Telegraph* reporter as I sprawled at his feet. He made me sound absurd. 'Miss Michèle Roberts, aged 22, dressed in men's clothes,' he wrote solemnly: 'said: "why shouldn't I be able to go in here after midnight with my girlfriend?"' I liked the idea of passing as a young masher, but I didn't make a convincing man: too curvaceous. Similarly, when I played Marvo the Capitalist Magician, in our play satirising Barbara Castle's 1970 Equal Pay Act (due to come into force in 1975) for its inadequacies, I donned trousers, a top hat and striped waistcoat, and painted on a curly black moustache, but could not conceal my hopelessly hour-glass figure.

The moustache reminded me of one of Nana's favourite stories about my father as a boy. Acting a pirate in one of the plays she wrote for the May Day festival in Hampstead Garden Suburb (she and Grandpa formed one of the working-class families for whom the Suburb was initially conceived), he had stuck on his black horsehair moustache with glue. Subsequently it would not abandon his top lip. Nana scrubbed away in the bathroom, to no avail. Finally it came off after liberal applications of spirit. Nana would have enjoyed our street theatre, I think now, but I didn't invite her along. I kept my family life strictly separate; in the background. I could love Nana, and know how much she loved me, and then I could go off and try to be a revolutionary.

We were right to point out the deficiencies of the Equal Pay Act: all these years later women still do not receive equal pay with men. Any young woman thinking feminism is obsolete just needs to look around her office and make some enquiries about salaries (let alone think about rape and how often it happens, because opportunistic young men know they can get away with it if the woman is tiddly and deemed to be asking for it).

On Saturday 25 September, 1971, we took up the invitation offered by the Festival of Light, run by prominent Christians such as Cliff Richard and Mary Whitehouse, who had a lot of power in the media, to attend their rally in Trafalgar Square. Their motto proclaimed: 'there's a solution for moral pollution.' Right-wing Evangelicals determined to stamp out sexual licentiousness, they nonetheless declared they wanted dialogue and debate with the opposition. Very well, then. Off we went to Trafalgar Square to debate with them.

We had decided to stage an event satirising the hypocrisy surrounding the bourgeois family. We dressed up as a family group, painting our faces clown-white, smearing on wide red smiles. I played the caricature mother, in a tweed suit and big flowery hat. Between two banners, one labelling us 'The Unholy Family' and the other proclaiming 'Fuck the F*mily', we walked along all chained to each other, singing 'God Bless the Master of This House', complaining at each other, grumbling, kicking each other down the father-mother-child-baby-cat chain of command. Our chains were held by two enormous white hands on poles, one hand labelled 'Church' and the other 'Capital'. We nodded hello to the gay men nearby who were all dressed as nuns and lewdly misbehaving.

Very quickly a bunch of militant male Christians joined on behind us and started shouting: kill a Commie for Christ! Others catcalled: give us an F-U-C-K. The crowd of angry, abusive men swelled but we kept going. We had hardly walked around three sides of the square before the police arrested us, put us in a van and took us off to Cannon Street nick, where we spent the next four and a half hours. They arrested the gay men too. At first they weren't sure where to put them: separately, or in with us? Chaps in habits and wimples were still chaps, the cops decided (we should have got them to arbitrate over Edith, the penis-swinging lesbian), and banged them up by themselves. They manhandled them far more roughly than they did us; they addressed us as harmless, pathetic ladies.

They'd only arrested us, they explained, in order to protect us from being beaten up by the muscular Christians. We whiled away the wait scratching 'Sisters Unite' on the walls of our cell with a hairpin taken from my matronly bun. Some weeks later we came up in Marlborough Street Magistrates' Court on a charge of Insulting Behaviour encouraging a breach of the peace, were found guilty and fined £3 a head.

Alison was our presiding genius, our chief writer. We wrote and rehearsed the plays as a group, but hers was the inspiring presence. She came up with the idea for our Situationist drama in the ladies' lavatories in Selfridges: appearing with only half our faces made up and sitting shaving the other half. She designed the costumes for our invasion of the Miss World competition at the Albert Hall: dressed in black, we paraded with electric bulbs strategically placed in our clothing to create flashing nipples and flashing cunts. When she went off to tour the States for six weeks, on a women's liberation bus, we marked the occasion by holding a dollybird auction in Hyde Park, an auctioneer with a whip selling us off, one by one, to the highest bidders in the audience. Passing blokes enjoyed it, shouting: it's that women's lib; you're crackers, not asking for money; what's the message, then? Then I dashed off to the Kienholz sculpture exhibition at the ICA, and then to the Poetry International Festival at the Queen Elizabeth Hall on the South Bank, which I found stultifying, full of safe, boring poets.

Going to live in Holloway among artists and radicals I had torn myself violently out of my family, out of what they expected and wanted for me. I felt I had to do this: less choice than necessity pushed me. Simply becoming a feminist in an intellectual sense was not enough. I could not imagine how to become an artist within the parameters of my strongly Tory and religious family. I had grown up, thanks to Catholicism, fearing my own body, distrusting my own feelings and thoughts; I feared and resented authority. Anger was labelled as wicked; equivalent to madness. I flattened all my turbulent feelings under a veil of cheeriness, expressed them only in poems, which I kept secret. Similarly, I tried to express what I felt in my diary. Writing was my soul-saver.

Like so many other young women, I had to rebel. It was speak out and leave and live differently and write – or die psychically. That is melodramatically put; but that is how I felt. This fight to the death was so painful precisely because rage and rebellion were twined up with love. I desperately wanted my parents to understand what I was doing and why. Simultaneously I wanted to reject them and what they stood for: safe Tory values; man as the head of the family; woman taking most of the responsibility but hiding her power. I wanted to support my mother, who was going through hard times after having been uprooted from her old home in Edgware when my father's firm moved to Bristol. Mum had had no choice, after months of arguing, but to go too. She was still struggling to settle in and make a new life. But she did not perceive my support. She saw only my rebellion, which she experienced as a personal attack designed specifically to hurt her. When she, Dad and Nana came to lunch at Fairmead Road, they were horrified by the untidiness and shabbiness, by the numbers of people sharing the house. I had stayed up until 3 a.m. the previous night talking to Yolanda, before we fell asleep in my bed, and had not got round to cleaning up. They saw nothing but dirt and squalor, the flouting of all rules about basic decency; anarchy; madness. Off we all drove to Stanmore to a pub called the Red House to celebrate Nana's ninetieth birthday. On came the house band, in red blazers. The singer, in gold lamé, crooned sentimental songs: 'Granma' and 'Appy Birfday'.

I continued my solitary walks around London. Crossing Westminster Bridge I saw a man leaning against the parapet, clutching his arm. Blood dripped from it on to the pavement. He explained he'd fallen down, and some old scars, from a lorry accident, had reopened. He'd discharged himself from hospital and was trying to get home to Sussex to see his wife who'd just had a baby. His first child had been killed at the mining disaster at Aberfan. Was he just pitching me a hard-luck story? Had he simply been in a fight? That never occurred to me, though I did realise he was drunk. I just enjoyed his liveliness and sexiness, his Welsh accent, relished the ferocity with which he talked, upbraided me as a poor weed for not getting all his jokes. Don't get me wrong, lady, he hastily added: I don't mean to upset you. I walked him to the bus-stop and gave him all the money I had: £1.10. Enough (in those days) to get him home.

Another time I walked along the Embankment as far as Monument, exploring shoulder-wide alleys ending in stone steps down to the river, and having a drink in the Ticket Porter ('the only pub in London to survive the Great Fire'): brown-painted plaster, velvet curtains draping the bar, watercolours of the local skyline, wooden stools and chairs, a bare floor. With Yolanda I walked up to Highgate ponds, to the Women's Pond: deep and reed-encircled, with ducks, lawns for sitting and sun-bathing, and marvellous old women quietly enjoying it. We stayed there all afternoon, picnicking on peaches, cheesecake and gingerbread men. One afternoon, loafing through Tavistock Square, I met a man who had sat there, on his little canvas stool, every day for the past thirty years, selling the sheets of handwritten poems and crayon drawings he pinned to the railings. He hated dogs, he said, because they crapped on his pavement works. He hated society in general because it crowded him out. I bought a picture of Napoleon swaggering in a greatcoat. Or I roamed the parks, discovering them one by one, kicking through drifts of fallen leaves.

Sometimes I needed to escape the collective house, the non-stop political discussions. I didn't fit in properly there, and I didn't fit into my family either. In the house I was too middle-class and in my family I was too badly behaved. I escaped up to Hampstead and walked hard and fast on the Heath, feeling the knot of tension inside loosen a bit. On these walks I flew some kind of flag, making me kin to other wanderers: I met tramps who chatted to me and offered me swigs from their bottles of booze.

Few trees or open spaces in Holloway. No fresh air in our house: the windows remained shut; gas fires burned the whole day. I had to get out. Holloway was raffish, chaotic, eccentric. Despite the men who followed me, shouting comments about tits, I loved exploring it, weaving in and out of its backstreets as I came home from the tube. I found a hairdresser: Mr Aladdin Bemrah; got a chic short haircut; and went off on holiday to Algeria and Tunisia with Terry. On my return I walked into a changed house.

My room had vanished.

During my absence Alison and Peter had decided, with the consent of their tenants, that the household should become a proper collective. We should no longer be defined, in a bour-geois way, by our possessions. We would construct our identities in different ways: collectively. Everything we owned would now be held in common (though not the actual house – Peter still owned that). Nobody would henceforward have a room of his or her own. We would share all our clothes and books. Along with everybody else I proclaimed this a marvellous idea. Given that it was a fait accompli there was not much else, short of moving out, that I could do. I decided not to leave but to stay. Once the shock of losing my private space had worn off, I wanted to try the experiment and take the risk. Did I panic secretly? Did I feel angry? I don't remember. In any case, at that stage of my life in the house I would have denied those feelings in public even if I had them in private. I wanted to belong in the group. It was uptight to worry about my identity vanishing along with my possessions. Very well, then, I would not be uptight. To prove this I took mescaline, then with Ali, painted the outside of the house black. We painted the stonework mushroom and the woodwork white. Ali bestrode the apex of the roof and fixed slipping slates. I watched her as I sat on the swing in the overgrown back garden: chilly grass, the pear tree and the brick wall against a flushed sky.

All kinds of communes flourished in London in the early seventies. Some were attached to different left-wing groups, or to hippy groups. Some, like ours, were owner-occupied. Some functioned as safe houses for Americans escaping the Vietnam draft, or for people needing to go underground, to flee the state authorities, for one reason or another. Some groups took over disused, boarded-up properties and squatted them: breaking in, getting the electricity and water turned back on and so establishing a semi-legal presence. A lot of landlords chose to leave their properties vacant rather than let them and allow their tenants their legal right not to be summarily evicted. The squatting movement was a response to the homelessness caused by these venal landlords. Local councils too left properties lying dormant for years, slowly becoming derelict, claiming they could not afford to restore them. Squatting therefore became a political act.

Our collective was not as keen as some to break down old bourgeois distinctions between public and private. One Islington household, which we visited regularly, had taken the doors off the lavatory and bathroom. It was reactionary, apparently, to want to poo invisibly. (A recent conversation with Lynne Segal, who lived round the corner from that particular house, clarified that in fact the lavatory door got left off through DIY laziness.) I took care never to need to pee when I went there. I was too naïve to understand some of what I saw. I thought the household formed part of The Angry Brigade (dedicated revolutionaries) but wasn't sure. They seemed so cheerful and normal apart from their open-air lav. Later on, members of this commune were arrested as terrorists, found guilty, and jailed.

Now, looking back, I can draw a parallel between giving up my identity, my clothes and possessions and room, and my earlier dream – inspired by my admiration for that great writer, Teresa of Avila, who reformed the Carmelite Order in the sixteenth century – of entering a Carmelite convent. Religious orders traditionally induced obedient behaviour through their entrance rituals, their rites of passage. Once you have had your hair cut off, donned the habit, kissed the ground, been humiliated into subservience, you are firmly part of the group, utterly loyal, unable to criticise it. Your obedience is not really a virtue: it simply benefits the Church which can make use of you, its willing instrument.

Saints like Teresa of Avila, of course, developed clever strategies for going their own way while pacifying the authorities. I wasn't as clever as Teresa. I blurted out what I felt then got put down. I liked being in a commune some of the time, loathed it the rest of the time. I assumed, as novices in strict religious orders might do, that it was my own fault if I was unhappy. I wasn't struggling hard enough. I'd ostensibly given up bourgeois morality but retained all my Catholic facility for continually blaming myself. I knew I wasn't educated enough in the new ways of thought. I didn't express myself in a sophisticated way. When the *Oz* trial began (*Oz* ran a cover featuring Rupert Bear with a huge erection and so the editors were arrested for obscenity), I expressed simple indignation. Pete cut short our discussion by telling me I was terribly naïve. I hadn't lived: I'd only ever read books.

Like professed nuns regularly welcoming each new batch of postulants into the convent with a special religious ritual, we held collective meetings which were supposed to bond us into a proper group. I remember we began one of these by playing games to engender mutual trust. In what had once been Ali's and Pete's bedroom, on the ground floor, we stood in a circle, fell backwards and forwards, caught each other. Then we tried to discuss the ways in which we put each other down! I felt unable to say I often felt barely tolerated. I still got paranoid about lack of privacy and space, other people not respecting one's things. I cherished my collection of books in publisher's cloth with art nouveau designs on the covers, my 1930s and 1940s crêpe dresses. I didn't want to give them up. We now kept our clothes in what had been Jo's and Kevin's room (they had moved out smartish in order to continue being a couple). Contradictorily, I felt possessive about my own clothes all right but nonetheless enjoyed borrowing other people's. Ali, for example, possessed a beautiful black velvet coat with frogging and velvet-covered buttons. Of course she fretted when I wore it: my shoulders were too broad and I split the seams. Large, burly Peter, whose clothes were too large for anyone else to want to wear them, and who anyway just wore jeans, would dismiss these petty feminine worries, smiling beatifically. In house meetings he would sit embroidering his spare jacket, to prove how much he was in touch with his feminine side.

Since nobody had a room any more, we all slept where we liked, in whatever bed, in whatever space we chose. So, having curled up on a mattress in what had once been your own room but was now the library, you might be awakened at 3 a.m. by some strange bloke crashing in through the door and rolling into bed with you. They didn't necessarily come on to you but nonetheless you didn't feel relaxed. If you protested, you felt priggish. I much preferred falling asleep with another woman. Rather than invading each other's space, we chose to share our beds. Ensconced, we could talk for hours. I hadn't shared a bed with another woman since childhood, aged six or seven, when night after night I'd hop into my twin sister's bed and we'd cuddle each other. Yolanda and I, curled up together, told each other stories. With Marie I talked about marriage, after we had attended a women's conference together up north in Skegness, at the miners' holiday camp there (the miners found feminists hilarious and teased us endlessly).

Once Pete took Peggy and me to bed with him as an experiment. All three of us lay on our backs. Dutifully Peter's fingers circled our clitorises. Dutifully we submitted. Finally Peggy and I caught each other's eye above his prone body. We winked and grimaced. I got up and left. Such absurdities! I was trying to experiment with freedom but it was within others' structures. I remember the pamphlet called *The Tyranny of Structurelessness* which circulated at the time. I was living out the pamphlet's critique. I imagined I had avoided the old hierarchies and rules but in reality I had merely exchanged my bourgeois patriarchal family for something that closely resembled it. The father-figure still had the power but did not have to admit it.

I wrote: 'life is a struggle at the moment and I am not always aware of the benefits for what I've given up. I know people care but I am not often happy. Only make jokes away from the house. Don't want to become a prig.' So, in order not to become a prig, I tried to go along with what was expected. I felt guilty for not being happy, guilty for feeling resentful, guilty for not being able to articulate my unhappiness. Oh dear. The nun in my head, that monstrous Mother Superior, was swinging her truncheon with gay abandon: thwack! Thwack! I had no idea, back then, that I could recognise her, name her, and deal with her. Nowadays, when I teach writing sometimes, I say to my students: thwart her with fickle love and flirtation, tease her, tickle her, dance the tango with her. But when I was young I couldn't do it. So teaching is reparative: trying to give the students what I didn't have myself.

For the time being I just stumbled on and coped as best I could. Somehow I protected myself. Thoughts of Nana helped a lot, because she was so honest, rude and rumbustious, so curious, so affectionate. Deep down, I survived.

My year as Library Scholar in the Department of Printed Books at the British Museum ended. My colleagues organised a small leaving party for me in Terry's room in the bookstacks. Ali and Pete attended it. On his way out, along the curving corridor walled with books, Pete, to prove his radical credentials (Property Is Theft) threatened to pocket a volume. I was silently shocked. The British Museum's books belonged to the nation, to everyone. But to Pete the British Museum stood for hateful state institutions, and he felt obliged to make a gesture, however childish.

I started at Library School at University College, part of London University. This formed the second half of my two-year postgraduate course. At the opening party one of the male academics, who would be teaching us, told me about a woman whom he'd recommended for a job on account of her beauty: well, of course, it matters so much with women because they go off so quickly. He was forty-five, with a pot belly and nicotine-stained fingers. I'd had to have an interview with him, back in the summer, in order to ask for help with the fees, which I could not afford, and I had been perfectly aware, after a minute in his presence, that he responded well to personable young students with curly hair and nice figures. Dressed in a blue Mary Quantish mini-frock, with white collar and cuffs, I had played the appealing young thing and been certain he would find me the money. He did. The Mother Superior in my head beat me up for playing his game. The mother in me says now: well, caught in a bind you did your best. At least you understood what was required of you and did it, and so you got the money you needed. Don't be so harsh on yourself.

The Library School was housed deep down in the depths of UCL. (When I went looking for it recently I couldn't find it – it seemed to have detached itself from its moorings and floated off.) I remember the women's cloakroom, dark and dank, with ancient cracked sinks. When you used a cubicle after one particular woman lecturer it always smelled of vaginal deodorant. This saddened and enraged me. In an enormous classroom, with high windows, we sat in rows at desks, like schoolchildren. Lecturers ambled in and out. We scribbled notes on bibliographical theory, cataloguing theory, classification theory, the latter supposedly a logical system of arranging books by subject so that you could easily find them in the library catalogue. Logic could conceal bias. The classification system used in British public libraries was the Dewey Decimal one, which divided knowledge into ten hierarchically arranged categories, broken down into subsections of subsections. Women were classified in a subgroup under Category Seven alongside

Lunatics and Gypsies. Men did not feature: as designers of systems they were assumed to be as omnipresent and invisible as God the Father.

For one special paper I chose to study Advanced Bibliography so that I could pursue my obsession with printing. For my special subject I chose female emancipation. I invented a new classification system, based on computer theory, which flexibly put women at the centre of the world, able to relate to anything and everything we liked. The high spot of the week was learning about practical bookbinding and paper-making with Sandy Cockerell at the Cockerell Press, about all aspects of printing. The lectures bored me. The other students were more committed and hardworking than I was. I made one good friend: Clark. He teased me. I asked him to go to bed with me. He refused: that would be a sin! We quickly regained our old footing of cheerful insults. Our comic, wry friendship kept me going.

At lunchtimes I escaped to the book barrows in Farringdon Road and searched for bargains, sometimes with Terry and sometimes alone. In the London streets I felt released. I loved their electric vitality, the crispness of the autumn air. I read the signs on buildings, the scrawls on brick walls, the graffiti on hoardings: the speech of the people making itself heard.

I realised I was not going to make a librarian when I did library practice in the local public branch at the top of Holloway Road. I disliked the librarians, frosty-faced ladies who spent too much time slapping down the black children in the junior library. Shelving returned books was intensely dull but had to be done. One afternoon I went delivering books to the old age pensioners around Islington. They all seemed to live at the top of many flights of stairs. Just getting up to answer the door left them breathless. But of course what mattered to them was not being shunted off into a Home. Most got through twenty romances a month and unerringly rejected those they'd already read. I saw a new Islington as we drove slowly around: these old blocks of crumbling flats, the new estates being built; the backsides of the Georgian terraces. Outside the last house we visited, a curly-haired workman sang in Greek as he painted stonework khaki. Our driver immediately launched into an account of how he'd tamed his over-exuberant Greek neighbours: they're as bad as niggers for having kids!

Afterwards I took a bus through Camden Town. I recorded later how, sitting in front on the top deck, I saluted and loved 'every crumbling brick, every peel of plaster with a passion renewed every time I pass'. I don't think the old age pensioners I'd visited felt quite so romantic about their run-down housing. On the other hand they hadn't yet been forced out. They were still independent. I got off the bus and explored along the canal a little way, then came back to the High Street. One house near Kanga's Exotic Vegetable Shop had a tiny basement area you could just see by peering over the pavement railings. It was smothered in urns of plastic flowers, gnomes on swings, rabbits skipping with puppies and ponies; all in plaster. I strode along singing out loud.

I continued to make new friendships. I met Frances Wood, who was an Assistant Keeper at the BM, rapidly becoming an expert on Chinese culture. She and her boyfriend drove me home from one party. We stopped in Kentish Town for fish and chips. Frances fizzed with energy and wit. She was beautiful, with silky black hair and rosy cheeks, fiercely intelligent, funny. In her company I felt real; ordinary; able to enjoy myself.

Conflict stabbed me. Should I leave the Fairmead Road house or stay? Should I become a librarian or not? Dear Mr Nixon, under whom I'd studied bookbinding at the British

Museum, rang me up to say he was pushing me for a job as second-in-command at St Bride's printing library. Peter, Ali and co. were keen to buy a local shop that had come up for sale, install a silkscreen printing press and get cracking making propaganda, run a café, bookshop, sound studio. We might copy the Black Panthers and run a food and clothes centre, we thought. For the moment, we established a food co-op.

I continued to make ventures into the public arena. I gave a lecture (courtesy of Pete) to the Saint Martin's Fine Art students, entitled 'Fashion as Bondage', and found that although I could be ideologically tough in a prepared paper, aggressive questions from the floor were much harder to deal with. I mounted another platform when, urged on by Selma James, the founder of Wages for Housework (a campaign with which I disagreed), I volunteered to speak at Conway Hall. A public meeting was held there to protest about the fate of Pauline Jones, a disturbed young woman who had kidnapped a baby and been slung into Holloway Jail. I went over to Selma's house to discuss our speeches. Selma was a charismatic figure, an impassioned speaker, who seemed to think she was Queen of the women's movement. When we took to the streets to demonstrate, she liked to stand on traffic islands, one hand on a bollard, and graciously watch the march past of the troops. On this occasion, an acolyte let me in, then told me to wait while Selma ate her lunch of plaice and chips. I sat opposite Selma, watching her clean her plate. I was hungry, but she didn't offer me anything to eat. A far cry from the traditions of hospitality in which I had been brought up. In France, a guest, unexpected or not, was offered an aperitif as a matter of course.

As part of the protest on behalf of Pauline Jones, the street theatre group briefly invaded Holloway Jail (via the former Victorian castle-like entrance to its courtyard) with banners, before being turned back. Selma later developed Wages for Housework into the English Collective of Prostitutes, with offices at King's Cross. Her argument was that women serviced men non-stop. Prostitution was simply sexual housework. We libertarian feminists supported prostitute women's campaigns for better working conditions but did not agree with Selma's cynicism: our belief in free love entailed valuing sex in a way that nowadays, when sex is more commodified and pornogrified than ever, seems perhaps hopelessly romantic. We believed in passionate sexual love between men and women, as equals. Men were our brothers and comrades, even when we fought them.

Terry held on to me and in some way I held on to him. His house was a refuge when things got too much at Fairmead Road. After one street theatre sortie, we came back to the collective house. Terry threw me on to the bed in the 'library' and fucked me. We looked up. There, outside the window, was Pete, perched on a ladder, repairing something, grinning and laughing as he peeped in. He cocked his thumb at Terry: good on yer, mate.

I found it very hard to study in the house. I was a crazy bookworm toiling over Library School notes when the others were out on the streets demonstrating or having impassioned discussions around the kitchen table over endless pots of tea. I fantasised about becoming a revolutionary librarian. I could radicalise the Fawcett Library, I thought. Or else start a women's movement library. Perhaps Germaine Greer would put up the funds?

The collective was no longer working well. Peggy, desperate for a room of her own, got allotted the space under the stairs where little Ivan formerly slept. Where did Ivan move to? I don't remember. Everybody was out all day doing separate things. We met only at night for dull suppers (lots of spuds, cabbage and parsnip chips) no one wanted to cook. I'd grown up in a family of good female cooks and missed good meals, just as I missed laid tables and tablecloths. Poor meals were matched by poor conversations. The secret power structure in the house created bad communication and little trust. For example, a new guy moved in without most of us knowing him or even being informed. Pete complained that Ali and the rest of us were 'draggy women' just talking endlessly about politics and being 'too heavy'. The house seemed full of strangers. I felt depressed, and often lay in bed and cried and then the Mother Superior in my head ticked me off for being a wimp.

I started to escape. One day, instead of going to a political meeting, I went with Peggy up to Highgate where we wandered in second-hand bookshops. On another occasion I skived off with Marie to the pub, then went to a jumble sale. Two chairs at 5p each, a silk Liberty print handkerchief for 5p, a handful of cutlery ditto. Then we went on to Lawrence Corner, an army surplus store: a canvas hammock, a tin soap dish. I had started buying things for a home of my own but didn't know it. That was not a wish I could make conscious. I had no money and nowhere to go.

Another outing was to the Isle of Dogs with Marie, Zoë and little Ivan. He wore his wooden-soled shoes and made a great clatter in the pedestrian tunnel running under the Thames over to Greenwich. We ate hot pies and drank cider, sitting in Greenwich Park. We played King of the Castle. An enormously fat Park Keeper (in those days Parks were Kept) bellowed at us: keep off the graaaass! It's the ruuuules! We went back across to the Isle of Dogs and roamed about. Deserted wharves, factories, pubs, narrow streets linking them. We tiptoed in and out of warehouses and sheds. It felt like another world: Mortmere; gothic and extraordinary. I remember a junk-heap of cobalt-blue cans and how beautiful I found them. We finished off with a party at a friend's house in Stepney. I was grabbed by a middle-aged West Indian man who held my arm in order to stroke my nipple, saying 'My little frizzle-fowl, you have a snub nose.' He took himself off so much all I could do was smile. His family sat around beaming over champagne cocktails and pilau. We went on to the second party of the night, given by Jenny of the BM. There, Ron, the indefatigable winder-up of feminists, compared relationships with women to dog-handling. Then I jumped on a bus to Terry's.

He was simply a dear friend now. I didn't want sex with him any more.

We cooked together, English food that recalled childhood meals at Nana's: thin brown bread and butter and watercress and shrimps; toad-in-the-hole; rhubarb pie and custard. Experiments culled from Saturday supplement food columns. I remember *escalopes de veau* with vermouth. I used to wolf down biscuits and cheese too. Trying to console need, to dull all kinds of wanting: emotional and sexual.

Intellectual needs felt easier to satisfy. I went on trying to educate myself outside Library School. I read Simone de Beauvoir's *The Second Sex*, Kate Millet's *Sexual Politics*, Frantz Fanon's *Black Faces White Masks*, James Baldwin's *Giovanni's Room*, and much besides. I worried about how I would earn a living, scanned what I called in my diary the 'disgusting' Women's Appointments ads in the *Guardian* (those were the days before such discrimination was made illegal), edged towards planning a definite escape. Looking back, I think I was like a young nun making up her mind to leave the convent: how difficult to go against a community you have chosen, ferociously loved and supported and now criticise. You feel you are betraying them.

We held a collective meeting. One of the women in the house had let it out I wanted to leave. Heavy going. I tried to speak my truth. The others invalidated everything I said by replying, But Michèle, we all feel that. I felt silenced and angry. Also I felt the stirring of my capacity to make a decision, to act on my own behalf, to consider my own happiness and to believe that it mattered.

I had a bad cold. There were not enough blankets in the house. I'd been, for peace, sleeping in Peggy's bed 'where the sheets don't entice anyway'. The next night Yolanda shared my bed. I couldn't sleep: she thrashed with nightmare. Next day I went with her for a walk in Tavistock Square. She said: I want to obliterate myself. We sat in silence, suddenly surrounded by a gust of pigeons chasing the crumbs of chocolate Yolanda had let fall. She hated the birds: why aren't they round anyone else? Birds don't eat chocolate. We moved to another bench. Windy day. Our slab of green turf frayed at the edges into black earth the gardener raked slowly. The miners' strike was happening, and the government had declared a state of emergency. Power cuts would take place next day. Buckingham Palace was luckily unaffected, a TV spokesman said.

I spent the night of 25 February 1972 crying while I packed bags and boxes. On Saturday the 26th I finally did it. My cousin and her husband came round with their car and moved me out.

Ali and I said goodbye only temporarily. We had seen each other through stirring and difficult times. Over thirty years later she remains one of my best friends.

Chapter Three

CLAPHAM JUNCTION

Chez Frances Wood, at St George's Square

I briefly rented a room over a little terrace of shops, in an old building, shabby and dirty, near the market at Clapham Junction crossroads. Other people's dirt always seems worse than one's own; that's the definition of dirt, perhaps. I didn't mind too much: that was just how it was.

My room was not only grubby but damp and cold, with a cracked and curling lino floor. The worn orange candlewick bedspread bore cigarette burns. A pair of someone's old knickers, yellowed and torn, stuffed a hole in the plastered wall near the window. A long mound of grey fluff, smelling sour as a dead dog, slumped on top of the wardrobe. The plaster fell off the walls when I scrubbed them. Nonetheless, the wretched little shelter was priced as a luxury flat because, although the shared bathroom and lavatory were two floors down, it featured a vinyl shower cubicle just outside the kitchen. The landlord's sons, wearing natty camel overcoats, generally arrived to collect the rent just when I was trying to take a shower, standing shivering under the spout, coaxing lukewarm drops from it. I liked the small, old-fashioned lavatory, though, off the landing at the turn of the stairs; it commanded a view over the railway cutting, its edges frothing with spring greenery and blossom.

I furnished my small room with my two junk-shop chairs, painted yellow, a pink 1930s faded quilt from a jumble sale, a table-top swing mirror that reflected my knees. No room for books; they went to live in Terry's loft. Terry had invited me to live with him but I firmly said no. I wanted my independence. Part of that involved sexual freedom: I wanted to be able to sleep with other men, in particular with the radical philosopher I had just met and liked a lot. We all believed in free love as a

73

theory but its practice could feel fraught with difficulty. Terry reproached me gently from time to time about what he saw as my infidelity. He was thirty years older than I was and gave me the love, praise and security of an ideal father in a fairytale. But that fairytale did not exist. I should have left him but I didn't know how to. It seemed too cruel. I was hurting him by sleeping with another man, but I didn't see that as cruel. The men I knew (Terry included) believed in sexual freedom. But Terry didn't want his own woman to be free.

I went on wrestling with studying, with my terrors of exams. I comfort-ate to dull fear and anxiety. I fretted about my relationships with Terry and other men. I tried to go on being involved with the street theatre group. I wrote poems in secret while paying lip-service to ideals of communal writing. I played with applying to do an MA, or a B.Phil. at Oxford. I wanted to edit a Middle English translation of the medieval German mystic Mechtild of Magdeburg, whose work I had discovered lodged in Duke Humphrey's Library in the Bodleian. At the same time, I knew I ought to be living in a more revolutionary way, whatever that meant. At night I lay awake worrying, then round about 5 a.m. took sleeping pills, so that I often overslept and missed my morning lectures.

Worry dissolved when I roamed London and forgot myself in exploring it. On the bus one day, sitting in my favourite seat on top at the front, I realised, as we careened through Vauxhall, that I'd travelled on the same bus the week before; I recognised 'I Love Victoria Vetri' scrawled above the front window. A child on the bus was grizzling all the way home. Be quiet, said her father: or I'll take you down to the police station and they'll take your drawers down and knock all your teeth out. When I got off the bus and walked home through the Junction a man, seeing me in my Indian kaftan, called after me: Jezebel! Jezebel!

With Terry, one Sunday, I strolled along the Mile End Road. We looked at the Eric Gill reliefs on the People's Palace, admired the Whitechapel Bell Foundry, explored the alley called Mile End Place with its row of cottages and small gardens, walked along the canal towpath. We bought pink and green sweetmeats in Pakistani shops. I gazed at pub signs, blue wooden benches daubed with graffiti, the lettering on the sides of warehouses, eel and pie stalls. I admired the East Enders. They seemed to know that they belonged to a place; that this part of the city was theirs. When I got on the bus, waving goodbye to Terry, the old lady I sat down next to began interrogating me: that your young man? You married to him? Why not? Isn't he hot? Does he want to letch into you? Mind, you didn't give in to him, did you? Christ, mate, don't go having no babies. I asked her, in return, about her own life. Her bloke had left her years before and she couldn't find him though she looked everywhere for him. Now she was an evening cleaner, living on her own with a bed and chair for company, and she chatted up all the blokes at the church clubs. She told me I should get married and get some decent clothes. My second-hand 1940s fur jacket, from the flea market in Brighton, was much too shabby. She shook her head at it. She probably would have disapproved equally of the treasures I bought off stalls in the Portobello Road: a green 1930s frock for ten pence, an old velvet jacket spotted with deep vivid orange, pink and purple and tied with a tassel, a yellow T-shirt.

Perhaps it was my strange, colourful outfits, not just my youth and sex, which attracted male drivers when I hitch-hiked, and got me lifts. I still went up to Oxford to visit my old friends there, could not afford train fares, rejected the bus. Once, coming back, I was picked up by a charming parson. He revealed that he had once worked with Chad Varah on *Eagle*

75

comic, for which he drew the Jesus strip cartoon. As a child I loved *Eagle*: full of boys adventuring. *Girl*, the sister paper, was more decorous, featuring simpering Belle of the Ballet in her pink *Sylphides* frock (perhaps I felt ambivalent towards her because I too had wanted to be a ballerina once but grew too tall – aged ten I wept all night when informed of this). The occasional heroic female missionary did surface. Since I identified with both genders I read both comics: simple. Chad, who founded the Samaritans, was an uncle of my elder sister Jackie's husband. I'd met him at family parties: tall and thin, with a cut-glass accent. The parson added that, now he had realised that people seemed to need him less for spiritual succour, he had started lecturing in management at Slough.

Another driver, on the way to Oxford, described to me, with relish, how he had bayoneted Germans in the war. I thought he might have a bayonet in the boot and start bayoneting me. I flinched as he swerved off the main road and plunged down a country lane. My luck held: he was merely taking a short cut into town.

Exams started at Library School. Manuscript Studies coursework was, I wrote in my diary, 'a real stinker'. We were given photocopied sheets of manuscripts to transcribe and commanded to identify the script in which they were written. The Renaissance humanists imitated the handwriting style of the twelfth century. You were supposed to know which was which. Caroline minuscule or not? Oh Lord. I turned to the second sheet. I vacillated between *protogothica* and *gothica Carolina*. All of us felt flummoxed and tried to help each other in whispers, squinting sideways, hissing suggestions. Very discreetly, I showed my friend Louise how to spot the *Incipit* ('Here begins') of the manuscript. Then, in desperation, I cheated outright. Since I was seated behind the star pupil in the class I found I could peep over her shoulder, thanks to my longsightedness, and copy her answer.

For Management Studies I wrote about how to forestall book thieves in libraries. Hmmm. Certain communards I knew would not have approved of that. Cataloguing was OK, because I'd so thoroughly learned it at the Department of Printed Books in the British Museum. Classification I could do, too, because it was a specific language, like poetry, and I'd realised how important it was. I scrabbled through the other papers. I passed. I became an Associate of the Library Association. One of the nicest students on the course, a fifty-year-old woman named Mrs Hempster, from the countryside in Shropshire, with whom I'd struck up a friendship, took me out for a celebratory lunch. She had done brilliantly. I liked her because she was determined, shrewd, independent-minded, strong. I wish I had got to know her better. She reminded me of Audrey at the BM. These unconventional women swam into and out of my life and made a deep impression on me. I admired the way they seemed to have the courage to be themselves and not mind desperately what other people thought.

My short-term tenancy in Clapham Junction having expired, I was homeless. I packed my bags, collected together my pots and sticks of furniture.

Frances Wood of the British Museum, who had by now become a friend, suggested I move in with her. She had a spare room in the flat she rented in Pimlico. I had had tea with her there recently and relished her relaxed, bohemian way of living, her capacity for enjoyment. On that first visit to St George's Square, which was tucked away close to the river in SW1, I had realised how much I liked the district when I walked through the market in Tachbrook Street, just round the corner. Rag-and-bone men drove little painted carts, pulled by ancient nags, up and down it. A china shop at one end spread its wares across the pavement, the cups and bowls all bearing joky handwritten labels. One read: 'made by a romantic policewoman: she never gave her husband arrest'. Racks of second-hand clothes swayed next to arrays of junk. I picked through a basket of antique dishes and bought a nineteenth-century soup-plate, painted with a red and pink stylised design of flowers and whorled leaves, from the factory at Sarreguemines, for fifty pence. I've still got it: one of my few remaining possessions from that time.

St George's Square offered seedy grandeur. The ornate classical façades of what had been individual mansions now concealed multi-occupied rented flats and bedsits. Frances lived on the first floor of number 24, in what must have been the drawing-room but which, on account of its size, we called the ballroom. This imposing space had been unevenly divided by thin partitions. Frances had a large room: I slept in the high-ceilinged shoebox walled off on one side of it. We both had access to the balcony, overlooking the square, on which Frances grew flowers in big pots. Behind our rooms, a windowless space led to the tiny galley-style kitchen, in the former conservatory, enclosed by old frosted-glass doors. A deep old porcelain sink nudged a 1950s cooker, opposite a bath which could be covered by a board in the daytime and function as a work surface. Clothes dripped from wooden racks hung from the ceiling. Frances displayed on shelves her collection of green and turquoise speckled and stencilled Chinese enamel mugs, plates and dishes. She made coffee in an alarming screw-up aluminium pot which, at the vital moment, had to be turned upside down if it weren't to spew boiling coffee across the kitchen. She cooked well: the peasant dishes then in vogue along with stripped pine and brown pottery, a certain view of rustic simplicity created by Habitat – which of course had nothing to do with how the real peasants I knew in my French grandparents' village in Normandy actually lived, longing for hot water, indoor lavs, central heating and carpets. When friends came to supper we ate proper minestrone, proper soup with *pistou*, proper Parmesan. Some of the highly educated, well-mannered male visitors were sexist in a particularly gentle way, deprecating the fact that so many really nice girls were unliberated and boring.

Frances, black-haired, clever and funny, wearing chic Chinese silk jackets and trousers, laughed and barked out jokes and challenges and tolerated the streams of male admirers drawn by her beauty, originality, way with words. She was the Lady of the troubadours, calling down to her knights: boys, boys, just form an orderly queue. Her large, low double bed sported an apple-green seersucker duvet. This bright green flag to me signalled Frances's unconventionality. The favoured chap of the moment was called Mark LeFanu. A postgraduate student and film critic (and cousin of the Mark LeFanu who ran the Society of Authors), he was as clever as Frances. They argued passionately. Frances could always go one better and drop into Mandarin to find good insults: you're not worth the stomp of a duck's foot! Mark's twin brother James visited and captivated me immediately with his bright blue eyes, twisted smile, energy and charm. He talked as rapidly as machine-gun fire. Just down from Cambridge, studying to qualify in medicine, an ardent Communist, he edited the Communist medical students' magazine *Needle*.

With my short hair, unmade-up face and feminist politics, I sometimes felt like the dragon who guarded Frances's door (of course, when I look back at photos of that time, I seem merely sweet and ardent, sitting cross-legged on a mattress on the floor, wearing a long skirt and a multicoloured striped scarf, arguing shining-eyed, clutching a spliff). Frances was the queen of the flat and I her handmaiden. This was a role I had played before and would play again vis-à-vis charismatic, powerful women who stood in, on one level, as mother-figures, however unmaternal (in the conventional sense) they actually were. I admired Frances. Sometimes I envied her. Sometimes I wanted to fight her. She didn't toss and turn at night agonising about the feminist revolution. She was deeply interested in the Maoist revolution taking place in China but also strongly individualistic: that was her appeal. She was from a solidly academic and upper-middle-class background and seemed certain of her place in the world: aiming to become a Keeper at the British Museum, perfect her knowledge of Chinese, work as a Chinese scholar. I was opposed to this 'straight' world and to the privileges it dispensed to those who inhabited it, even though, of course, I had briefly been part of it. My politics would not allow me to re-enter it.

Deeper than politics was the sense, hardly articulated, that I was, in any case, shut out from it. It wasn't just class; that I came from a more ordinary middle-class background than Frances, Mark and James. In terms of class I was, indeed, privileged compared with many others: I had won a scholarship to grammar school, been encouraged to take A levels and S levels and apply to university, and had got through Oxford helped by a grant from the state, which my parents topped up, and by my own earnings from vacation jobs. I could subsequently have got a 'good' job, got a mortgage, but had not done so. Why was that? Why had I chosen to stay outside the system? Why did I feel outside, in the wilderness?

My disquiet had more to do with my sense that I had removed myself from being loved and accepted by my parents. I had left the Catholic Church, did not believe in God, had become a feminist and a socialist, refused to get a proper job, had lived in 'squalor', was determined to write, whatever the cost. Nana sent me a sweet letter: they will always forgive you, whatever you do. I didn't believe her. The Mother Superior in my head snarled that I was wicked because I was trying to think for myself, follow my own desires, find out what I wanted to do and act on it. I tried to ignore her. She surfaced at night, in bad dreams.

I applied for Social Security to tide me over temporarily while I tried to decide what job to apply for. Messages came from the Holloway communards reminding me that radical projects awaited. The free school was going well. I was supposed to be helping start a research centre and library, wasn't I? Nonetheless the collective at Fairmead Road was collapsing. People were deciding to go their own ways. The house would be sold.

A Social Security inspector came to interview me at St George's Square. I was out. Mark answered the door. The inspector asked to see the rent book in order to verify my claim. What rent book? asked Mark. The inspector said: so she's living with you, then? If you were a woman who shared a flat with a man you were assumed to be having sex with him. You therefore did not qualify for Social Security: the man would be keeping you in exchange for your giving him sex. I had been paying Frances rent every week but neither of us had bothered recording our transaction. I realised I would not get any Social Security. I'd better find a job quickly.

But what job to get? How to live? My attempt at loving a man of my own age, rather than a father-figure, was not going too well. Taking my radical philosopher lover to Paris for the weekend was disastrous and precipitated our break-up. He was more interested in seeking out a particular aftershave, made with juniper berries, on the Boulevard St Michel, than in having sex with me. He stayed aloof. I came home in tears. We stopped being lovers but continued our intense friendship. At last it dawned on me that he was actually gay.

Sarah LeFanu, the younger sister of Mark and James, came to stay in St George's Square for a couple of nights. She captivated me. She read voraciously, she was a feminist, she was very clever, she was very pretty, with a pale, pointed face, red curls tumbling to her shoulders, green eyes. An undergraduate at Cambridge as her brothers had been, during the summer vacation she was working nights as a waitress. She would come home at 3 a.m. and we would sit on the balcony, looking over the square, and she would eat sausages and drink cider (cheaper than beer) and tell me of her adventures in the restaurant. She was very honest. She always told the truth and openly said what she thought. I admired that. With Mark, I went up to see her in Cambridge once or twice. I remember a lunch-party in a big back garden, with a live rock band. We danced all afternoon and evening. Sarah saved up her wages in order to go off to Greece on holiday with her friend Jill Nicholls. I watched her pack. Her bag was too full and too heavy. No room for books. She opened the bag, took out half the clothes in it, put in volumes of philosophy in their place. Starting to love Sarah included believing that the intellectual life did matter. I knew I wanted to put writing at the centre of my life but did not yet dare admit it openly.

Friends invited me to go and squat with them in Camden Town. I hesitated. I still loved the peace and space at St George's Square. Mark and I would sit together in the evenings, drinking cider and chatting, waiting for Frances to come home from dinner with her hopelessly infatuated supervisor. Or I would go to the cinema and watch Godard movies. Or simply lope about the streets. I didn't know how to tell Terry that I wanted to end our relationship. I didn't know how to admit to the communards that I wanted a break from intense radical activity. I didn't know how to fund myself while I began writing. I felt trapped.

I picked up the *Guardian* and looked at the Jobs section.

Chapter Four

BANGKOK

With Sarah Dunant
and Sue Maingay

Bangkok airport, in the late evening, teemed with people, most of them much smaller and shorter than I. Exhausted and disorientated after my long flight, I stood guard over my suitcase in the middle of the vast, anonymous space of the Arrivals lounge, and waited for the British Council official due to meet me. I felt conspicuous, not only because of my height but also because of the sailor's trousers, from Lawrence Corner, that I was wearing, with button-up flap front. I had dyed them bright yellow. Here, all the tiny Thai women hurrying past, impeccably well groomed and neat, seemed to be wearing navy knee-length skirts and floral blouses with puff sleeves. I was wearing a blouse too, but a tatty second-hand Russian-style one, beribboned and smocked in scarlet. And instead of delicate slingbacks or sandals I was wearing boots. I was the only white giantess on the busy concourse. At least the Council colleague would have no trouble identifying me.

A young Thai man in a dark blue uniform, carrying his peaked cap under one arm, hurried up. Are you waiting for someone? he asked. The British Council, I replied. Fine, he cried: I'm so sorry to have kept you waiting. The car is this way. He picked up my case, ushered me out of the terminal.

The car turned out to be a jeep. In the back a crate of beer sat next to a pile of LPs. I got into the front seat. We roared off into the night: black, humid, smelling of dust. We zipped along a motorway planted on either side with dark, spiky shapes of bushes; oleanders, I guessed. Sparkling lines of traffic streamed in both directions.

My companion switched on the radio. It bleated pop music.

He began chatting away in American-flavoured English. What was I going to do in Bangkok? Would I travel over all of Thailand? Would I go to Pattaya beach? Most *farangs* went there. He grinned at me, with a sort of swagger.

I sat back in a cocoon of tiredness, barely conscious of what was going on around me. The hot plastic seat, the tinkling music, my companion's fresh-faced good looks, hardly registered. Nonetheless, unease began creeping through me. For several kilometres I ignored it, like the itch after an insect bite. The feeling persisted. Something was wrong.

I did not want to admit it. I did not want to find out that I was in trouble. I did not want to face the fact that I had got into the wrong car with the wrong man driving it.

Where the hell were we going? What was he up to? I roused myself and chatted brightly. Meaningless phrases to keep him happy while I thought about what to do. Plan A: if I pretended everything was OK and just played along then nothing bad would happen. Plan B: I would anticipate trouble and pretend it wasn't trouble and in that way keep one step ahead. This was the technique I had used on the streets in London when men harassed me and I was afraid they would turn violent if rebuffed: keep cool, humour them, wait for the moment when you can escape down a side street. Here in the speeding car on a foreign motorway there were no escape routes and I felt terrified. What would happen? Did he want to rob me, rape me, murder me? How could I have been so stupid as to believe him?

For a few more kilometres I stayed silent, sweating and worrying. Then, at last, I gathered my courage and broke through our joint pretence.

I've come to Bangkok to be the librarian for the British Council, I said: you're not from the British Council, are you?

No, I'm not, he said: I was one of the stewards on the plane.

88

You didn't notice me but I noticed you. I'm taking you to a party.

There's been a mistake, I said: please take me back to the airport.

He shrugged. I waited in terror. He sighed. Then he complied, doing a swift U-turn at the next junction. He had decided not to be a kidnapper after all. What would he turn into next? We roared back to the airport. It was dark and hushed; shut for the night.

Please take me to the British Embassy! I cried.

That, too, was closed and dark. Not a soul stirring. I had hoped for guards, or a porter, but blank gates faced us. Locked.

We drove off, down impersonal boulevards lined with tall office blocks. We tried the British Council building, with identical results. I got the young man to take me to several hotels, one after the other, but they were all full. I had no Thai money with which to pay a hotel bill (no credit cards in those days), no contact telephone numbers (no mobile phones in those days, either, as I've said before). All I had was a piece of official notepaper, the address of BC headquarters at its head: the letter I'd received in London telling me I would be met by someone from the Council.

We'll go to a motel, my companion finally said. I did not argue. Why was I so meek? I should have escaped when we stopped outside an hotel. But I was too scared of the strange town to run away into it on my own. Terror had made me passive and docile. I had given up believing I could sort this out. To stand up to this smooth young man felt impossible. He might be a psychopath; he might pull out a knife and stab me and throw my dead body into a canal. The force of his will had transfixed me. I might have feminist principles but I did not know how to stand up to a man at close quarters.

Ancient habits of obedience to authority-figures reasserted themselves.

We drove towards what the young man said was Chinatown. We entered a courtyard. The gates opened and then closed automatically behind us. Our headlights cut the dark. A pair of green plastic curtains swished round us, sealing us off from the outside world into a tiny alcove. We got out of the car. A door at the far end opened. In we went. We pay in the morning, my companion explained.

The space was bare and impersonal. Double bed, armchair, ceiling fan, shower cubicle with lavatory. I kept my clothes on. I took a sheet off the bed and wrapped myself tightly in it. I spent the night curled up in the armchair. Every time the young man approached me I croaked: I'm not going to sleep with you. I clutched the Gideon Bible I had found in the bedside table and read it in order to stay awake. The air-conditioning roared. My companion dozed on the double bed. In the early light he taught me to count up to five in Thai. Then he drove me through the traffic jam of rush-hour Bangkok. Wide, modern streets, lined with bland, modern shops. American-style advertisement hoardings. Buses, crammed with passengers, some of whom hung on to the footplate, the bumpers. Horns blared. People shouted. Policemen at junctions blew whistles. Sweat poured down me.

We got to Siam Square, a small, neat development of shops and restaurants. Here was the British Council, which we'd visited in the darkness the night before: a modern, pretty building, in pink-washed concrete, its low façade pierced by a row of round portholes instead of windows. I hopped out of the jeep. The young man drove quickly away. I picked up my suitcase, went inside. Air-conditioned coolness. I climbed a staircase curving up through a concrete well, spoke to a Thai receptionist in the foyer at the top. I must have looked a wreck: red-faced, dirty, sweaty, in crumpled and peculiar clothes. The receptionist politely directed me to an office next door. Here a white man in a short-sleeved shirt looked at me coldly. I'm the new librarian, I faltered. He spoke, with the same cold expression. Where have you been? People have been driving around half the night looking for you. What happened? I spent the night in a motel in Chinatown with a strange man I'd never met before, I explained.

The British Council and I soon realised we were not meant to stay together. Like mismatched lovers, at the beginning we had not imagined things would turn out badly. Everything had seemed so promising. I had convinced the three middle-aged men who interviewed me, at the London HQ, that I was the Right One. I was well educated, passionate, eloquent, a bit unconventional. I could talk the talk and walk the walk.

I had applied for the job, advertised in the *Guardian*, on impulse, almost whimsically. I was desperate to escape from the complications of my life in London. Here was a possible route out of trouble. The ad required a trained librarian to work in Bangladesh. I was considered too young to cope, so was sent to Bangkok instead, and the Bangkok librarian was sent to Bangladesh. The office gossip I picked up later on implied she had been banished after having a love affair with a married man on the staff. He, of course, did not get banished. I did most things wrong. I sent the King and Queen of Thailand stern reminders that their library books were overdue. I ordered *Gay Times* for the Periodicals section. I refused to wear makeup, high heels and smart mini-skirts, as requested, but strode about in cheesecloth draperies, hippy sandals and a semi-crewcut. I learned to speak Thai, which was not considered necessary. I hobnobbed with Thai people. I smoked Buddha grass. I argued with my misogynist white male colleagues who boasted about their adventures in the local massage parlours and brothels. Nor did I fit in with their wives, who, forbidden to work, held coffee mornings at which they boasted about their jewels and complained about their servants.

The British people in the office all considered themselves good liberals. Nobody took my politics seriously: they merely tolerated them. Colleagues yawned when I openly opposed the American war in Vietnam, criticised the American servicemen who came for rest and recreation to the Bangkok red-light district, questioned the way that the Council automatically had to tiptoe after the Foreign Office and support the American government. At the moment we were backing America not only to invade Vietnam but also to bomb Cambodia. My woolly socialism began to firm up. I opposed the Americans' war. So what the hell was I doing here?

My alternative lifestyle (too many parties involving 'dubious' locals), loudly expressed incorrect opinions, and lack of restraining male influence, were bound to get me into trouble. I was eventually suspected of drug-smuggling, I found out much later. Apparently (so the possibly apocryphal story went) someone was passing heroin via the BC library, using cut-out sections of *Gray's Anatomy* to pack the drugs into. The Foreign Office, I was told, kept a tail on me.

They'd have seen me exploring the food markets, the canals, the temples, going on outings with Thai colleagues to sacred sites, learning from my female colleagues how to cook Thai food. When I remember Thailand it is through visual images, brightly coloured details; the part standing for the whole. An old Chinese woman on a packed bus, in faded blue, freshly ironed smock and trousers, her hair in a small grey bun, holding my basket for me on her knees because I was standing up.

The printed labels on bunches of joss sticks, matchboxes, bottles of Tiger beer. Saffron-robed monks, seated in a circle on the ground, being attended to by an outer ring of barbers. Topiary elephants, monsters, snails, and squirrels by the side of a dusty road. Tiny wooden hotels perched above the river on stilts. A purple bed-curtain printed with blue flowers. White jasmine petals in the dusty corner of a temple courtyard. A huge golden Buddha lying on his side on the ground, propping his head on one hand. Smells too: frangipani and jasmine; dry dust and river water and rotting rubbish; durian fruit and chilli and coriander.

When I arrived at the Council that first morning, and blurted out my tale, I was immediately packed off to a hotel for three days. This was standard practice, to enable one to recover from jetlag. The hotel room, its big plate-glass window veiled in nylon, was huge and bleak. I could have been in any large city in the world. I opened the wardrobe to stow some clothes away and a cockroach leapt out, long feelers waving. I screamed then smashed it with my shoe.

A basket of bananas, bearing a welcoming card, stood on the table. For three days, nobody came near me or spoke to me; I felt I was in solitary confinement. I was exhausted and jetlagged but could not sleep. I felt too ill and too scared to venture outside. I ate the bananas and tried to read. I was still in shock after having been kidnapped. I kept feeling I had dissolved, melted into the grey nylon curtains.

On the third night I was summoned to a drinks party at the Council, held to celebrate the opening of an art exhibition. In the hotel boutique I bought myself a smart new outfit: a long brown wrap-around batik skirt, and a yellow wrap-around top like a dancer's cardigan. Off I went in a taxi. In the large upstairs salon, with its pale wood flooring and long blue curtains shutting out the evening, we drank tall glasses of whisky weakened with much soda and ice. I was passed from group to group of local academics, teachers and businessmen: here at last is the new librarian. I smiled and nodded and chatted. I don't remember the art we were supposed to be celebrating; I was feeling too strange. Everybody was immensely well dressed and polite. A blur of calm faces. I met two English people of my own age: Sue and Peter Maingay, both teaching English for the Council. We eyed each other and knew we would make friends. Another young teacher, Arthur, short, very wirily built, with a shock of black hair, swept me up. The party was ending. We should eat. He took me off in his small sports car to the late-night food-stalls in the market to eat mussels. Obviously trying to impress me, he drove very fast. I hung on as we skidded around corners. The market certainly impressed me: the corrugated-iron food-stalls, the open-air cooking, the shouting and arm-waving, the total lack of white people. Arthur spoke fluent Thai. He joked with the serving-man. I had hated his driving but admired his language skills. We ate mussels with chilli, in steaming broth, extremely fiery, lemony and delicious. Everybody wiped their mouths on wisps of paper napkin which they then dropped on the ground. We sat in a litter of greasy white paper and cigarette butts. Smoke swirled from the grills. Strings of light bulbs swayed overhead. The dark night smelled of fried fish and jasmine and burning charcoal. Drinking a beer, I felt happy. This was the real Bangkok.

Violent pains began to stab my insides. I clutched my stomach and said nothing. Arthur paid the bill. His air grew proprietorial. He clearly expected to take me back to his house and fuck me but I begged to be driven back to my hotel, saying I felt very ill. He shrugged and looked angry, but did as I asked. All night I felt pierced by daggers. I threw up, had diarrhoea, threw up some more. I phoned Reception through veils of pain and begged for a doctor. He came at last, in the middle of the night, when I was almost unconscious with agony, and diagnosed food-poisoning.

I spent a further three days at the hotel, unable to get out of bed. Arthur phoned one night, saying he had been convinced I was lying when I'd said I felt ill: just a coy ruse. On the third day I got into work. Everything and everybody was very shiny and bright, very sharp, with edges that felt stabbing, like the food-poisoning. I'd been floating all over the place, ill and lonely. I had to bring myself back, get things into focus, stay alert, behave professionally. I could do all that. But life in the air-conditioned concrete Council bunker went on feeling completely unreal and I went on feeling deeply unhappy. Briskly my colleague Beryl told me that culture shock afflicted whites abroad: you just had to get over it. Beryl was tall and long-legged and looked good in mini-skirts. She had rosy cheeks and dark curly hair. She tried to be kind to me and make friends but we were from different planets. She had learned to be jolly and merry. She chaffed the men and pretended not to be offended at their anti-women jokes. You had to be a good sport and not let them see that they had hurt you. Beryl had been hurt quite enough in her life, she told me in a rare moment of self-revelation. She had built her defences of becoming a chap among the chaps, a competent bureaucrat. She had no time for people being emotional and oversensitive. She played along and so should everybody else.

The Council had arranged for me to stay in my predecessor's flat on the Sukhothai Road, a couple of kilometres from the office. Accordingly, I moved in. Once my trunk arrived, wobbling up on a little tin rickshaw-lorry, I pinned up my Cuban revolutionary posters, laid out my brown pottery coffee set, made the bed with my brown sheets. That stylish 1960s colour seemed all wrong here; when I looked outside, at least. The little garden behind the block of flats blazed with scarlet and purple and pink blossoms. The tiny swimming-pool sparkled turquoise. Climbing the concrete stairs to the second floor I left all that brilliance and light behind. The flat was gloomy, with heavy mahogany doors and polished dark wood floors. It boasted two sepulchral bedrooms, big plate-glass windows draped with floor-length fir-green curtains, a balcony, a dining area complete with formal table and chairs. The antique air-conditioning system roared.

Even more overwhelming than this sombre interior was the presence of a maid. She begged me to keep her on as she so desperately needed the money. I complied, but felt very ashamed of having a servant. It seemed immoral that another woman should have to take care of me. She went to the market for me and cooked my food as well as doing the cleaning. After a few months she vanished, along with my few bits of jewellery and all the money in my purse. I learned afterwards she was known to gamble heavily. I did not hire another servant. I did not miss the embarrassment and shame I had felt at being a rich white *farang* but I did miss the sapphire and pearl ring she had stolen. It had belonged to my French grandmother and my mother had given it to me. I felt bad that I hadn't properly taken care of my mother's gift.

Every morning I went in to work along the Sukhothai Road, which whirled with dust and construction works, seethed with traffic. The weather was extremely hot and humid. If I walked, skipping up and down over the uneven pavement and potholes, I arrived red-faced and soaked in sweat. The buses were always crammed so full that I did not dare try to board, people leaning out of the windows, bunched on the bumpers, the front steps, clinging to the handles of the door, waving as they went by, laughing at the panting, scarlet-cheeked giantess. I gave up and took taxis. You bargained for the fare and then got in. Sometimes I hailed an official yellow taxi, sometimes a motorised rickshaw. We swerved and lurched along, nipping back and forth around lorries, switching lanes at a second's notice. The hectic car ballet was punctuated with blaring horns. This was a dominant version of modern Bangkok: a steamy traffic jam. On arriving at Siam Square I entered another world: hushed and chilly. The office was air-conditioned; I shivered in my little back room. Unless I invented excuses to leave it and go upstairs, perhaps with a query or an armful of files, I saw scarcely anybody all day long. I sat behind my desk and stared at the closed door and jumped every time the phone rang. I was just pretending to be a proper librarian. Sooner or later I'd get found out.

Gradually, learning about the job, I discovered that I wasn't free, in any case, to decide what books to buy for the library here in Bangkok, what books to send up-country or to the libraries in Cambodia and South Vietnam for which I also had responsibility. Everything was already mapped out. I was helping dish out government aid according to particular, precise political and economic constraints. That was the Council's *raison d'être*. To be of political use to our government and our dominant partner North America. The Thais would benefit as a side-effect. Roads, for example, would get built if they were of use to the Americans or to big business. In the end I came to realise you did not have to decide much at all. You had the illusion of free and independent decision-making. The structures already existed and you just had to gallop within them, a charming beribboned pony between the shafts of the Council chariot. For example, one of my jobs was dishing out British Government books aid to Thai universities. So my deputy librarian, Khun Pat, arranged my visits to libraries and accompanied me and I just smiled and shook hands with the relevant people and then put the relevant file in the Out tray.

I hung on for seven months. I'd probably have got the sack if I hadn't given in my notice first.

I collapsed early one morning. Having resolved to learn Thai, I went to a 6 a.m. class, along with a few Unesco officials and a couple of men from the British Embassy. I had become quite friendly with one of them, a middle-aged Scotsman called John. Together we chanted our verbs. When the teacher wanted us to practise 'I do not like' by singsonging 'I do not like Communists, I do not like the Vietcong', I refused and firmly said I disliked dried shrimps. John raised his sandy eyebrows. He liked chatting to me, though. Sometimes he gave me a lift to the Council after class. He introduced me to his son Fred. Aged sixteen, Fred had run away from public school. Now nineteen, he was drifting around the world, following his father from posting to posting, while he tried to decide what to do. He would come to my flat in the late afternoon, when I got back from work, and smoke Buddha grass with me. He brought along LPs. He introduced me to The Velvet Underground and David Bowie and lent me his copies of *Rolling Stone*. In return I gave him my *Oz* trial T-shirt, emblazoned with the picture of Rupert Bear sporting his huge erection. Fred, lanky and golden-haired, was very easy to be with. In his company I felt peaceful and ordinary. We had a sweet, calm friendship, lolling in stoned silence, just listening to music. When we did talk, I knew he trusted me to listen to his anguished tales of childhood and not repeat his secrets. He was not close to his father.

When I suddenly burst into tears in the Thai class one morning and could not stop crying, John offered to drive me home.

He saw me up to my flat and waited while I opened the door. Before I could get inside and shut it again, he jumped me, kissing me and pawing me, trying to pull up my shirt. I shoved him out and slammed the door and burst into tears all over again.

The doctor diagnosed culture shock and provided tranquillisers. People in the office sent Get Well Soon messages. I knew I was not ill. I was unhappy and angry, full of conflicts I could not yet cope with. I downed the pills anyway. They calmed me, soothed my ever-present mosquito bites, which were always turning into tropical ulcers and causing me agony, and helped me to sleep at night.

I sat in my flat with the air-conditioning turned off, the windows open, the humid air crawling over my hot skin, wrote my diary, tried to sort out my thoughts. I realised that my two lives were tearing me apart. Neither of them corresponded to what I thought of as my 'true' self, whatever that was. Perhaps there wasn't one? But something buried inside was trying to break out. I covered it up by performing two roles. By day I pretended, and more or less succeeded, to act as the BC librarian, smiling and nice and reasonably efficient. I had bottled up my distress when, in the course of my brief visit to organise books aid to Cambodia, I visited one of the refugee camps in Phnom Penh and saw the havoc caused by the American bombing, the suffering of local people. I had miserably accepted that I was part of the machinery that let the bombing raids happen. I poured out my anguish and anger to my diary. Then by contrast, at night and at the weekend I lived like a hippy, wandering around Chinatown and the Thieves' Market, the back alleys and wharves and waterfronts, smoking dope, holding wild parties which upset the landlord, swimming nude with friends in the pool at night, which upset him still further, hanging out with people not on the Council circuit: artists, dealers, musicians, travellers. With my few Council friends I tried to straddle both worlds. With Sue and Peter Maingay I discussed psychology, politics and the counterculture, went on holiday to Laos, to Burma. With Arthur I also discussed politics a great deal. With the Maingays we went away for weekends, explored the national parks. Back in Bangkok, travellers, alerted by the grapevine, came to stay. I cooked for them. My housework was rudimentary. I didn't notice the cigarette burns on the edge of the coffee-table. This upset the landlord yet again.

The person I felt closest to was Sue Maingay: very intelligent, wryly humorous, unconventional, subtle, discreet. Small and slender, with silky brown hair, she had an enchanting wide grin. We talked to each other a lot. Sue observed my various foolish sexual adventures with kindness and went on being my good friend.

In those days many people (middle-class ones, anyway) seemed to think that only men were interested in sex. It felt difficult being a young woman aged twenty-two seething with sexual desire. The Catholic Church divided women into evil temptresses or holy, sexless mothers. I had been taught that pre-marital sex was wicked, that adolescent sexual desires were wicked. Girls supposedly did not have desire, but had to control and prevent boys' desires. As a feminist I loved, desired and also resented men. I didn't believe in marriage, was fed up with men harassing me, thought I was anti-romantic, yet longed for a sexual companion.

I began a love affair with Bertie, a colleague in the office, eight years older than myself.

Bertie was warm, sensual, loving, playful, sweet. We had a lovely time in bed. I discovered I wasn't frigid after all. Bertie understood and liked women's bodies. With him I found it was easy to come. He was the first lover with whom I had real pleasure. I think I was his escape from the Council as he was mine. I was his refuge from having to be a proper grown-up, a proper, repressed, unemotional, respectable white chap. In bed we could be two children playing whatever games we wanted; no holds barred. Bertie had read the *Kama Sutra*. Right. We experimented, knotting ourselves together, trying out impossible contortions, playing dares and forfeits, putting on silly costumes, acting erotic theatre we invented at whim, laughing. I cut my hair even shorter, pretending to be a boy, because that turned Bertie on. I had seen Suzy Seven-Up in a bar on Patpong smoking seven cigarettes through her cunt at once: I showed Bertie that I could do the same. We wrote each other poems and love letters, gave each other tiny presents: pebbles, feathers, single flowers. Sex astonished me: so passionate, easy, happy, sometimes joyful, sometimes comic. We larked about rather than talked too much. I steered clear of our political differences, which did not fit my fantasy. We smoked a lot of dope and drank a lot of champagne. Inside our tiny world, wholly centred on bed, we were equals, innocents, and there were no clichés. Adam and Eve dancing naked in the paradise garden; before the Fall.

Another traveller turned up asking for use of the guest room. Sarah Dunant had been given my address by an old friend from Oxford. She had been working as a bar hostess in Japan and was now on her way through South-East Asia, making for Bali. She arrived just as I had given a month's notice. She was small, sexy and vivacious, bubbling with hippy slang. Women were ladies. I gave her a buzz. People could be very fine. They shouldn't be heavy. Sometimes she got the blue meanies. Bertie and I were getting it together. This new language took me into a new country. I fell in love with what Sari represented:

lightheartedness; adventurousness; the uncomplicated search for pleasure.

Sari moved in. Both of us, in secret, examined the other's clothes. Sari's rucksack was crammed with brightly coloured long skirts, little wrap tops. She approved of the embroidered jeans I wore when away from the office. She and I got very close very quickly, staying up for hours talking, smoking dope. She joined in my escapades with Bertie, coming out for extended lunch hours, perching on our bed with us and chatting, arranging funny poses for nude photos *à trois*. This was a threesome (not a sexual one, though) that worked, perhaps because we played friends not father-mother-daughter. Sari sat about in my office half the day, talking. For my farewell sherry party at the Council we made each other dresses out of pages of *Oz*. How pleased the Council staff must have been to see the back of me.

I scooted away with Sari, on the overnight train to Malaysia. We travelled mostly by bus after that, through Kuala Lumpur, Malacca, Jakarta, Bali. We called ourselves travellers, because we stayed in cheap, basic guest-houses rather than hotels, but of course, like any other white Westerners on the hippy trail, we were tourists: far, far richer than the local people. For a while I tried to ignore the contradictions of my life, just as I had in Bangkok, and to give myself up to hedonism in the way that Sari did. She called me Mimi (my family name) as Bertie did, and I liked this new self the nickname revealed: affectionate, happy, irresponsible, unafraid. I liked my new disguise: wide, long trousers in thin cotton, long-sleeved Indian thin cotton shirt, flat sandals, straw hat. I wanted to be unobtrusive; not a voyeur; to see but not to be seen. Sari was more flamboyant and more impatient of male-defined dress-codes governing women in Muslim cultures. In Malaysia she sometimes went braless;

bare-legged in shorts or a mini-skirt. Small boys followed us in gangs, throwing stones. Each time we had to run away. Women on their own, inappropriately dressed for male sensibilities, were deemed to be asking for it, just like in London. On Bali, with its animist Hindu culture, a place in which the local women often walked around topless, it was all right for us to sunbathe half-naked on the beach. But, wrapped from throat to knee in a sarong, walking back to your hut, you often got jumped by Indonesian soldiers and had to fight them off. The male hippies we met told us to cool it, babes: these guys can't take it.

Many local people showed us exquisite kindness and hospitality. Mr Low, in whose shabby, very pretty guest-house we stayed in Kuala Lumpur (after booking into a brothel by mistake and wondering why the room had swing doors and kept being barged into by strange men), lent us a map and gave us cups of sweet sludgy tea, clove-scented cigarettes, good advice. The plaster walls of our room were washed in faded amethyst, lavender and peacock. The stained-glass window held panes of pale strawberry, lime, orange, mauve. A flowered woollen sheet covered our hard double bed. We kept our journals, and our cups of tea, on the marble-topped round table. The dressing-table had china-handled drawers. A frieze of ants raced around the walls at waist level. Mr Low took us out for fried noodles and showed us the market. I loved the street furniture: the banners and awnings; the ice-crushing machines in cast iron painted pale green and pink and decorated with wrought-iron fish and swans; the bright brass urns, adorned with brass bees and eagles, which dispensed a honey drink. Mr Low dispatched us to mosques, to temples whose floors were patched with prayer rugs; under colonnades square stone pools, filled with green water, sent flickering reflections up on to the underside of the roof. Mr Low's kindness and gentleness made up for the bullying of the gangs of men who followed us around, shouting angrily. I began to shout back, eventually, scared of provoking their violence but unable to take the hassling any more.

To record all these images I bought exercise books, from the market stationery stalls, with cloth spines, squared paper and marbled blue cardboard covers with green corners, blue-edged labels on which you wrote your name. I wanted to write everything down: impossible. I learned that you had to discriminate, choose, trust your own perceptions. I went on writing poetry as well as keeping a diary, drew up lists of short stories I planned to write. The experiences and conflicts of the last year began to form themselves into ideas for a novel which I scribbled down and kept secret. A journey, I discovered, was like writing: pushing into narrative. You had to invent it (invent from Latin *invenio* – 'I come upon'), step by step, faltering into the unknown. What tugged you along? Chance. Your own desire. Others' nudges.

We lived for six weeks in a straw-roofed hut on Bali beach, hiring motorbikes to ride up into the hills to see temples and watch village productions of the *Ramayana*, ecstatically tripping on magic mushrooms, experimenting with opium, making casual friends in passing. I left Sari with this new gang of people and returned for a brief visit to Bangkok to enjoy a stolen trip to the seaside with Bertie. We stayed in an old colonial hotel surrounded by flowering gardens. We argued, cried, talked. I was often what Sari called 'heavy'. I was not ready to make a long-term commitment, much as I adored Bertie and adored the lovely times we had in bed. Bertie didn't like my feminism when it led to my becoming anguished and didactic. He didn't like what he felt was my pompously expressed socialism. He didn't like my poetry either. Too complicated, darling.

I decided I needed to return to England.

The dear Maingays put me up temporarily in their little house on stilts, complete with pond, reeds, kingfishers. Bertie would arrive and slide into bed with me very early in the morning, under the mosquito net, in the exquisite coolness just before dawn. Another bubble; time suspended; no real world. Then, after that tiny world of delight got broken up by clocks, he would have to go and I would read or wander the streets. I explored the neighbourhood evening by evening; full of ordinary Thai people going about their lives; very different from the nouveau smartness of Sukhothai Road. Peter, Sue, Bertie and I went to Thai and Chinese films, to a Thai boxing match, ate at cheap food-stalls, hung out with Thai artist and teacher friends. On one occasion Bertie and I picnicked in a park, watching old ladies perform martial arts with wondrous dexterity, and then, drunk, we hired a room for an hour in a motel. Swisher than the one in which I'd spent my first night in Bangkok, with a mirrored ceiling. Afterwards we went for a massage. The sexes were shown into different parts of the parlour. My massage was done with a sort of rolling-pin. You lay naked under a sheet while the bored masseuse thumped you. Bertie said, later on, that he'd been offered the full sexual relief service. Then we went to the late-night food-stalls and ate fiery Lao chicken.

A few days later I took a taxi to the airport and got on the plane home. In the transit lounge at Hong Kong an elderly Chinese man, very well dressed, with a mahogany face, chatted me up. He needed a new live-in mistress and thought I would do. I was very slender and brown after the weeks on Bali beach. I was young. I was wearing one of Sue Maingay's mini-skirts I'd walked off with. He promised me a flat and a diamond ring. I said no.

Chapter Five

CAMBERWELL

Launch of 'A Piece of the Night', with
Ruthie Petrie, Rosie Parker and Alison Fell

Returning to England in December 1973, I hitched to Bristol to visit Mum and Dad. I spent a few days at home with my family; seeing how they were; collecting the suitcase of clothes and belongings I'd stowed there. Nana had been very ill. Mum was exhausted from looking after her and from work. She and Dad were appalled that I had given up a safe, secure job as a librarian and chosen instead to make writing my priority. How could I be so mad as to dream of becoming a writer? I would never make it. I would fail.

Despite their disapproval, however, I felt determined to stick to my decision. Looking back, I know I felt driven to write. Writing meant voyaging into the unknown and having adventures; asserting myself and my capacity to tell tales. I had written ever since I was five years old. Perhaps the Catholic notion of vocation helped. Your own individual desire (which the Mother Superior inside you disapproved of) could be linked to the idea of something bigger than yourself urging you on.

Dad had dreamed of writing, once. Immediately after the war he had written some humorous stories about army life which he showed to me, when I was nine or so. I was baffled by the stories' long-winded style. I realise, now, that Dad, like many self-educated people, believed that he had to prove he was intelligent by showing he could weave elaborate sentence constructions. He had educated himself through reading. The bookcase in the sitting-room was stuffed with classic novels, also with tales of masculine derring-do such as the *Stalky and Co.* series by Dornford Yates, the Hornblower series by C.S. Forester, *Beau Geste* and *Beau Sabreur* by P.C. Wren and with volumes of history by Winston Churchill. Dad would have loved to have gone to university but didn't get the chance. He didn't get published, either. His stories had been rejected, one after the other. Dimly I felt his sadness. I couldn't say to him what I felt, neither in elaborate sentences nor in simple ones.

I took the train back to London: properly December-cold; grubby and grey. 'Doris Lessing grime,' I wrote in my diary, remembering her descriptions, in *The Four-Gated City*, of London after the war. I felt like her heroine Martha Quest, a stranger arriving in unfamiliar streets. Like Martha, I wished for adventures. First of all, though: some winter clothes. I unpacked my old black woollen Biba trousers and put them on. How scratchily odd to be wearing heavy wool once more. Like going back to school after the summer holidays and donning a serge skirt. That same shock of difference.

London quickly became home again. My friend Lin, from the street theatre group, gave me temporary accommodation in Finsbury Park. She and her husband Roger shared their tall terrace house in Ridge Road, walled with books, with two other women friends from the street theatre group. Lin had just given birth to her daughter Elly: we gathered around, adoring god-mothers. The atmosphere was gentle, domestic and intellectual. Roger, who taught philosophy at Middlesex Polytechnic, seemed to enjoy, rather than just tolerate, living with a group of feminists. We gave him plenty of debating practice, over plenty of wine at supper, and he was always able to pull down a book from the shelves to back up his argument. The house was very much his and Lin's domain, but we all helped cook and clean. I signed on briefly at Wood Green labour exchange while I looked for a job. Wood Green was charming, a sort of industrial village. I admired the redbrick architecture: the Barratts sweet factory, the small Victorian terrace of houses with a clock-tower in the middle. The railway cutting sliced through the small local parks. From the top of Lin's house, on its high ridge in Finsbury Park, sticking my head out of the attic window I could see the Ally Pally on its own hill, crisply outlined against the clear, bright sky tinted with pink and blue. Bristling black trees. A swarm of red roofs rushing downwards.

Sarah LeFanu's brother James had become a friend. He had written me occasional letters while I was away, one, in response to my enthusiasm over Marcuse, denouncing him as a senile old wanker, and another announcing his resignation from the Communist Party. What were the reasons he gave? I don't remember. Anyhow, he was now a stalwart of the Labour Party. I went over to Stepney Green to visit James and his friend Bob in their squat, chosen because it was near the London Hospital where they both trained, and ended up spending the whole weekend with them. Carnival time. We played uncomplicatedly: walking past the docks, drinking in riverside pubs, burying James in leaves at Blackheath, listening to a steel band in a pub and then dancing at a party in Brixton. After the party, back at Stepney we got stoned, danced rock 'n' roll, dressed up and played more invented games. James and Bob acted a boxing match for me, bringing on not hefty punches but hefty volumes by hard-hitting left-wing thinkers, Marcuse duly vanquished by Marx and Engels. The burlesque went on most of the night until, worn out laughing, we all fell asleep on the floor. In the morning, arm-in-arm the three of us went off to Brick Lane, where I bought a 1920s Charleston dress and James and Bob bought black nightshirts. Lunch of curry puffs and sweets in a Pakistani café, then on to the bus and back to Stepney for more cups of tea, a fashion parade, more dancing. Later, Bob gave me a lift home on his motorbike. Roaring through the east London night I felt ecstatic.

Sarah LeFanu was squatting nearby with friends in Mayola Road, Mile End (her street has now vanished under the greenery of the new park). Evenings out together meant the local pub. Sarah got into trouble with barmen because she drank pints and they felt it wasn't ladylike. They tried to serve her in daintily stemmed half-pint glasses, which Sarah indignantly refused. Sarah was now working as a fund-raiser for the British Hospital in Vietnam, a charitable organisation based in the anteroom of a church near the Portobello Road. Ladies draped in black lace mantillas crouched over their rosaries at the Virgin's altar, looking like curled wisps of black ash. Beyond them shone Sarah, a rosy-faced angel with a mop of red-gold curls. She bicycled everywhere. She rode a splendidly old-fashioned woman's bike, which let her wear 1950s frocks without hazard and transport treats in the big basket. Sometimes, if we'd been out to a party together and come back late, I'd spend the night at her squat, and in the morning we'd loll around together in our white Victorian nightdresses, drinking tea and talking. The house was cold and damp, with an outside lavatory. I remember the kitchen best, where we sat and talked over the supper Sarah cooked up. We were fond of huge platefuls of spaghetti carbonara: fuel for all the cross-town bicycling we did.

My method of earning a living while I started writing greatly upset my parents. I had managed to get two part-time temporary jobs: one as a clerk at a unit that did sociological research, and one as a pregnancy tester for the Pregnancy Advisory Service near Cavendish Square, a charity which helped women get abortions if they could not get them on the NHS. Abortion was legally allowed on medical or psychiatric grounds, if two doctors agreed that the pregnancy threatened the woman's physical or mental health, but many GPs were against it. Desperate women therefore turned to sympathetic doctors in the private sector. Mum, as a devout Catholic, opposed abortion and was appalled I chose to work for the PAS.

Frances Wood's new boyfriend, Tim, an Oxford don, had bought a house, as an investment, in Talfourd Road, on the borders of Peckham and Camberwell, and needed tenants to pay off his mortgage. Tim offered me a room at £5 a week, which seemed a cheap rent (less than I'd paid in Regent's Park a few years earlier). Perfect: I was saved from the slog of finding somewhere I could afford. I accepted immediately. I took the bus down to south London to have a look.

Foreign parts, these; dangerous, even. North Londoners did not cross the river; dared not venture into the wilderness beyond Waterloo; held it in contempt. The urban myth named south London a fearful place, full of villains. Camberwell Green looked placid enough as we trundled through it. I admired a Greek taverna on one corner, the doorway festooned with pink plastic roses, grapes, fishing-nets and wine bottles. Just as I got off the bus, two men, walking along in front of me, suddenly stopped short in their tracks then shot backwards and hid behind a hoarding. Armed robbery in the mean streets! A horse came galloping along riderless, its bridle and reins flying free, and headed off towards Camberwell Green, three panda cars in pursuit. The Lone Ranger was nowhere to be seen.

Tim's house turned out to be run-down, very shabby and dirty, mice-ridden, lacking a hot-water system and a kitchen. That didn't deter me. Beggars can't be choosers. I was being offered a home. I grabbed it.

Talfourd Road comprised two facing rows of solid, late-Victorian terraces interspersed with a little housing estate, filling in a gap made by wartime bombs, and a pub. At the end of the street the fine Edwardian fire station reared up, and on the far side of the main road you saw the squat redbrick façade of Camberwell Art School. Just around the corner was Kennedy's Sausages, one of a small local chain of butcher's shops, with a splendid 1920s sunburst window. You could buy meat pies there, over the marble-topped counter, and yellow slabs of Cheddar, and tins of baked beans. I used to dash down to Kennedy's to buy a slice of cheese for lunch, whizzing past the singleted firemen playing volleyball in their yard, whistling and catcalling as I sped by. Men on the Camberwell/Peckham borders seemed not used to young women in jeans, with short hair, a springy step. If I dawdled, or stopped to look at a shop window, they would sidle up behind me and hiss: lesssbian!

Tim's house had a big pillared porch, a basement area, a lean-to bathroom and lavatory, and behind it a long garden in which Frances planted honeysuckle. Backing on to our garden was that of Mr Salmon, an old Cockney who seemed to have lived here since at least the eighteenth century; to be history incarnate. He leaned over the fence and watched me mark out and dig a vegetable patch, fertilising it with horse shit from the local police station stables (where, doubtless, that riderless horse belonged) and with lime. Mr Salmon pointed to his walnut trees and described how they had once formed part of an orchard. The farm on this spot was long gone. He told me about Camberwell Green's dairy, how Londoners used to come out here to buy milk and eggs, how cows used to graze on the Green in the olden days, how it had been used as a mass grave in the last war. When you walk on the Green you're walking on layers of human bones! He was a dedicated gardener. He called plants 'subjects' and talked about them as though they were people. Gentle and funny, he accepted me in a calm and unquestioning way. He reminded me of my beloved Londoner grandfather, Grandpa, who smoked a pipe, cracked jokes, enchanted me by accepting my gifts of drawings and placing them in his inside pocket over his heart, and grew rows of sweet peas in his little back garden. I recorded Mr Salmon's words and later put them into the novel I'd begun writing. I wanted to remember him and putting him into a book seemed a good way to do it. Mr Salmon died a couple of years after I moved into the district, and his house was sold.

People die but their words go on, as long as someone's listened to them. The words last inside our memories of each other. We knot ourselves into the past, further and further back. We push through death; story loops back into story; we encounter the dead. Today my mother tells me tales of her two grandmothers, Thérèse and Pauline, and they come alive for me, and the room seethes with dead people talking. That's what history means to me: listening to the voices of the dead, feeling connected to the dead, that they are still here with us now. Writing means bearing witness to other people's stories as well as my own. Searching for those lost others. It begins in infancy. The mother vanishes and the child calls out for her and so speech begins. The child tries to lure her mother back, tries to capture her in a net of words, angry and passionate and tender. The child weaves her myth of belonging and not-belonging. The web of words breaks. The child starts telling another story. She searches for and finds mother, grandmother, great-grandmother, ancestor, neighbour, acquaintance. She makes them up: finding means inventing. Loving people means receiving their stories. Hearing their stories makes you love them. I've shuddered all over with delight when doing research and I've heard voices swim up out of seventeenth-century Inquisition records, out of eighteenth-century law records. Ordinary people talking. Their stories are not lost. Writing (the transcripts of the authorities trying them in lay or ecclesiastical courts) has preserved their voices: here they are, talking to me. I become their witness.

That love of language from the past took root in secondary school, when for English O level we read extracts from John Evelyn's diary. I couldn't believe it: a man from the seventeenth century was talking to me and telling me what he thought about gardening, his son Dick's death, the ladies of Venice in their high-heeled pattens. No wonder I went on to study the history of the English language at university. The voices of the dead sprang alive and one form of the Old English language evolved into another, Middle English one, and (with a fair bit of struggle and slog) I could try to understand all these different languages.

No wonder I loved my chance encounters with people in the streets. Strangers afforded me moments of intimacy, let me glimpse their lives. I cherished these meetings. They seemed pure; not filled with my need and hunger for love (I still couldn't always approve of those). Londoners' turns of phrase delighted me: so original, deft, witty. Their tales fell on me like showers of presents. The people I met by chance and talked to then walked away or got off the bus but their words stayed with me and then later on I wrote them down. My casual encounters with Londoners made me feel connected; not an alien outsider but part of the human race. People gave me tiny vignettes of their lives and I carried these home with me and treasured them. These short conversations broke me out of myself and joined me into the great web of the city. First of all the words were in the streets and then they moved into the house, into my diary.

My fellow tenants were much fiercer than our gentle neighbour Mr Salmon. Celia, one of the other former inhabitants of Frances's flat in St George's Square, moved in, and her good friend Dani, another Australian. Dani was small, blonde and neat, with little gold-rimmed specs. She was an ardent feminist, also ferociously Marxist and ultra-left. She denounced Tim for being an absentee landlord living off rents, exploiting people's need for housing. She denounced bourgeois ideas and art forms; a con to lull the masses. She denounced Samir, her Lebanese lover, when he moved in, for his weakness and passivity in the face of her ferocity. She denounced Sari, who had returned from Bali and moved into the attic floor with her artist friend Jude, for being a hippy, a hedonist, a liberal. Sari wisely lived a separate life upstairs, with Jude tucked into the small room next door to hers. In their plant-filled domain the pleasure principle reigned: dope, laughter, loud rock music, incense. Weekends away with gangs of friends on the Suffolk coast. Parties every Saturday night. Outings to open-air Van Morrison concerts. Sari would sit cross-legged on her big low bed, stitching away at her patchwork quilt, writing her diary in her big A4 notebook in her distinctive square black handwriting, and cheerfully ignoring politics. Keep on trucking! Peace and love! Sari was training to be a radio producer at the BBC and believed in enjoying herself. I did too, when I wasn't racked with guilt at my bourgeois individualism. I would run upstairs to be a hedonist in the attic, then run downstairs to be a proper revolutionary in Dani's room.

I allowed Dani to dominate me. I didn't know how to stand up to her. She took over the job of Mother Superior in my head, acted as an authority-figure who despised me for my personal inadequacies and political confusions. For Dani everything was clear-cut. She had begun reading Lacan and Althusser. Everything I enjoyed was apparently Only Ideology. What about when you walk down the garden in the indigo dusk and smell the flowers' scent and think rapturous thoughts? I asked. That's Only Ideology, Dani said firmly.

Her politics did mean she gave people practical support. She made friends with the Chilean family across the road in the council estate, plonked there by NALGO, the trade union who'd sponsored them, who were isolated, lonely and spoke little English. They had gone into exile after Manuel, as a trade-union organiser, had been tortured with electric shocks under Pinochet. Manuel was often, unsurprisingly, in a bad nervous state. I don't think any help was offered him. He would come round and talk for hours in broken English. One day he and I discussed cocktails, which he dreamed of drinking. On Social Security he could afford a single pint of bitter a week. We fantasised about holding a cocktail party. Sometimes we would all go across the road to have supper with him and his wife Elva and his mother, in their cramped flat. A poster called 'The Dove of La Paz' showed a dove flying along barbed wire, jagged splashes of blood spurting behind it. The windowsills jostled with house plants in big food tins still with the paper labels on.

Our new Chilean friends lavished us with hospitality. If they offered a cup of coffee, it came with a plate of sausages and beans. They cooked us big meals of fried chicken and peas. While the two small children played, and her mother-in-law was safely in the kitchen washing up, Elva whispered how hard it was to make love. The old lady didn't like hearing her and Manuel, and would thump the thin bedroom wall. Later, Elva got a job, and Manuel felt more lonely than ever. His depression distanced his children, who preferred their lively mother. Manuel yearned for his male comrades, many of them still in prison in Chile. We all went on the big Chile demo in mid-September 1976. Earlier that month, on 9 September, I noted in my diary, Chairman Mao had died. That was a big political moment, but the politics of knowing Manuel and his family meant more to me.

Dani also took in Kim, a Cambodian refugee of perhaps eighteen who seemed completely deracinated, very excitable, prone to panic attacks and great anxiety. We kept an eye on him as much as we could. Sometimes he painted in watercolour: wistful, sentimental posters of flowers and birds. Pretty doves; not blood-spurting ones. Dani also extended hospitality to travelling Australians who needed rooms, putting out mattresses for the overflow. Practical, determined, organised, she took charge of the house.

Dani's occasionally harsh tongue frightened me. I didn't see enough of her ordinary human side. That emerged when her friend Helen (another Australian) visited: the two of them would laugh and talk in their private Australian, political world. I knew Dani cared about clothes. She loved good food. She could cook a decent ratatouille. She liked the sweetmeats Samir's aunties sent from the Lebanon, the little pastries packed with honey, almonds, pistachios and hazelnuts. Her friend Laura described to me how sweet and funny Dani was. She sighed: you two just don't understand each other. My political ignorance irritated Dani. I was too emotional for her, as well.

I was struggling to write. That implies believing in yourself: that you have got something to say. I didn't always feel confident. Sometimes I felt insecure. This was the side of me Dani saw. She didn't want people to have weaknesses. These frightened her, I think. She needed to feel in control of herself and so tried to control others. She did better, in those days, with tough people whom she couldn't dominate. A few years later, bumping into her in the street, I discovered that, like Laura, she was about to train as a psychotherapist. Oh how nice, I said politely and hypocritically: I am sure you'll make a very good therapist. God help the clients, I thought bitchily to myself.

One of my theories about beautiful female therapists is that they are often people who need a bit of distance. The job suits them perfectly. But then I would say that, wouldn't I? Dani was cool and distancing. I was very emotional and hungry for affection. We were bound to clash.

Celia organised the disposal of rooms. I couldn't have the downstairs front room, she explained, because we would need that for communal living. I don't remember resenting Celia's bossiness, but even if I had I wouldn't have let myself say so. I didn't have the power in the house. I didn't see that I could fight it. Celia, like Dani, enjoyed organising people and space. She eventually became a social worker. Some years later I saw her on TV, in a documentary about old age. Celia radiated health, beauty, youth. Her big dark eyes shone with ardent self-belief. She had reorganised an old people's home, turning it into a commune, because she thought it would be so much better for the old people to join in with each other more. The old people protested that they didn't like it one bit. They wanted their privacy and their own space, thanks very much. I was maliciously amused. Celia had not changed.

Celia allocated me a small first-floor room at the back. I liked it because it was mine. I liked my view. I put a table under the window. Throwing up the sash at night, in the intervals of writing, I shivered enjoyably with cold, gazed at the stars, the streetlights twinkling in the distance. London throbbed and hummed. Mr Salmon's walnut trees were massive black shapes. The air smelled of earth and compost and petrol. Sometimes I would sprint out, along the dark street, to the cigarette machine opposite the fire station. Smoking kept me going while I struggled with words.

I was writing about a French childhood, a London present, a British imperialist past, linked by a story of hidden identities only revealed right at the end. The novel emerged both urgently and with painful slowness, in bits and pieces. Twisting words then paragraphs together, sentence by sentence, felt like working in wrought iron. Rather than describe what I already knew I was trying to write about what I didn't know: what a woman might be and why she was as she was. I wanted to discard naturalism in favour of something truer because deeper; mined from below the surface of things. I foraged down into the unconscious to discover new images and phrases; progress felt difficult, often painful, chaotic. For a long time I didn't know what my structure would be. Heaps of paper lay around on the floor, and from time to time I shuffled them into new patterns of order. Finally they began to hook up into a structure composed by the main character's memory process. The novel turned out to be about memory, storytelling, the struggle for truth. Necessarily it zigzagged as consciousness does under pressure from the unconscious. At last I had found my form.

I carved out my own space in language, and also in the house. I painted my room's floorboards pink, stripped the painted fireplace back to the original marble, put up bookshelves. Did I get my books back from my ex-lover's attic? I must have done but I don't remember. This new lodging (one of Nana's words, that) quickly filled up with books, mostly second-hand. I bought books on all aspects of what came to be called later women's studies, and I bought quantities of novels and poetry. I began to collect Temple Classics, because the bindings were so pretty, and Victorian books on women, very nicely bound in boards; publishers' bindings. I found sticks of furniture, such as my table, in junk shops in the Peckham backstreets. I bought a mid-nineteenth-century Quimper plate for tenpence. I helped the others sort out the ground-floor communal room (lots more paint-stripping) and fix up a makeshift kitchen behind it. Tim installed rudimentary water-heaters in the shed-like bathroom next to the back door and in the kitchen.

One Saturday, while we were all out, he nipped in and painted the kitchen pale purple. We deplored his taste and hung up lots of concealing pictures. Sari contributed a big fake shuttered window, in raised moulded plastic, as a sardonic image to hang above the kitchen sink. Groups of friends came in to help us redecorate. In between slapping on coats of paint we drank bottles of beer and smoked dope. We sanded and varnished the floors. We bought second-hand squashy Victorian armchairs in faded green velvet for a fiver apiece, second-hand Victorian tiles for the brick fireplace surrounds (the originals had been ripped off), second-hand curly iron grates to replace those torn out in the sixties. We felt we did Tim proud. He wasn't so sure. He'd wanted to help us out, establish a nice, friendly group of tenants with whom he would get on well, and he'd ended up with a houseful of would-be revolutionaries whose leader, the indomitable Dani, thought nothing of telling him that he was, shamefully, getting our restoration work for free. Frances did some painting, but she and Tim, daunted by the sharp tongues and the revolutionary atmosphere – political posters in every room – came round less and less.

Dani, like Lenin, believed in organising the party members. She divided up the household tasks and pinned up a rota in the kitchen. Men and women alike took their turn, performed an equal share of household jobs. Samir cleaned the lavatory like everybody else. We all did the cooking. I remember Dina, who lived with us for a while and who was a member of the small libertarian group Big Flame, making us breakfast to hearten us one chilly morning before a Troops Out of Ireland demonstration: scrambled eggs thick with bran. Who needed body

armour for protection against truncheon blows? We were for-
tified by character armour: breastplates of bran. Dina's lover, we
discovered later, an amiable chap who ambled about after her
like a devoted spaniel, was in fact a Special Branch spy, set on
to her to infiltrate the revolutionary group and act as an
informer. Less a pet than a bloodhound; a sniffer dog. Served
him right that in order to spy effectively he had to endure
Dina's breakfast special. The Full Trotskyist.

South London erupted into my dazzled vision as a new
country. Peckham and Camberwell opened up to me as magical
places. I wandered the backstreets endlessly. Nineteenth-
century builders seemed to have gone wild here, putting up
houses decorated in flamboyant Gothic, neo-Venetian, neo-
Byzantine style. Few neat terraces and instead a village-like
jumble: little rows of late Georgian cottages, front gardens
spilling with roses and flowering creepers; different, highly individual little villas, set in secret squares and alleys. Their names
enchanted me: Artichoke Place, for example, and County
Grove, which the local children had (of course) changed into
Cunty Grove. I used to smile every time I saw, from the top of
the number 12 bus, that blacked-out o on the sign. Found language! The unconscious erupting on the street! Thanks,
children. Here and there lurked pockets of mysterious wasteland, old wartime bomb-sites, flourishing with weeds, tangles
of convolvulus, buddleia sprouting from the crevices in tumbledown brick walls. Old factories, old industrial buildings,
were masterpieces of design. One former wash-house had on its
side a big mosaic of a Camberwell Beauty butterfly. Here in
Camberwell Ruskin had courted a girlfriend, who later jilted
him. He had designed a window in the local church, and was
immortalised in the name of a little local park, entered through
an arching wrought-iron gateway, where now solitary men sat

and drank. Muriel Spark had put her hero Dougal into Peckham Rye. Hadn't an angel once appeared near here to William Blake?

I loved the district because it wasn't all tidied up. Exploring it, peeping at it, touching it, you could get hold of its history; make it speak. London was a body, a beloved body, that let me clamber all over it, play with it, caress it, talk to it. Sometimes I walked over to Brixton, where the décor of streets was wilder: walls painted in ice-cream colours, shop fronts spilling cornucopias of sweet potatoes and yams on to the pavement, fenceless front gardens, luscious with weeds, with cars parked inside them, rose bushes planted in old rubber tyres. Women shouted and sang to each other from clothes stall to clothes stall. Reggae belted out from the second-hand record stalls.

We didn't begin, in Camberwell, as a commune, exactly. Just a group of people living together. We were different enough to be visible: an odd household. Nonetheless, our working-class neighbours showed us great tolerance. Even when, in summer, we sprawled on the long grass out back and played loud rock music, they didn't complain. The Caribbean family on the left were friendly; apparently accepting of us though strict with their own daughters. These girls used to slip out at night to go dancing and come home very late. Their front door having been locked by their father, they'd try to climb in through the front window, which required clambering from the side of our porch on to their front windowsill, clinging to it spread-eagled, hanging on, with one hand, to the top of the sash, and fiddling with the window-catch with the other. The deep basement area yawned beneath. I used to come down and lend them a hand. Mrs Williams was always very busy. One day I met her in the launderette. The machines churned and frothed and creaked. Mrs Williams finally kicked the door of hers and shouted: come on, machine, ain't got no time to waste!

The white family on the other side kept their house shiningly neat and eyed our shabbiness disapprovingly. They saw us as foolish, hopeless ragamuffins (rapscallions, rogues, rascals, ruffians, all those good insults beginning with r). Nonetheless they were kind. In the pub they handed us parcels of old clothes their own daughters no longer wore. With exquisite sensitivity they wrapped these discreetly in brown paper so that we wouldn't feel embarrassed. Mrs Clark said to me on one of these occasions, shortly after Bertie had stayed for a week while on leave: terrible nightmares someone has in your house, I hear her shouting and shouting, I thought I should come over, but my husband, he said to me, you leave her be, she's all right.

The neighbourhood was changing, as the old working-class communities began to disintegrate. High unemployment meant that families got torn apart as people had to move to find work. Many of the old streets of small houses people loved had been razed and skyscraper housing estates put up to replace them. The Breton onion-seller, complete with beret, striped T-shirt and bicycle, might still tootle past; locals still might gather for a singsong in the pub on Saturday night; but middle-class people like ourselves were beginning to move in. Tim got a conservation order put on the tall, ancient plane trees at the end of the road. Dani shrugged. Ecological concerns featured low on the list for most lefties in those days. Standing under these trees, one snowy morning, I watched construction workers, eighty feet up on scaffolding, playing snowballs. Someone in the Town Hall with a literary cast of mind had named the nearest council block Voltaire. I thought this was merely fancy, then found out that Voltaire had indeed once visited London, in 1726, when he was temporarily exiled from France because of his subversive opinions. He had lived briefly in nearby Wandsworth, but not, as far as I could discover, in Peckham. The painter David Hepher, whom I met twenty years later when he taught at the Slade, lived near us, in Camberwell Grove, and lovingly painted our local tower blocks, transforming them into huge near-abstracts of squares and oblongs. I got a shock seeing these paintings; these grim places transformed into art.

Since my two jobs took up most of my time, I did a lot of my own work late at night. Writing, mining new combinations of words from deep in the unconscious, making new shapes with them, went on feeling chaotic and disturbing. You had to fly off from the known into the unknown; jump off the edge of the world. I think I used to fear I'd get lost in the unconscious and never find my way back. Keats talked about a writer's need to hover in not-knowing and un-reason; to wait in the darkness. Sometimes I feared to fly, thought I'd plummet through the air and crash on to the rocks and die. I'd happily launched myself into the unknown when I prayed to God, as I did all the time as a child. Now, God wasn't there any more. I launched off into empty space with nothing to cling to except my own desire to find words and to make something.

Writing at night meant I could hide what I was doing. Writing a novel, a private, individual project, still felt necessarily a secret activity. I salved my conscience by going to lots of meetings called by local tenants' groups and women's groups. These were practical, to organise campaigns around local housing, women's health issues, the need to set up local rape crisis centres, to plan demonstrations, to set up information networks. Other groups I took part in were for reading and discussion. With Sarah LeFanu and friends I began reading Marx and Engels and discovered that Marx told good jokes.

With Sarah, in a little group of two, I began reading Freud. We wrote each other analyses, notes, questions. What excitement! Armed with the notion of ideological struggle, at last I was learning to think for myself. Dani, by contrast, did not encourage me to study with her. I was too much of a beginner. When the comrades visited she took them upstairs and shut the door in my face, telling me that these were closed groups. I felt snubbed and angry. I could tell the closed door that, if not Dani. Perhaps they were plotting how to outwit the Special Branch. More bran in the scrambled eggs?

Encouraged by Ali, I had also begun to write political journalism. She wrote for the underground paper *Ink* (launched in response to the *Oz* trial and part of the *Oz* empire), for the alternative local paper *Islington Gutter Press*, for the independent (that is, non-party) socialist-feminist *Red Rag*, and for *Spare Rib*, the women's liberation magazine. I published pieces in *Ink*, and in *Spare Rib*, using a chopped-up, collage form to present ideas on romantic fiction and on fashion. Zoë Fairbairns, already a published novelist, had been *Spare Rib*'s poetry editor. When she gave up the job, the magazine collective, after duly interviewing various candidates, offered it to me. I took it. The collective had just moved to premises on one floor of an old school-suppliers warehouse in Clerkenwell, in a curving side street round the corner from Clerkenwell Green, near the Marx Memorial Library. Other floors were occupied by the Readers and Writers collective, the radical Publishing and Distribution Collective, and *Undercurrents* magazine.

So ultra-idealistic had I become, politically, that *Spare Rib* seemed quite tame and middle-of-the-road to me. One of its editors, Rosie Parker, was actually married. Heavens above! My disapproval masked envy: I imagined she had a man to help her, whereas I struggled alone and was very hard up. But *Spare*

Rib sold well and was popular, reaching women who wouldn't have dreamed of reading *Red Rag*, let alone all the small magazines rolled off duplicating machines (a long-winded, messy procedure) and distributed at meetings and in pubs. For my part I refused to read the *Morning Star*, the Communist paper, because I thought it merely reformist, and I wouldn't touch the *Socialist Worker* newspaper because Tony Cliff had refused to allow women in his party to organise independently. I went on reading novels, poetry and biography as voraciously as ever but I also devoured the floods of pamphlets and booklets the feminist presses turned out, devoting many pages of my diary to reflecting on all these new ideas, to wondering how I should live. Sometimes rather pompously and priggishly, I am afraid. That seems to have been my way of smoothing over the contradictions between theory and practice. They were supposed to be dialectically related. I didn't always see how that worked. I would fall back on idealism, and when that failed me, on earnestness. I squirm, now, reading some of those diary entries, and I smile, too. Good for me! At least I was committing myself to something and having a go.

Spare Rib ran a clever mix of social and political comment, interspersed with poems, stories, lively graphics and photos. It was threatening enough to the status quo for the straight media to continue to mock and vilify it, but I felt nothing but contempt for those silly bourgeois journalists. I felt light-years away from them with my vision of a bright new world in which no one would dominate or exploit anyone else. At *Spare Rib* we tried hard not to dominate each other but to respect our equality. Everyone was an editor, with an equal say. Marsha Rowe, the founder, had no more power than stalwart members of the collective: Jill Nicholls (Sarah's friend), Ali, Rosie Parker, Ruthie Petrie, Angela Phillips, Ann Scott. All decisions were made collectively. At editorial meetings, accordingly, I showed the group the bunch of poems I had chosen for possible publication that month, from the hundreds that poured in, and waited while they were solemnly discussed. These meetings took up a great deal of time. In the end I got fed up with not being allowed to make my own decisions on which poems to publish, and wanted to spend more time writing, and so eventually left. Ali, fierily committed, original and inspiring, deeply involved as both a writer and a commissioning editor, hung on in there.

Having waved my flag as a would-be writer, I was invited to join a newly formed feminist writers' collective whose aim was to create and publish a book of short fiction. I was immensely flattered and said yes straight away. This group comprised Michelene Wandor, Zoë Fairbairns, Sara Maitland and Valerie Miner, all of whom had already published. We met in each other's houses, most often in Michelene's, so that she could keep an eye on her two teenage sons. Over a couple of years we did indeed produce a collection of short stories, interleaving these with essays in which we discussed language, politics and aesthetics. Rejected by the newly founded commercial feminist presses, Virago and The Women's Press, our collection was accepted by a small, independent socialist publisher (run by a man – heavens!), the Journeyman Press, and came out in 1978. We called our book *Tales I Tell My Mother*. Not all our mothers wanted to hear all our tales.

Our group was one of the first of its kind, although, obviously, such groups were springing up everywhere. The establishment literary world was thoroughly male-dominated (the only exception being Claire Tomalin, literary editor at the *Sunday Times*), ruled by masculine, middle-class ideas, masquerading as objectivity, of what constituted good writing. Men's writing was given far more attention than women's.

Coolness and irony were fashionable; ways to escape exploring feeling. We simply sidestepped these rules of conduct. We were going to make up our own minds. We were experimenting with different kinds of narrative voices, uncovering new, raw, angry subject-matter. We wrote collectively, in that we criticised each other's work, gave each other ideas, discussed everything minutely and exhaustively, but, whereas in the street theatre group we had tried to write together, as a committee, in the *Tales* group we each took responsibility for our own stories. During heated conversations we tried to bash out a new aesthetic. I began to learn how to give and receive criticism. That was difficult for the beginner I was, my over-reverence for others' authority and experience conflicting with and concealing my own driving sense of purpose and ambition. Ruthlessness in female artists was respected neither by the straight world (you were not a real woman) nor by the left (you were not a real revolutionary), so I kept mine hidden. The *Tales* group bravely addressed and challenged these questions.

I grew fond of Sara Maitland, intensely intelligent and ardent, who had already had stories published in *Bananas*, the experimental magazine founded by Emma Tennant, which also published Angela Carter. Sara's passionate, intellectual Anglicanism intrigued me even as I disagreed with it. I had given up my faith with ease, and had no idea how deeply its attitudes were rooted inside me, how much importance I still accorded its rules even as I thought I'd broken them. Sara drove an old Citroën *deux-chevaux*. With great kindness, she often gave me lifts home. Sometimes our conversation grew so animated that even when we had arrived at my house we would sit on in the car for another half-hour, furiously swapping perceptions and ideas. Sara's husband Donald, a vicar, looked after their small daughter Mildred on writers' group nights. Sara was beginning to construct a feminist theology. Evenings at the vicarage involved passionate smoking, passionate gin-drinking, passionate challenging of conventional sexist religion. Donald gave as good as he got and hung on in there.

With Michelene I formed a second writers' group, a group of two, to edit and publish a small anthology of feminist poetry. We called it *Cutlasses and Earrings* (a quotation from one of my poems) and included work by Astra Blaug, Sheila Rowbotham and Ali as well as our own. Ali and I were in yet another poetry group, with Stef Pixner, Tina Reid and Ann Oosthuizen, to do likewise. We called our first collection *Licking the Bed Clean* (a quotation from one of Tina's poems). We put drawings and cartoons alongside the poems and designed our own cover. We self-published. This was both a radical and a practical decision. The straight poetry presses did not want our sort of poetry. Later on, of course, when we had established ourselves as writers, giving readings around all the alternative circuits, the establishment condescended to hear us. When our group was finally invited to give a reading at the Poetry Society's headquarters in a Georgian house in Earls Court, Ali spotted the busts of famous male poets on the mantelpiece, Milton, Dryden, Shakespeare et al., and swiftly turned them to face the wall. *Spare Rib* understood our project and let us use their office at weekends. There, we designed, typeset, cut and pasted our pages. Ali, ex-art-school, was chief designer.

London seethed with cultural revolution, swirled with gaiety. Alternative arts events, of every sort, took place every night. Compendium bookshop, near Camden Lock, hosted many talks and readings. It offered an unparalleled array of left-wing books, foreign languages books, international magazines, weird comics, and journals, and had a large, excellent poetry section.

Centerprise, in Dalston, Hackney, formed a centre for working-class groups to write and publish a new sort of history, a new sort of autobiography: the lives of ordinary people. Various black groups fomented equally varied and passionate forums of publication and debate. We all dashed about. Our revolution was gleeful and public. People didn't stay in their homes in neat little couples shutting out the world. They went out to get involved, whenever possible taking their babies and children with them. Women, no longer confined to the home, were urgently at the forefront of shaping our brave new society. Young mothers were revolutionaries. We called it the move from rocking the cradle to rocking the world.

I still felt very fond of Bertie, and missed him. We saw each other irregularly, when he came back on leave. During our times apart, though, I let myself take other, more casual lovers. I also began to get emotionally involved with Michael, a colleague at the sociological research unit, an ardent left-winger. Bertie did not fit into my libertarian life and I did not fit into his desire for marriage. We tried to fit ourselves back together. After Bertie came back to the UK we went on holiday to the South of France. As long as we were alone together in our little bubble, as long as I did not burst out and harangue him about politics, we had sweet times. He could not see the need for revolution: people should just be nice to each other.

We roamed around Provence by bus, staying in cheap hotels. I've got a photo of myself in Cannes, wearing scarlet boots, a little black zip-up jacket, a scarlet sweater, a grey pencil skirt. I've swung my feet up on to the bench I'm sitting on, to show off my red boots. I've got very short hair, I'm waving a Gitane, and I'm grinning at the camera: the picture of outward cheer. We travelled light. In Nice airport I bought face cream, a strawberry-scented shampoo. Even thirty years later, the scent of strawberries brings back the sensual bliss of that week. Cold winds and hot sun. We tramped the roads between Lourmarin and Cucuron, dawdled alongside olive groves and vineyards. I remember a tiny village, high up above Grasse, where we stayed briefly, called Bar-sur-Loup; its icy, invigorating mountain air; the village bar into which we dived for warmth, an ancient, cave-like place cut from the rock, very dark, full of old men with bony brown faces playing dominoes, nodding at us as we hovered by the stove. In a backstreet restaurant in the old town in Nice a hardworking prostitute danced for us and for a bunch of local men. One of them tore off her blonde wig and donned it himself, then pleaded with her not to let his wife know he was there. The *patronne* threatened to throw them all out unless they piped down, then served us, for twelve francs each, a feast of *salade niçoise*, escalope with *haricots verts* and garlic, Cantal and apples, a carafe of wine, and coffee. Plum brandy she gave us on the house. We weaved back to the Hôtel des Etrangers, to our *grand lit*. Sex was as tender and loving as ever but I didn't once come, all that week. I had begun leaving.

We had final forays together around London. I took Bertie through the foot tunnel at the Isle of Dogs, where lorry drivers slept in their cabs, into Greenwich Park, into my favourite riverside pubs. I showed him the Peckham Sainsbury's, surely the last one left in London with long marble counters, ornate shelving with toffee-coloured tile surrounds, muslin-turbaned assistants cutting the cheese, the manager seated alone in a little wooden pavilion at the far end. When Bertie and I did make a complete break, he left the Council and went off to Argentina, where he fell in love with someone else. When he returned to England he found a companion with whom to settle down, happily married, and at last have the babies he so longed for.

I had refused to live with him and have babies. I was determined to write novels. Not just any old novels: novels evincing a radical new form and language and sensibility that would take huge amounts of time and emotional commitment to write. Deep down, when I admitted it to myself, I was extremely ambitious. How could I possibly write while looking after small children, earning a living, and running a house? I didn't think Bertie wanted a lover who wrote, as he didn't want one who was a feminist, either. He seemed to want someone uncomplicatedly maternal, whose husband and children would form the centre of her world. I felt split in two. Thanks to my Catholic heritage I divided creativity from sexuality, the life of the soul from the life of the body. Nuns or mothers. Writers or mothers. Intellectuals or mothers. You couldn't be both. As a feminist I questioned this enforced choice but couldn't find a way through it. Very well, then. I made my choice. No children. You had to make sacrifices for art: this was mine.

I did, however, get pregnant soon after leaving Bertie. I had embarked, during Bertie's absence abroad, on a brief relationship with a man called Ben. This had to be conducted on his terms, which meant only seeing him when he suggested it and not being jealous of the two other women with whom he was also having sex. Occasionally the three of us met in cafés and conducted very serious conversations about how we greedy women mustn't oppress poor Ben with our heavy demands. Poor Ben was very charming and handsome and nice to go to bed with. Poor Ben thought we were all very charming and nice too and saw no reason why he should have to pick just one of us to be nice to him. I had assumed responsibility for contraception all the time I was with Bertie. I didn't trust men to do so and most men didn't like condoms, anyway. I didn't want to mess up my hormones by using the Pill. That left a cap. Caps were not completely reliable as birth control, however, and I hadn't had mine refitted after losing a lot of weight in Bali. Now my period was two weeks late. Rather than face going to my GP, a Polish Catholic, and trying to persuade her that I qualified for an NHS abortion on social grounds, which I thought impossible, I chose to have one done illegally at home. A feminist paramedic whom I knew came to Talfourd Road and did it for me: easy, quick, painless, safe. She jiggled two straws inside me and dislodged blood, a small blood-clot. That might have been a foetus, she said. I didn't know whether I'd been pregnant, not having had a pregnancy test; but felt hugely relieved.

I had left the research unit early that day and explained to my colleague, Michael, why I was going home. I made myself sound cool and unconcerned. Michael said: oh you seem to be taking that very lightly. Impossible to explain to him how I felt. Michael was supremely intellectual, his left-wing politics theoretical rather than practical. His structure of thought was hard, rigid, inflexible. Little place for women's liberation in his worldview. I saw him as a challenge and argued with him passionately. Lunchtimes in the pub got longer. A second pint, and then a third, as we tussled over how to model the questionnaires for our research. I questioned all the assumptions built into Michael's model about good and bad mothering, the way that ticking boxes one to nine (nine for 'don't know') got nowhere near understanding women's lives, the way that some of the social workers (part of our study) often wrote so disparagingly about their clients, the objects of the questionnaire, completely failing to understand the harshness of their lives. There was one social worker I loathed in particular. She saw not poverty but personal inadequacy. She wrote mockingly how one single mother was clearly very immature because she was pathetically grateful for the gift of a pair of tights.

After a year of arguing, and not filling in very many research forms, I got Michael to agree that his research model was flawed. He wrote an immensely long paper setting out the theoretical reasons for his change of mind. He read this to the social workers when they came for their annual meeting. We met in the house in Camden Town of Jill, another colleague. The social worker I disliked was fed up, Jill told me later: she'd been hoping to pop into John Lewis and look at curtain material and here she was stuck in a small hot room while Michael droned on about sociological theory in words of four syllables. Served her right, I thought.

Half my week was spent doing the pregnancy tests at the PAS. Our small team of testers worked in a shabby basement, unobtrusively entered down a steep flight of steps. We took the urine samples, did the tests, gave the women their results, and filled in all the necessary forms. I was given no counselling training. Presumably it wasn't thought necessary, since our instructions were to tell the woman her result (in private, of course) and ask her, neutrally, how she felt about it, in case she wanted to talk. If a woman with a positive result said she wanted a termination, we referred her to her GP. (Abortion on demand does not exist in the UK and it is not easy to get an abortion: two separate doctors have to be convinced that the grounds for abortion exist and permission has to be given by both of them.) If for any reason the client felt unable to consult the GP, or had done so and been refused aid, we referred her upstairs, to the trained counsellors who helped women make decisions about what to do.

Some women, receiving their test results, expressed delight, because they wanted to get pregnant, and rushed away. Some were grateful for the contraceptive information we gave them. Others were devastated to be told they were pregnant, burst into tears and then poured out their unhappy stories. Of course I listened. I could not possibly show women to the door while they sat in front of me weeping. They recounted tales of male doctors' and boyfriends' callousness, indifference, brutality. I did not know so much suffering existed. I did not know how to listen in a detached way: I took the women's grief and anger into myself and carried it home with me.

Opponents of abortion like to think women skip off to have abortions as lightly as they try on shoes in the sales. Not so. I witnessed women facing up to a major moral decision but not being destroyed by that. What I didn't witness was the women's relief after the abortion though I knew it existed. I didn't see the clients again after I had referred them to their GPs or to the health workers upstairs. Day after day I encountered women feeling traumatised, panic-stricken, unhappy, desperate. Many had financial problems as well and of course the PAS charged for its doctors' services. Sometimes women felt forced to go through with unwanted pregnancies because they hadn't enough money to pay for an abortion. Working at the PAS I saw the underneath of our culture; its façade ripped off. Women had to endure such misery. The world seemed a tremendously cruel place. One morning I just collapsed into tears. I wept into the urine sample I was testing and ruined it and the woman who'd given the sample had to go and supply another one and was understandably annoyed. I was told to take the day off. I went home but didn't know how to cope. I just went on crying.

Work at the sociology research unit was demanding in a different way. I couldn't just fill in numbers on computer forms and then zip off home. I felt obliged to engage in my verbal wrestling matches with Michael. He represented male power to me; inflexible, unyielding rules about the way of the world.

Battling with him intellectually, I was setting up in opposition to centuries of male domination; I felt I was fighting for my life. At the same time, I liked the sexual frisson that began to accompany our impassioned discussions. We started what we called then a relationship; we never used the term love affair. True to our politics, we tried to discuss it rationally between bouts of fucking. To my diary I admitted that I was powerfully drawn to Michael partly because he was an authority-figure like my father. The rules of honesty by which we lived dictated that we talked about the situation for hours. Michael felt trapped by me. He rejected me continually. I could not let go. I did not want to give up our highly erotic, pleasurable hours in bed. Orgasmic sex meant I could freely express my need to show and give love. Michael found this too much.

I think, looking back, that I probably poured out the very love to male lovers that I wanted to receive; they could not always reciprocate. Many men in those days felt they needed to be completely in control of themselves and of women.

In Michael's authoritarian theoretical discourse I was over-emotional and intellectually incorrect; women's liberation was not necessary. I felt trapped in Michael's attitudes, was trying desperately to fight my way free. Michael's reading of Lacan meant he saw women as having no real self or desire. Only men had that. His views enraged me, but I felt caught in a bind. I fought his authority yet accepted it; could not just walk away from it. I still kept on trying to explain myself to him, justify my views. I couldn't assert myself in Michael's language because it denied me a self, a voice, any desire. His language castrated women. We were speechless lumps of flesh. Although he was by background Jewish he was articulating the views of priests in my Catholic childhood. Women were holes of nothingness.

I did not yet fully know my own power. That would take

years to develop and it would happen through writing. I would discover that power to me meant creativity, writing novels and poems, and had nothing to do with institutions or wealth or worldly position. In my mid-twenties, however, I floundered suddenly. Despite committing myself to writing, I felt inarticulate still, silenced by the man with whom I was in love. I was full of anger but did not know what to do with it. Eventually I learned to name it as an energy to use in writing: put it out, put a form on it, play with it, shape it.

Michael helped turn me into a writer: I had to retreat from him and learn to value my inner world, my own mind. My time with him was so shattering that I nearly broke down. I was mourning many losses. The loss of my parents' approval, and, I feared, their love. The loss of a true love: Bertie. The loss of fantasies and illusions. The loss of a skin or two. I had protected myself with what felt, sometimes, like a glass shield of niceness and brightness. Sartre and de Beauvoir called the shield bad faith; a form of hypocrisy. Now my anger began to crack that shield apart. I thought I was cracking up but it was the shield breaking. Perhaps how a snail feels without its shell. Finally I realised I needed to back away from fighting, turn inwards for a bit, acknowledge the necessity of doing that.

I had wanted and tried to be a hero on other people's terms. Now, feeling bruised, I left the battleground and hid in a cave. I decided I needed some help and went into therapy.

I didn't know what to expect. Therapy eventually turned out to mean admitting openly I felt angry. Recognising this was a very scary process at first. I had picked up as a child the notion that expressing anger, and so losing control, was proof of madness. I babbled non-stop to prevent Sandra, the therapist, from getting anywhere near me and discovering what I was convinced was the terrible truth of my insanity. After many sessions of this she briskly suggested I was boring rather than mad. So then I got on with the therapy, which meant the much less dramatic, long and difficult slog of admitting and owning all the emotions I felt but which scared me so much.

The abstract words we use for naming feelings cannot begin to convey the physical turbulence that emotions are, particularly when expressed to someone standing in for your authority-figures. I felt I was a tiny ant confronting a huge goddess (that Mother Superior again) who could slay me. She had total power. She would kill me if I opposed her or felt angry with her or upbraided her for not loving me enough. Gradually I realised that Sandra, the therapist, was a human being sitting opposite me. I was not a monster who had to be slain. It felt astonishing to sit and talk openly to someone who listened carefully to what I said and didn't think I was mad and bad but who did question and occasionally criticise me. Sandra listening to me so carefully taught me how to become a good listener to other people. Showing me this kindness, she showed me I was worthy of it, and simultaneously encouraged all the love and joy I so often felt to come out.

It seems obvious to me now: if you squash down anger you squash down love too. But back then I felt like a child learning an alphabet of feeling. The true grammar of love.

I muddled on. And of course my friends knew I loved them and went on loving me and we told each other so and so we all kept going. And so we learned to love each other even more deeply, knowing each other well, tolerating each other and fighting and larking about and having lovely times. We became a tribe and that tribe still strongly exists because we have seen each other through.

I came home one day and saw a large parcel, addressed to me, on the porch steps: the first copies of *Cutlasses and Earrings*.

My first ever publication in book form. I felt speechless with delight.

Sandra, who was in a writers' group herself, encouraged me to go on writing. If I brought poems into therapy she listened to them. Alongside my novel I continued to write poetry and through poems I discovered a sort of language that let me live, the language of the body, expressed in metaphor. Metaphors connected the inner world to the outer world, opened them up to each other, connected conscious to unconscious. City could flow into self and self into city. That was how I experienced life, walking around. Now I was beginning to find and make forms that could manifest that.

Pursuing friendships, I developed new, intense relationships with women, for example Sue Draney (another travelling Australian), whom I met at the PAS. We would sit in Italian-run Marine Ices, Londoners' favourite ice-cream bar, near Chalk Farm tube, and talk about sex and creativity. On Whit Sunday (when the Holy Ghost, the Paraclete, came down upon the apostles and gave them the gift of tongues) we relished a Bomba Paracleto. We went to Columbia Road flower market together, delighting in the large burly Cockney men stepping along proud as brides clutching enormous bouquets, and Sue would tell me tales of her recent travels in Maoist China. One day, after a long chat on a bench in Cavendish Square, we kissed each other goodbye. A middle-aged man stopped and said, in a heavy mid-European accent: women kissing on the streets, is rain. We laughed, and he said: you are husband and wife? No, said Sue: just wives.

Sue had lived in Peckham, and knew all the clothes and junk stalls around the corner from East Street market in Walworth. I told her about the church near Camberwell Grove and its gloriously crazy notices. The current one used roman and gothic typefaces all mixed up, upper and lower case in higgledy-piggledy confusion. 'Come and vote,' the notice read, 'for the stewards of your church, to supervise it's [sic] running and extend the kingdom of God in Camberwell.'

The kingdom of God was within me too, I began to know that. I was a *flâneur* walking about and bursting open with love for the London streets; then the internal and external worlds would fuse and I would experience the bliss that mystics feel, self all gone, just this flow of alive delight.

One day I walked from Liverpool Street to Peckham, zigzagging through Southwark en route, registering horrible cages of jerry-built flats with the odd concrete play space attached fenced in with tall wire walls like a concentration camp, but also delighting in how at the end of every street the horizon altered, the perspective shifted. Here were empty, half-ruined neo-Grecian churches, sudden enormous swathes of green surrounded by miniature art nouveau brick terraces, yellow council blocks next to exquisite Queen Anne cottages. The skyscape was cluttered with cranes, factory chimneys, steeples, spires, columns. Wastelands enclosed with corrugated iron would suddenly part and allow a glimpse of tree-lined narrow streets of neo-Byzantine blocks of houses, each entry with a painted front door, iron bootscraper and little wood and tile porch. The old workplaces were being pulled down. Streets were being laid waste. You could still trace the old communities architecturally but it was all coming down. When I got home at four o'clock I felt the outside come in with me. My room felt light and blowy. I could see through the fireplace into a wasteland beyond and the window dissolved into the garden which was all bareness, space, light.

Bliss was bicycling home, stoned, after supper with Sarah in Mile End (those big platefuls of spaghetti carbonara), through the City at night, the air soft after rain and smelling of warm dust, potatoes, flowers. Trains rattled overhead as I shot under the blackness of bridges, the darkness streaming behind me like hair. Once, at a traffic lights, three youths on motorbikes, two blokes and a girl, studied me. Is she a punk rocker? asked the blokes of one another. No, replied the girl definitely. They roared off. Then an old man saluted me: eh, my lad, you're handsome all right, bet you've got all the girls after you. At the next bus-stop I passed, a nun (or a person dressed as a nun) was passionately embracing a man. And at the Elephant and Castle roundabout, a black woman in a bride's long white dress and flowing white veil crouched over a very small bicycle and pedalled furiously onwards.

The summer of 1976 was a scorcher. The heat soaked me as I rode through tunnels of hot winds, the green leafy backstreets of Notting Hill, on my way to visit Sarah at work. The streets smelled of the fruit on the market stalls, of drains, hair oil, chips. You gave way to sweat and just enjoyed it flowing down you. We would sit on the kerb outside the pub, beers in hand, and talk. Or I would bicycle up to Islington to visit Ali, now moved into Lynne Segal's libertarian-feminist communal house. On one occasion Pete was there, dressed in a shirt with gold threads. He told me tales of going rabbit-poaching in Devon with seven dogs. Lynne's wild green garden contained a clump of fruit bushes. Ali wrote a wonderful sexy poem about that garden, entitled 'Picking Blackcurrants'.

Back at the house in Peckham, we spent a lot of time outside. Sometimes Manuel and family came to have supper with us. On one particular warm night we carried the table outside, laid it with an Indian paisley bedspread as cloth, a pot of daisies. I made a proper *tarte aux fraises* with *crème pâtissière*. We played reggae. Gradually various neighbourhood children sloped in, helped themselves to Newcastle Brown, ate every-thing in sight and then danced and played hide and seek in the basement. One night I went to the Mayflower at Rotherhithe, on the river. I drank in the river smells and noticed the sad loss of life in what had been docklands, skyscrapers taking over from the wharves. The French (pub) in Dean Street was another favourite stopping-off point on my bicycle rides. However many pastis I drank I sweated them off the moment I got back on my bike. I liked the French's décor: the black and white photos, the cast-iron lever for removing wine bottle corks, the silver and glass urn, with little taps, for water. I liked the clientele too; lots of elderly actors in overcoats ordering pink champagne. The Pineapple in Leverton Street in Kentish Town was another favourite. I went to the street festival in Leverton Street, where Michael was now living in a communal house. Sideshows, fire-eaters, clowns, a rock band, a jazz band, and all of us dancing in the street. Later we all piled into the Pineapple. I sat on the kerb with Jody, an art student, from Michael's house. The Aberdeen Pipe Band started playing. She threw off the Chinese pink silk jacket she had bought for 10p off a stall, got up, began dancing. She'd grown up in Aberdeen.

Feeling joyful often happened around Sarah LeFanu. One day she bicycled over from Hackney to visit me for lunch, car-rying fresh peas in a twist of newspaper in her bicycle basket. I cooked omelettes to go with them. We sat on a rug in the back garden to eat, surrounded by toppling grass and flowers, tried to read Marx but kept falling asleep in the sun, then took some cocaine, hopped on to our bikes and sped across the river, making for Islington and a party. We rode abreast so that we could chat as we went. After dancing for a few hours at the party, we bicycled on up to Forburg Road in Stoke Newington, where Sarah's boyfriend Chris (another medic, a friend of James and Bob) had a room in a communal household. The house looked dark. We bunched up our skirts, climbed up on to the dustbin and thence to the front window and broke in. We found Chris in bed, rolling a large joint. We sat together, smoking and chatting, then I crashed out on the sofa downstairs. In the morning we went to a birthday lunch, ate strawberry tarts, danced some more. Sometimes Sarah and I would meet up with James, and we would just put records on and dance. There was always a party somewhere. Benefit gigs for left-wing causes always included dancing to live bands.

One of the best outings that summer was to Bournemouth with Sarah. We were so hot that we bought ourselves skimpy, low-necked sleeveless T-shirts off a stall, then sat on the beach with a large bottle of red wine. We hired a rowing-boat (named *Sea-Wolf*, as though it were a German destroyer), and set off, tipsy but confident, swigging wine at intervals, daring ourselves not to stay too close to the beach. Very soon the rip tide swept us briskly out to sea towards the horizon. The beach vanished behind us. We managed to turn the boat around and rowed furiously. Just hard enough to stay in one place. With every vigorous pull on the oars my bosom leapt out of my T-shirt and had to be stuffed back. Sarah gave up and lay in the bows, laughing. I rowed harder, until at last we reached the shore again. We sat on the beach and ate hot dogs. Then Sarah threw up into a waste-bin. She said: I should have remembered I am definitely a moderate. I behaved like an ultra-leftist. A moderate would only have eaten one hot dog.

I tried to keep up with politics. I went on going to meetings on every subject under the sun. I joined in with friends when we protested against the National Front marching through Lewisham in a show of strength to try and frighten the black community. The police, on horseback, charged us, to drive us back. The male stewards, from the SWP, had cunningly put the feminists at the front, perhaps thinking that would deter violence, so we took the brunt of the charge. How huge those horses were, trampling and kicking. We were only as high as their knees. The police lashed us with truncheons. The National Front beat us with batons. I was so terrified I shat my trousers. I remember cowering in someone's front garden behind a rose bush. Next to me Jill Nicholls, Sarah's friend, was even more terrified than I was, and I noticed, with interest, that I forgot some of my terror shielding her.

In February 1976 I had been on the Troops Out of Ireland demo. Again, the National Front attacked with sticks and stones, this time before we moved off. Some of the men dashed to the back. Anti-authoritarians like Laura, Dani's friend, surged to the front. We walked back from Portobello Square, where the march ended, to Samir's car, accompanied by a man called Brian, from the south-east London branch of Troops Out. He told me he used to be a stuntman, riding horses. He stood in as Robin Hood on the TV series, and also played a Roman centurion in *Cleopatra* in the part shot in the UK, which was afterwards scrapped. There he was, so well-spoken and neat, dressed in a smart tweed coat and muffler, holding off the National Front and then sliding along the icy backstreets of west London past houses decorated like wedding cakes. When it began to snow he draped his scarf over his head and looked like an orange-whiskered Virgin Mary.

Sari and Jude had both moved out. Our lives had become very different. Both of them wanted to travel more. We lost touch for a long time. In their place had come Dina, and Paula. Dina, very idealistic (hence her membership of far-left Big Flame), very gentle, very keen on wholefoods (and bran in her scrambled eggs), joined me in gardening. We produced splendid

crops of marrows, potatoes, tomatoes, runner beans and lettuces. When we turned our backs and forgot to pick the
produce, we discovered six-inch-long radishes, beans as big as
bananas, a tree of tarragon, run-to-seed lettuces swivelling like
helter-skelters. I used to fight my way to the washing-line
through a forest of weeds, Jerusalem artichokes looming overhead. Our walnut tree produced fruit, and I remembered Mr
Salmon. Paula was usually too busy to garden. She worked as a
public librarian. She was merry, both childlike and maternal, full
of humour. She had short dark hair, rosy cheeks, a face per-
petually creasing into a smile, a voluptuously rounded body. She
was left-wing, independent, but you felt her taking the revolution with a good pinch of salt.

We all cleaned, cooked, gardened. The house briefly became
a real commune. A real home. We laid new (old) carpets. I
moved downstairs the pine dresser I'd bought for almost nothing in a junk shop and then stripped, put my 1930s plates and
tins on it. With Paula I cooked bread, cakes and pies for parties.
We went to buy new (old) bikes from the junk man, visited
friends squatting a local disused church, visited Paula's friend
Sean, an ex-monk, throwing a party to celebrate his new
motorbike. We went to the Waste in Hoxton and sat in a café
with a menu painted on a wall, chocolate-coloured wooden
partitions which concealed bearded men in overcoats standing
over people, whisking up their sleeves to reveal lots of gold
watches, offering them in low voices as terrific bargains. We
went to the Ladies' Pool, the bordering lawn crammed with
women because of the heat. A notice by the entrance gate read:
'ladies, your devoted attendants request you not to bathe topless.' None of us took any notice. We swam, and read, and ran
about, and picnicked, and talked to each other.

Dani, with the house now full of her friends, was gentler,

mellower. New people dropped in to visit. A seventy-year-old friend of Dina's, called Doug, came to breakfast before giving us a hand with the gardening. He had fought in Spain during the Civil War. The Young Communist League members were very keen, he told us, and wanted to shoot everybody on morning parade who had dirty buttons. One of their officers phoned up one morning from the hotel where some volunteers were stationed: it's bad enough when they're drunk but when they're naked as well!

With my new friend Jody, the art student, I hung around the run-down house in De Beauvoir Square, Hackney, she now rented with other artists. I modelled for her, lying on a chaise longue drinking cherry brandy and listening to Billie Holiday. I went away on brief trips, to see Sian, who was teaching in Norway, to visit Laura's old chums in Copenhagen, compare their squatting campaigns and women's centres with ours. One afternoon two of her women friends and I ended up in bed together. I enjoyed it very much. On my return I fell into bed with Jody, and enjoyed that very much too. She was pearly and pink and plump as a Velázquez nude.

I dropped into bed with quite a few other women around that time. Then I dropped into bed with Paula, and that continued and became a real love affair.

Goodness: I'd become a lesbian. I celebrated, going to the *Spare Rib* birthday bop. People spilled out all across the street. The local lads turned up and joined in. The band Jam Today was playing. Music bounced off the brick walls, the well of streets and warehouses. Sweat and satin and beer and noise. A line of women dancing arm in arm. Back in the house in Camberwell Dani, Paula, Laura and I dragged a mattress to the opened window as a thunderstorm banged and crashed, lightning lit up the sky, and we played Albinoni and Handel and Haydn very loud.

August 1977: the bathroom ceiling fell in. Our landlord Tim decided this was a portent: it was high time we all moved out. He wanted to sell the house to his newly wed brother, who needed a marital home. Dani urged us to resist. We were sitting tenants, after all. We had rights. Tim should not make us homeless. She wanted us all to squat the house, and exchanged ferocious messages with Tim to that effect. I didn't have the courage to stick with her line for long. I couldn't cope with being so aggressive towards someone who was still some sort of friend and who had been a pretty good landlord when all was said and done. Dani and I confronted one another. I stood up to her. We had a row. She and Samir withdrew from group life.

The commune had fallen apart. Time to be off. We all made our separate plans for moving out. Or didn't. I sat in the pub with the son of Mrs Clark next door. He bought me a pint and urged me to work for the Post Office, same as he did. How sweet he was. He really cheered me up.

Travelling by bus from Peckham to Victoria, to catch a bus to go and see my parents, I scribbled down what I could see from the window, as a way of saying farewell to the neighbourhood I think. An old man, beautifully dressed in a dark double-breasted suit with spiky lapels, inched his way across Camberwell Green, clutching his Zimmer frame. Between the Green and the Oval many houses were being pulled down. Coltsfoot bloomed bright and feathery amongst the rubble. Front doorways and porches gaped. Buddleia grew lopsided on shattered windowsills. From my vantage point on the top of the bus I could look down over the corrugated-iron walls separating the street from all the mess. A scrawled message read: 'corrugated iron is the character armour of the council.' A man cleaning milk bottles in the Unigate factory at Vauxhall looked out of his window, caught my eye, and smiled back at me. Another message, near Vauxhall Bridge, asked: 'what shall we do when the vortex opens up?' A different hand had written: 'send for Zardoz.' Someone else had signed himself everywhere in precise red and yellow lettering as the King of Elfland. Underneath was scratched: 'it's only rock 'n' roll.' Behind me on the bus two men were talking about hats. One of them wanted to know what he could buy himself for twenty pounds. A sombrero, the other man urged him: buy a sombrero. It'll keep you warm, it'll keep you cool, and you can collect rainwater in the brim.

On my return from that journey I handed in my novel to Stephanie Dowrick of the newly founded Women's Press. I'd heard through the grapevine that the Press was looking for contemporary fiction and decided to chance it. Then I packed a couple of suitcases with clothes and china. I organised selling most of my beloved books. I had to sell them. Too many to transport to the new flat I was going to share with Paula. I gave my collection of religious and mystical texts, many of which I'd bought on the upper floors of Thornton's in Oxford, to Sara Maitland. I had once written an essay on Lactantius's poem about the phoenix, and how this fiery bird turns up in medieval poetry, for Rosemary Woolf, my tutor at Somerville. Now Lactantius and his phoenix went off to the vicarage in Hoxton, where Donald now worked, and I rose from the ashes as a lesbian phoenix and flew off to join Paula in Peckham Rye.

Chapter Six

PECKHAM RYE

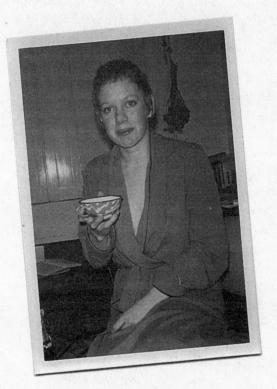

My Amazonian haircut

Paula and I found our flat by looking at ads in local newsagents' windows. We moved in autumn 1977. Where was it? Alpha Street or Scylla Road or Choumert Road? Such good names in Peckham. I don't remember the name of the street (one of my diaries for this period is missing; lost in the move) nor the name of the landlady. Let's call her Mrs Benson. She lived alone, and was a widow with too many rooms, renting half of them out.

Mrs Benson's house fronted a hairpin corner where two streets met. She lived on the ground floor and let part of the upper two. My room, on the first floor, was a high-ceilinged shoebox for giants. Brown dimpled wallpaper to dado level; cream dimples above. Brown velveteen curtains shut out the street. Shiny brown lino reflected back the cold. The gas fire couldn't shift it. I rattled in that room, a single pea in an over-large brown pod. I spent most of my time upstairs, either in the kitchen or in Paula's big, low-ceilinged room opposite it, which was warmer, with Paula's own carpet and rugs laid down, floor cushions, and with a more efficient gas fire. We saved our fifty-pence pieces to feed the meter. We made a pretty kitchen, despite the pokiness of the attic space, with a floor I insisted on painting pink, rose-coloured wooden chairs, my little dresser stacked with my French plates, pots of blue hyacinths. I put a blue glass vase of pinks on the table, a bunch of paper anemones – purple, red, pink and blue – in a green glass flask.

The colours echoed those in the surrounding streets. Walking around, exploring, I saw these gleam with hallucinatory intensity. The pavements were red and green. Houses were tinted banana custard yellow, pale raspberry, pale cocoa.

A frilly stone porch was holly-berry scarlet and the pale blue of hair-ribbons. I cherished the colours of cars, vivid after rain, in the grey streets: streaks of yellow and crimson and sapphire.

Paula owned a car. She provided my first sustained experience of driving around London for fun and I adored it. We whizzed through Trafalgar Square. We whizzed around Hyde Park Corner. We whizzed around south London, exploring the backstreets of the Rye and East Dulwich and Nunhead; utterly foreign and mysterious and secret and magical. We gawped at the higgledy-piggledy mixture of architecture and styles: bungalows, prefabs, faux-rustic 1920s cottages with verandas, villas, blocks of flats; all mixed up.

In some places modernity seemed never to have arrived. A woman called Sherry, whom I met via her lover Colin, a colleague at the sociological research unit, lived in an ancient mansion block set well back from the main road near Stockwell tube. Completely unmodernised, near-derelict, the flats still felt inhabited by their nineteenth-century tenants. Sherry's tatty but splendid domain in the basement boasted gilded marble columns, art nouveau marble mantelpieces, a range, wooden shutters, gas lighting. Many of the flats were squatted; the council had got rid of most of the old tenants in order to do renovation work (you just knew that they would destroy everything that gave these dwellings their charm). Behind the crumbling building the communal garden stretched large and rambling, surrounded by big old trees, with a stone urn at the centre of the unmown grass thick with weeds. At dusk, one evening when I visited, children's voices threaded the blue air with shouts and laughter as they danced around a bonfire.

Sherry told me tales of the flats' other inhabitants, for example Mrs Cosgrove, born in Java into a circus family. Aged fifteen, she met her future husband Billy, who went to sea at twelve and joined the circus at thirteen. She bled every time they made love, so Billy wouldn't let her have children. They kept cats and dogs and budgerigars instead. They had retired to the flats twenty years previously, with all their pets, Mrs Cosgrove with blonde hair down to her waist. She washed her jumpers in paraffin and her hair in peroxide. She still demonstrated tumbling and somersaults to all the children around. After Billy died, she wouldn't admit he was dead. The animal shit piled up in the flat, and the Social Services came and put her away in a mental home. Sherry said she'd always been crazy; that was her way of coping, and she coped well; Sherry knew if they took her away she wouldn't survive. Mrs Cosgrove didn't: the nurses dropped her in the bath one day and she broke her hip and died.

Sometimes at weekends we drove into Kent or Surrey to go walking. Up Box Hill we climbed (thinking of *Emma*) and then zipped to the pub. Sometimes we drove up to north London. In Hampstead, we went to Humboldt's bakery on South End Green to buy plaited chollah bread (the delicious bread of my childhood, bought from Grodzinski's in Edgware) and to admire the old biscuit tins on the shelves. Large and square, decorated with gold arabesques, these bore legends in gold lettering: petits fours and *langues de chats*. The pâtisserie down the road boasted feather-light choux and tarts served on round tables covered with blue-checked cloths. At other tables Russian men sat playing chess. (The bakery in Peckham at this season sold gingerbread crowns to mark the Queen's Jubilee, gilded with yellow icing and stuck with currant diamonds.) When the weather was warm, in spring and summer 1978, we went to that favourite place, the Women's Pond at Highgate, to swim and sunbathe to the music of woodpeckers, to picnic on wine and olives and *dolcelatte* and grapes. Forget-me-nots crowded along the wooden fence; cow-parsley frothed under the edging trees. We went to a watercolour show at the new and fashion-able Zanzibar in Holborn, where we drank gin fizz with lime and cream, and to classic lesbian clubs such as The Gateways where we drank gin and tonic and danced.

I got to know Paula's friends. One of them, a small, delicate man called Cloud, cooked us a Japanese supper in the kitchen of his flat before performing a cabaret for us in his sitting-room. He seated us in leather armchairs, then retired behind a curtain concealing an alcove. Twenty minutes later he reappeared dressed as a geisha, with elaborate kimono and a white mask of a face, and did a fan-dance for us. Later, he advised me on clothes, sending me pairs of jeans he thought would suit me. He supervised my sewing of a frilly skirt made of old lace table-cloths I then dyed pale green.

I didn't want to conform to media stereotypes of lesbians. I wore skirts when I wanted; a pair of airmen's padded trousers I accessorised with gold high heels; my red 1940s crêpe frock. I went off to meetings of Lesbian Left wearing these outfits with my LL badge proudly pinned on.

Paula cocked an ironical eye at my earnest forays to feminist-socialist-lesbian meetings. She mostly put her political energies into trying to be anti-racist at work, then came home and wanted to enjoy herself. We had lots of friends in common, and I made new ones of my own. Lesbian Left was fun some-times, very intense at others. We debated all aspects of sexual politics and socialist politics. We discussed camp, fascism, kitsch, art. We went on picket lines to support strikers, such as the Asian women striking at Grunwick's, the film-processing factory, for equal pay. We liaised with gay men's groups. We wrote articles. We wrote sketches and skits for revues. We went to supper at each other's houses and played reggae and jazz records and danced.

Some of the women in the group shook their heads at me: you're not a real lesbian. I was indignant but they insisted I was just passing through. Being a lesbian in those days wasn't a question of ironic postmodern games or roles, as queer theory or the modern media might have it. It was serious. For a start, you might well lose your job if you came out. You would certainly lose your children. Straight women dipping a toe into lesbian waters were much disliked, as were would-be groovy bisexuals who took few risks. Most of the gay women I knew were in faithful couples. Serial monogamy, we called it. When couples broke up, as of course sometimes happened, it was especially anguishing for the women involved since there was no social recognition of the relationship having existed at all. Lots of the gay men I knew believed in complete freedom and went cottaging as a matter of course. Plenty to argue about at joint meetings.

Despite friends' doubts about my authenticity, I came out to my parents. My horrified mother declared: you must be mad, you need a sex-change or a lobotomy, there's something terribly wrong with you. Then she looked at my short hair and relented. She shook her head: and you must get terribly cold in winter. She cast on and knitted me a stripy hat. I wore it with pride; a sort of lesbian tea-cosy.

I loved sex with women. I relished the strangeness and delight of there being no fixed roles. You could do absolutely anything you wanted and you could be active or passive and you could swap around and take the initiative or not. You could be extremely sensual for as long as you wanted, as quick and fierce as you wanted. I also relished the closeness which you could experience, which I'd found with no man except Bertie. But he and I had had to live inside a bubble to achieve that, and there were parts of me he hadn't wanted to know. I felt that

Paula and I knew and accepted each other completely. Over-simple and over-romantic, this myth, but it nourished me well for a while. Loving another woman physically, coming with her, made me feel really good about being a woman for the first time in my life.

Paula sometimes needed to back off, to turn silent, to push me away. We had to create boundaries between ourselves because it did feel easy (to me) to become almost too close, to blur the lines of separateness. With men, I came to see, you could invoke the physical difference (the phallus as cliché) as an immediate way of knowing you were two separate people. With someone who seemed to be the mirror image of yourself you had to construct the necessary difference. The other person's character and tastes mattered a great deal as part of that. I think, now, I tried, unconsciously, to turn Paula into a mater-nal figure (a good mother who pushed away that Mother Superior). She was older than I was. More experienced in life. Wiser in some ways. Less intense and less splurging with emo-tion, uncomplicatedly liking pleasures of all sorts. She had given me fantastic support all through the lonely months when I was writing *A Piece of the Night* and got churned-up about it. She would crack a joke and all would be well again. Once, I began worrying about the odd structure of the novel, its back-and-forth zigzag (perhaps a commonplace nowadays but back then something I felt I'd invented): did she think I was crazy? No, she said impatiently: you're just a modernist. Then we had cups of tea. Sarah also gave me great support, reading and criti-cising various chapters, egging me on. She pushed me to regard the novel less as still a part of myself than as an external object which could be judged, altered, changed, rewritten.

Stephanie Dowrick of The Women's Press (backed by Naim Attullah, that *soi-disant* lover of women) agreed to publish my novel on condition that I rewrite it. Formally, it was a bit too experimental for her, a bit too wild and all over the place. I dropped some aspects of my experiment with the structure, the tricksier bits, but kept to the main spine of the protagonist's memory and flashbacks alternating with the present and with a narrative set in the past. Originally, the opening paragraph contained the image 'Mary Magdalene wiping Christ's arse with her hair'. Stephanie insisted this be changed to the conventional wiping of feet. I named chapters 'sections' because I saw the text as a body that had been cut up and damaged (one male reviewer crowed with delight that no chapters meant no chaps, ho ho ho). Stephanie didn't like my use of thriller motifs, my jokes about dead bodies/dead books in libraries, originally a structuring device, and made me cut them.

The novel opened with the words 'There is a dead nun in the school chapel.' I didn't realise then that the dead nun was my adolescent self, not yet independent and articulate. The novel ends with an image of women talking subversively to one another. That's certainly what brought me back to life and enabled me to live. I don't care how po-faced that sounds. It is true.

While I slogged away at a final draft I supported myself by working as a clerk for Latin American Newsletters in their office in Cowcross Street, Smithfield. My previous two part-time jobs had come to an end. Jane, one of the editors at *Spare Rib*, worked there part-time doing promotions. She put in a word for me when a rush clerical and mailing job came up and more hands were needed at the pump. I got on with the columns of figures I was given, finished on time, and so seemed to have passed some sort of test. The company took me on.

I was given a regular three days a week putting contributors' details on to the computer and dealing with subscriptions. To record these we filled in dockets, circling numbers by way of translating figures into computer-speak. Repetitive work; easy to become bored and tired and make mistakes. Upstairs, on the floor above, worked the journalists, writing the copy that resulted in the weekly newsletters detailing Latin American politics and commodities. Roy, the office manager, nipped up and downstairs between the two office floors. The hierarchy was otherwise strictly maintained. I worked with a group of women from Essex, all old friends of each other's. Two of them were twins, doing the book-keeping. Their parents came in as office cleaners every night, and told me tales of going hop-picking down in Kent when young. That explained their remark when someone got anxious: don't topple your hop-basket.

I liked Roy very much. Young and handsome, from Newcastle, he went everywhere on his racing bike. He was highly politicised but never used jargon; only his own words. He was honest and funny; good to talk to. I fancied him too. Not much I could do about it since I was A Lesbian, and had a badge to prove it. I remember Roy squatting down by the side of my desk one day, when I'd mentioned lesbianism, and saying: well, you see, lesbians do make men feel a bit left out. The other man I liked the look of was Anthony, one of the journalists, black-haired, with a thin, clever face and curious dark blue eyes, rather sad-looking. Roy found himself a sweet Parisian girlfriend called Pascale, dark and slender and quick. They moved into a communal household in Queen's Park. Pascale became a good friend and we all went to parties together or out to pubs to hear live rock music and dance.

I respected my women workmates. I saw how hard they worked, first in the office and then at home. They were from old East End families now moved into Essex. When I visited them at weekends in their little modern houses sparkling with cleanliness and neatness, I understood what a feckless creature I must seem. They cared for their men, children, grand-children. They were proud of their immaculate gardens, their new cars. They were equally proud of how well they worked for LAN. They didn't seem to give a toss for the division of labour that awarded the middle-class journalists higher status and fatter wage packets. They accepted it. That was the way of the world. They knew they were indispensable, expert, utterly professional. They tolerated me, the bohemian girl, as long as I did my job properly and didn't mess about. They shrugged at the journalists, mostly male, who spent quite a bit of their time chatting and gossiping. They were not socialists. They shrugged at feminism too: that was for middle-class chicks wanting to get into the middle-class men's world.

Yet, slowly, inch by inch, over the months we drew nearer, politically as well as emotionally, to each other. I learned from them the realities of their tough lives, which they felt could not change. They conceded that they could do with a spot of domestic help from their husbands. We talked carefully, some-times over a snatched lunch. They brought in home-made sandwiches, to save money. Roy and I sometimes went out to the cheap Italian cafés thronging the area. My favourite was the one at the top of Cowcross Street, just opposite us, where you could get, for practically nothing, thick bitter coffee from a hissing urn, and breadcrumbed, fried escalope with spaghetti and tomato sauce. This particular dish I have never eaten in Italy; not regional so much as 'Italian'; perhaps invented for the Brits; but delicious nonetheless.

Smithfield in those days was simply a working district, not a fashionable, consumerist one. Not residential; no lofts; no galleries or restaurants. The meat market, sawdust-floored and stinking of blood, bustled with porters hefting carcases on to wooden barrows, wheeling them rapidly this way and that. Dead animals flopped redly in pieces, heaped up on display, not hidden in vast refrigerators. People shouted and whistled and pedestrians had to mind their backs as they scurried through: strange little vehicles like mini dumper trucks whizzed about. Doctors from Bart's ran back and forth too, and we used to joke that you couldn't tell the meat porters from the doctors; both lots wore white coats covered in blood (in those days one saw few women doctors and certainly no women porters). The pubs opened early in the morning, so that the market workers could get a drink when they needed one, then packed up by lunchtime when the activity faded away.

I prowled the neighbouring streets, exploring. I did my shopping at the stalls in Leather Lane, went to the Italian delis, noted the Scuola Guida Italiana (Italian Driving School) with its tricolour shopfront, and the Italian church. Founded in the mid-nineteenth century to support the Italian immigrant community, this blazed inside with golden light fittings, racks of votive candles, mad baroque splendour: all gilding and blue plaster ceilings and statues of saints in ecstatic swoons. I could nip over to Clerkenwell Close in five minutes, and visit my friends at *Spare Rib*. I could wander up the Farringdon Road, admiring the fine Victorian industrial buildings, and salute the neo-Byzantine office block in which my father had once worked. I saluted him in The Quality Chop House (whose frosted window read 'Progressive Working-Class Caterers') where he had taken me, aged ten, to eat steak and kidney pudding and drink London's Noted Cup of Tea. Now of course the chop house is a fancy restaurant charging fancy prices.

One afternoon I arrived home from work earlier than usual, dashed upstairs to find Paula, and discovered her in bed with a middle-aged man I'd never seen before. He turned out to be an old friend of hers (whose name I have forgotten), whom she'd vaguely mentioned from time to time. They were in the habit of spending an afternoon together now and again, apparently, but Paula, in the course of our eighteen-month relationship, hadn't got round to telling me. She explained that they just cuddled rather than having full sex, but nonetheless jealousy devastated me. I didn't want to admit we'd been having diffi-culties. I only wanted to think I adored Paula. I retaliated by inviting myself around to Anthony's flat in Stepney Green, drinking a lot of wine. I must have been overwhelmed by anger and grief because rather than try to work things out with Paula I simply fled. I accepted Anthony's invitation to use his flat while he went away for a month to Rome. I shrank down my belongings, throwing away old papers and letters and giving away books. I packed a suitcase and moved out of the flat one weekend. I sold the possessions and furniture I couldn't take with me. Paula hung on to my dresser for me. Goodbye to another collection of books. Anthony's flat was tiny. No room for extras.

Paula was cast by some of our lesbian friends as the Wronged Wife and I as the cold-hearted Bisexual Bitch who Betrayed and Abandoned Her. I thought this unfair but kept my mouth firmly shut. Being lectured by those moralists felt like being thrown out of the Brownies. Rip off that Lesbian Left badge and give it back! Other lesbian friends simply told me to do whatever I thought was right. Their warmth and kindness touched me. But I wasn't able to sit down and think about what was right. I was muddled and driven and just felt I had to run.

Cressy Houses in Stepney had been built by the East End Dwellings Company, Victorian philanthropists wanting to house respectable working-class tenants and also get a return on their investment. Next door, overlooking Stepney Green itself, was Dunstan Houses, once (in the early twentieth century) packed with German Yiddish-speaking anarchists, who worked as artisans in the East End. One of them, Rudolf Rocker, had played host to Kropotkin when the latter visited. Later on, tenants became Communists.

The tenement blocks formed a square around a courtyard with a disused bath-house in one corner. Flights of stone steps led up to iron-railed landings which formerly housed the out-door lavatories, one to each group of three flats. Now people grew flowers here in pots, chained up their bicycles, set up racks to dry their washing. Most of the flats had had hot-water systems installed, but one old lady was still drawing water from a cold tap under the outside staircase. Now that the Company had been wound up, the flats were allowed to be sold. They were starting to go to middle-class owners. Anthony had bought his after his divorce. He told me that it was the cheapest flat he had found in the whole of London. His former girlfriend, Liz, a very intelligent, sweet woman who was a classicist by trade and later became a novelist, lived in a flat upstairs.

Anthony's cold, dank flat, with its slits of kitchen and bathroom, tiny sitting-room and bedroom, seemed cramped for only one person, let alone two. Yet, of course, whole families, with numerous children, had originally been housed in these dwellings. I felt bad for complaining to myself, but nonetheless I felt lonely and frightened in this dark, strange little place. I went out to see friends as often as possible. With Sarah LeFanu I talked about books. With Ros Carne, who wrote theatre reviews for *Time Out*, I went to shows. Ros generally wore a big army greatcoat in which she looked very splendid. My dear friend Sarah Benton, a Communist and a journalist, whom I had met, as I had met Ros, through the women's movement, came over to visit me one evening. Ardently intellectual, she was bracing to talk to. Our conversation went on so late that Sarah stayed the night. She slept on the very short sofa with her feet hanging over one end.

At Easter I went out to Rome to join Anthony for a few days. After fighting off the taxi driver who tried to rape me, I eventually found Anthony at the address he had given me, a former flat on one floor of a small palazzo, an opulent place tucked in a side street near the bottom of the Spanish Steps. His ex-wife (whose name I forget – I'll call her Maria) lived here with their daughter in an atmosphere of luxury, warmth, scented darkness. She worked as a painter, and let us sleep in her little studio. That was a fraught visit. She and I got on remarkably well, but all kinds of tensions bubbled and seethed below the surface for everybody. Her friend Roberto turned up on Easter Sunday morning and we all ate Easter lunch together: a feast of baked stuffed artichokes followed by roast lamb and almond tarts.

Back in London I battled on in therapy, still lurching about, flailing my arms and protesting. Sometimes I wanted to run away and live a calm cool life of total repression. But I hung on in there, feeling, most of the time, that therapy was helping me. In particular, I was discovering that the unconscious was not only a mode of thought but a magical and visionary place, like a kingdom under the sea, alive with images, fragments of stories, memories, strange invented people and animals. A real treasure-trove for a writer to enter. I ceased to feel scared of it and went down to it eagerly.

I corrected the proofs for *A Piece of the Night*. Sara Maitland, who remained a close friend, had a first novel coming out too: *Daughters of Jerusalem*. The *Tales* group was looking forward to the publication of our book of short stories. I didn't show my novel to them. I kept quiet about my excitement.

Early June 1978. I didn't know where to go. At this point James LeFanu, Sarah's brother, stepped in and offered me a room in his recently purchased house in Stoke Newington. Sarah had moved there when he bought it. But now she and Chris had decided to go off to Mozambique for two years, and work as volunteers for the *revolução*, and her room was vacant. I gratefully accepted and moved in. We held several farewell parties for Chris and Sarah, most at Forburg Road, the hall cluttered with tea-chests full of books. The best party was held the night before they departed. The group of close friends ate supper together in the garden, in the cool, damp darkness, with a lamp on the table that Chris had fixed up, the flex snaking out of the kitchen window. I said farewell to Sarah for two years. I said a second farewell to Paula. We'd been seeing each other, remaking our friendship, but now she decided that was that; enough. Painful for me, and scary to recognise her anger, but I had to accept it. The day after Sarah left, and after that meeting with Paula, I went to see Lin from the street theatre group. She had had breast cancer for some time, a double mastectomy, did not know how long she had to live. I walked through green leafy streets towards her house. Then, after our sad conversation, away again, trying to come to terms with her death.

It felt sweet moving into Sarah's little room on the first floor at the back of the house. I thought of it as her room; not as mine. I liked that. In the mornings I sat up in bed and drank tea, smoked a cigarette, enjoyed the fresh air blowing in through the open window, looked out on to greenery and roses, listened to birdsong. Very tranquil, here, next to the Abney Park cemetery so overgrown and voluptuous with green. The cemetery, curving, with a complex arrangement of paths, seemed completely circular. Whenever I went in there for a walk I got lost. It spun; the wheel of death. At night I'd sit up with James, chatting. I would roll and smoke a joint. Then he'd play music, Eric Satie, perhaps, and study while I sat and read. Very peaceful and companionable. James was a darling to live with; funny, wild, original, affectionate. He had masses of friends. Women queued up to spend time with him, fell over themselves to fall in love with him. His current lover was Serena, a Roman beauty, an academic specialising in English literature. We would all go to the pub together. Stoke Newington Church Street in those days boasted just one restaurant (today it has perhaps thirty): the Anglo-Indian. Since this lovely curry-house was unlicensed, you gave your order, went round to the pub, and then they came and fetched you when it was cooked. James and I took Serena, and other visiting Italians, to hear punk rock bands playing live at the local pubs. The Italians did not understand punk rock and grew bored and had to be taken home.

Serena departed back to Rome. Other female tenants, in succession, occupied her room. James loved being surrounded by women. Our company cheered him up: he had failed his Membership (medical) exam and was feeling low. I wrote in my diary: 'he feels he has failed to be a hero and a genius. Very high standards he has: exemplified by Lenin, Thomas Mann and Bob Marley at the moment.' I wanted to comfort him but there was little I could do besides listen. I sometimes felt (unreasonably) jealous of his charisma and attractiveness to other women but always touched by his affection towards me. We went on playing, partying, dancing, walking around London, as we had always done. I went on seeing my old friends. Sian had moved to Leeds, to a communal house in Chapeltown. At weekends, when I visited her, we walked in the Dales, sat in pubs talking for hours, went to parties, went out dancing at the Polish Working Men's Club. Whenever two or three of us got together in each other's homes, for a drink or supper, we would end up dancing, as I've said before. Every Friday and Saturday night there was a party somewhere and off we would go, for the dancing.

Through *Spare Rib* I had met a woman called Polly. One day she told me that there was a spare room in her house in Holland Park. She and her husband Sim, and Alex, the male friend with whom they shared the house, were looking for a fourth person. Would I like to be that person? Why didn't I come to supper and meet the others?

Much as I liked living with James, much as I loved him, my room was extremely small. The single bed tucked under the window left little space for possessions. James was a delightful, eccentric being; he had been very kind to me. He was like a brother. I was scared I'd fall in love with him if I stayed on, and that then I'd be extremely jealous of all his girlfriends. So I decided it was better to go, and stay good friends at a little distance. The arrangement had always been named a temporary one, in any case. Time to move. James was annoyed at first, because I'd become part of the household, and then accepting.

I could not have afforded a commercial flat rent at this point, because I was still determined not to take a full-time job, not to go back into librarianship. I had to earn a living somehow, but I needed to make time for writing alongside. Living in another communal house, sharing expenses, might not be ideal, but seemed the only way to survive financially.

I felt sad and lonely. I missed Sarah, and I knew I would miss James. '*Courage, ma vieille,*' I wrote in my diary: '*espérons. Forwards!*' Off I went to Holland Park.

Chapter Seven

HOLLAND PARK

Sarah LeFanu and Portobello market

Polly had inherited wealth and been able to buy a big house. Generously, she opened this to others; she wanted to share what she had. We did not pay rent. Polly was my benefactress. I was relieved and delighted at being offered a home in which, apparently, I could stay as long as I wanted.

Once, as a child being driven down Holland Park Avenue in the car with my parents (en route to friends in less glam Wimbledon) through the tunnel of tall, ancient plane trees, I had fantasised about living in the neighbourhood. Now I had stepped inside the fantasy. Behind low white stone balustrades, sparkling like sugar, the well-tended front gardens spilled with flowers, blossoming creepers, graceful trees, planted in that romantic English style of the tamed wilderness. Fullness and frothiness of texture and colour and shape. Polly's district curved around the side of a little hill, on which a racecourse had formerly stood. The crescent-shaped streets, lying one below the other, followed the oval of the track, communal gardens, enclosed by the houses, curling between them. The houses reared up adorned with columned porches, tiled steps, Dutch-style pediments. The façades were painted in sweet-pea pastels: dusty pink, pale blue, lemon; and in smart dark shades of navy, fir green, scarlet. In summer, people kept their long front windows open to the night, rectangles of gold releasing the hot clatter of jazz. The smoky blue nights would tug me outside to walk, and the air would be full, inexplicably, of the scent of fields: of cut grass, and of lilac and jasmine.

In the fifties, this had been a district where poor people lived. Landlords had let out these mansions as rooming-houses, cheap flats. I discovered from the published volume of her letters that

173

Jean Rhys (poverty-stricken, often on the flit from lovers or trouble), a writer I much admired, had once rented a room in 94 Elgin Crescent, a neighbouring street. Black people had arrived from the Caribbean during the fifties and established their community. Colin MacInnes had written about the race riots of Notting Hill in his fifties novel *Mr Love and Justice*.

Now, owner-occupiers were moving in and doing up their properties. The once-shabby houses, until recently the haunts of liberal upper-middle-class bohemians, were becoming more Tory and more expensive. Grilles veiled them at night. Burglar alarms sprouted above every front window.

Turning off Holland Park Avenue, out of the shade of its towering plane trees, you entered what seemed an Italianate garden framed by stucco; a riot of roses through which moved the occasional car. Portobello Road was five minutes' walk away. Above us, at the peak of the hilly end of Ladbroke Grove, St John's Church poked its spire aloft. Early-nineteenth-century cottages hid in the narrow backstreets around Pottery Lane. The local pub was tucked away in a side alley. Julie's Wine Bar, a bohemian den furnished with armchairs and sofas, carpets and wall-hangings, lurked down here too.

Inside Polly's house, the walls, hall and landings were painted eau de nil or white. Brown fitted carpets ran throughout. The big basement kitchen was flanked by a laundry room and a TV room. On the ground floor a drawing-room stretched from front to back, where, beyond French windows, a little balcony gave on to the tiny private garden, surrounded by a flowering hedge, leading, via a gate, into the big communal one. You couldn't see the ends of this slice of melon-shaped parterre; they curved out of sight, hidden by bushes and trees. A narrow gravelled path curled around the edge of the big garden, linking all the little ones.

The yellow-painted drawing-room's parquet floor was strewn with kelims; framed nineteenth-century embroidery samplers on the walls jostled modern art; old white wicker garden furniture mixed well with a chaise longue, lots of green plants. Crammed bookcases and white-painted cupboards, waist-high, ran all round the room. The effect was airy and playful, somehow like a ballet. Polly had a desk here, overlooking the street. She and Sim slept on the first floor, their bathroom alongside Sim's studio, in which he kept his knitting-machine. He designed and made sweaters for fun; by day he was a research scientist.

On the second floor, Alex had a bedroom and, above it, reached by a circular iron stair, a study space under the roof. He had access to the roof via a ladder and trapdoor. I moved into the front bedroom, next to Alex's, and we shared the adjoining bathroom. The long, low window paralleled the bath. You could lie lapped in water with the casement open, feeling fresh air blowing over your skin, seeing clouds skim the waving greenery of the ornamental maple just outside, listening to birdsong, the combination of coolness and warmth inducing bliss.

From the roof, when I had asked Alex to let me through his space, I could watch the sunset melt into blue-grey night, pick out the coiled lazy snake of the motorway, creased and glittering with cars, the oblongs of tower-blocks pitted with gold. Above me, jets trailed jewels. Cool air on my face, the backs of my hands. I'd peep into the lit rooms of the houses opposite where the warm blue eyes of televisions blinked. I liked being alone up there, hidden in the darkness that rushed past me like a great wind.

We agreed I should move in for just a month to begin with, to make sure we all got on. On probation, I kept to my best behaviour. My only faux-pas during that time was at breakfast, which we all took together, sitting at the refectory table in the basement kitchen, enjoying Alex's home-made bread toasted to perfection. Alex, always in clean cords and properly ironed shirt, would turn towards me and courteously enquire if I would like the marmalade, or the butter. No thank you, I would reply, and carry on drinking my coffee and reading my book. I didn't realise that in turn I was supposed to offer the marmalade and the butter to him, and that in fact he had wanted them all along only hadn't been able to ask for them outright. This was the convoluted, self-denying form of manners he had learned at boarding-school but in which I had not been trained at the convent.

I found Alex alarming. Tall, lean, broad-shouldered, unsmiling, he appeared dry and reserved, and spoke in clipped sentences only when strictly necessary; revealing no emotion. He hovered, watching me for mistakes. The first time I used Polly's sewing-machine, he materialised from nowhere and stood at my shoulder, silently observing as I fumbled, to see whether I knew how to thread the bobbin correctly. When I asked him to show me his bicycle route into town one morning he agreed, saying sternly: just mind you keep up with me. On my mettle, at the very first junction I overtook him and sped off so fast that I lost him completely. He came home amused that night, and I saw him smile for the first time. He was an excellent cook, going very carefully by the book. He often made classic French country dishes: quiche lorraine, crème caramel, cabbage stewed with ham and sausages. On Saturday afternoons he would sometimes come downstairs from his writing and whip up feather-light scones. On these occasions I would sit and chat to him about his research into architectural design. You had to coax things out of him. Then he would talk about pseudo-vernacular in the suburbs, or lath-and-plaster Victorian walls, or the symbolic function of basements, whatever that was. Eventually we made friends; tentatively; I would open my arms to hug him and he would give me a swift peck on the cheek. He was always busy; no lolling around daydreaming. Not in public, anyway. On spring weekends he fixed up his boat, kept at a yard in Essex, and then on summer weekends he went off sailing. Sometimes his friend Alistair came round and they played chess. Alistair and his wife had a child. After an afternoon at their flat Alex returned exhausted: you have to watch children all the time!

Sim, a bearded, relaxed American clad in baseball jacket and trainers, was easier to make friends with. He, like Alex, enjoyed cooking, and introduced me to dishes such as tuna chopped up with spring onions and mayonnaise, BLTs, home-made baked beans. One day he served us asparagus: to me, a luxury. Sim was as shy as Alex in his own way, never talking about himself, but quite happy if I joined him to watch football on TV while smoking joints. As long as I didn't start making elaborate deconstructive analyses while stoned. I would start going on about balletic masculinity and poor Sim, fed up but polite, would shrug and pull on the joint. Like Alex, he bicycled to work, but at weekends he drove an old ambulance. I used to accompany him on bulk-buying trips to the wholesalers, where we stocked up on tinned food for the household and tinned catfood for the cats. I'd never gone shopping by ambulance before. I enjoyed zooming across west London and the easy, careless way in which we filled up our enormous metal trolley with multiples of everything. Sim also used the ambulance when he acted as roadie for his rock band, The Resisters. He played rhythm guitar. The band did the rounds of all the bops and benefit gigs for left-wing and libertarian causes. Their songs had socially aware lyrics. One chorus went: 'oh the pain oh the pain when you go insane oh the p-p-p-p-p-p-p-p-pain'. Sometimes the band practised in our basement and then stayed to supper.

Polly, dark-haired and fine-featured, with delicate, arched eyebrows and big dark eyes, did not recognise her own beauty and was very modest generally. She worked as an art historian, writing books on art by women. She cooked when it was her turn. Rather than rustic French dishes, she favoured the (*plus*) *haute cuisine* taught by Julia Child in *Mastering the Art of French Cooking*. She impressed me by whisking up hollandaise as a matter of course whenever she served fish. When Sim's American family came to stay, Polly, worrying about the amount they ate (they were all fat), nonetheless felt obliged to produce the big roast dinners they loved, the meat loaf and tomato sauce, the apple pies and cheesecakes.

What did I cook? A mishmash. A bit of everything plus a lot of aubergines. On Saturday mornings I raced off to the fruit and veg market on Portobello Road, armed with two big baskets, and bought cornucopias of fresh vegetables. Mind yer backs! The market, hurly-burly, rang with cries and shouts, snatches of song. Rotten vegetables, vegetable peelings, orange wrappers, blue tissue lining-papers, shallow plywood boxes, littered the ground, silted up the kerbs. The air smelled of fresh greens, of ripe fruit, of rot. I became a regular, chattering to other shoppers as we jostled in the queues, greeting them each week. I got to know my favourite stallholders quite well. They bawled jokes to each other as they twisted bags full of spuds, parsnips, carrots, and spun the bags exuberantly by their brown paper ears. Here you are darling! They would tease me: what sauce are you going to put on them artichokes? And when I replied: cream, probably, they'd invite themselves to dinner. At the end of the day, when the stalls, festooned with strings of yellow electric light bulbs, were dismantled, and the wooden barrows wheeled away, clattering on iron-rimmed wheels down the uneven street, the nuns came foraging for scraps in the hills of waste along the kerbs.

I usually bought more vegetables than strictly needed, partly so that I could demonstrate to the others I was contributing sufficiently to the household, partly just for the pleasure of it. Our step-in larder was huge. The fridge was large too. This atmosphere of easy amplitude was permissive, made me feel generous and capable; I rejoiced, feeling I could cook anything I wanted, splash the olive oil around, drink lots of wine. Polly did not display her wealth in any ostentatious way. Quite the opposite: for example she dressed (very elegantly) in second-hand clothes. Nonetheless one felt (and enjoyed) the presence of money: the size and number of rooms in her house; the pieces of antique furniture dotted around; the lack of shabbi-ness. Two bathrooms plus a downstairs lav! Everything was clean (we all shared the cleaning) and in working order; unlike any of the houses in which I'd lived before. The neighbours, less bohemian and chic than Polly, were all well-off too. I loved spotting Holland Park woman, with her navy cashmere jumper, navy tights, navy pumps with gold bars, her well-cut tweed skirt, her striped shirt with the collar turned up, her string of pearls. Women here were crisply spoken and crisply ironed. The banker-husbands too.

The district, at the end of the seventies, still had plenty of small local shops, and only one trendy, overpriced deli, Mr Christian's, which I scorned to enter. Garcia's, on Portobello Road, sold Spanish produce at realistic prices, and I went there to buy salami and cheese and to ogle the tall, wry-faced boy with curly dark hair who worked behind the counter. Round the corner, the old-fashioned grocer's shop still sold corned beef, custard-powder, digestive biscuits. There were no wine bars up here (Julie's was further west); just pubs. A branch of the Body Shop had arrived; I thought its post-art-nouveau frontage pretty tacky. Just along the road, the butcher, in his striped blue and white apron, acted as therapist for his queue of women customers, cheering everybody up with jokes, suggesting delicious cuts. Trips to the launderette were enlivened by chats to the manageress. She had lost many of her teeth, although three long, narrow ones remained, sunk separately in her lower gums. She once described to me going to the dentist: private, so it hurt less. He was so sexy he could have taken her head off and she wouldn't have cared. Fillings, now, were another matter. She'd told him she couldn't stand the pain; better to whip them all out and have false ones put in. She was going to a party, Americans, they were bound to offer her a glass of wine so she wanted to look nice. The bloke's got a ballerina staying with him, you should just see the jewellery she leaves lying around, well. I'll be handing round the wine and so on at this party, I only work here because it's over the road from where I live. She looked at me: do you work?

Indeed I did. I went on working at Latin American Newsletters, earning just enough to live on, and started a second novel. My first, *A Piece of the Night*, had come out in autumn 1978; the first piece of original fiction published by The Women's Press. All my friends came to the launch. I was very proud that *A Piece of the Night* was joint winner, with John Lahr's biography of Joe Orton, of the *Gay News* Literary Award 1978. I framed the certificate and hung it on my bedroom wall. Reviews divided between praising my imagination, muscular prose and inventive story structure and deprecating my obvious wish to destroy Western civilisation. The poet Blake Morrison (who twenty years later became a friend) said stern things about over-the-top poetic language employing (oh no) domestic imagery: clouds like apricots, well, really.

Many of the young men I knew despised feminism. James banned it as a subject one night when I went to supper, criticising me for wearing a women's-symbol earring: gratuitous nonsense. The noble struggle of the workers was fine, less so the noble struggle of women. Dunc, another medic friend there that evening, a trainee psychiatrist, insisted that feminist ideas were just weak rhetoric and polemic and feminists incapable of sanely living their lives day to day. My earring showed my exhibitionism and my pleasure in femaleness my narcissism. However cheerful, unneurotic, well dressed and men-loving I might have been feeling when I arrived, these stern critics knew better. With friends I could always fight back and defend myself, however, and I went on loving my dear friend James, and indeed cherishing his ferocity, his sternly expressed, uncompromising views.

Now that I was a published author, Alison Hennegan, *Gay News*'s literary editor, started giving me reviewing work, enabling me to lap up books by Maureen Duffy, Judith Kazantzis, Monique Wittig, Aphra Behn and many others. I got to know the editor, Denis Lemon, and had supper at his house a couple of times. He wasn't a bit like the gay men I'd made friends with through Lesbian Left. He was a right-leaning, hard-headed businessman. A right-wing furore, engineered by Mary Whitehouse and her supporters, erupted over his decision to publish a poem featuring a gay centurion fantasising about Jesus on the cross. The poem suggested that Jesus understood gay suffering all too well. What was the fuss about? I could see that right-wing Christians would not like the links made between masochism, Jesus and gay sex, but the poem was a bad one, crude and sentimental, lacking real subversive power. People should only get upset about bad poems' badness, I thought, not their content. Only good poetry could be really challenging. Whitehouse and co. were idiots. So I scornfully decided. Nonetheless *Gay News* was successfully prosecuted for blasphemous libel.

Polly and I had lots of friends in common through the women's movement. With different groups of these friends, including Ali and others from the writers' group, I went on holiday several times during these years, renting houses in Provence (still cheap in those days), and then reading, walking, swimming. Polly's friend Ruthie, a Canadian with a deep, rich voice and chuckle, who had started off at *Spare Rib* and now worked as an in-house editor for Virago, did much of the driving. She had once been a chauffeur to someone she described as 'my old madame' and swept us confidently along motorways in her *deux-chevaux*. I cowered in the back, alarmed by her habit, while cruising at speed, of meditatively lifting both hands off the steering-wheel.

On one of these trips we stayed in the hilltop village of Bonnieux, in an old, dark, high-ceilinged and cavernous house, which belonged to a highly intellectual lesbian friend of Ruthie's, much given to writing earnest essays on Lenin. In those idealistic days, one didn't expect Marxist-feminist revolutionaries to own second homes. It was what a Leninist would call a contradiction. Ali, making the bed one morning in the main bedroom, discovered a whip underneath it, with little metal bits knotted into the thongs. One didn't expect Marxist-feminist revolutionaries to own whips, either.

My room in that house had flaking, dusty-pink shutters, a red-tiled floor, a straw-seated chair, a sagging bed. Crickets sang outside. The heat beat at the closed shutters like fists. During the siesta time I dozed and daydreamed, smoked untipped

Gitanes, wrote poems, caught hold of threads which would pull me further into the labyrinth of my new novel.

I was unhappy and tense much of the time, worrying about things. The usual: money, work, love, family. My mother had loathed *A Piece of the Night*, finding it ugly, cruel and disgusting, and believed I had written it deliberately wanting to hurt her. To mock everything she believed in. To destroy her. I felt sad and angry. I wanted her love and approval but realised I couldn't have them if I wrote the wrong sort of book. The price of independence was to feel unloved and lonely. My child self mourned and felt squished. My bloody-minded adult self gritted her teeth and got on with things and kept going.

I thought more than ever about mother–daughter relationships. Did the daughter's struggle for freedom have to be at the mother's expense? What did mothers really feel, deep down? I was struggling out from under my mother's shadow, and we were beginning to talk to each other. My mother started that conversation, by denouncing *A Piece of the Night*. She could have been coldly contemptuous and said nothing, but she spoke out and said exactly what she thought. I spoke back in my book's defence, tried to explain it. So we lurched on. Fighting, I now see, is very intimate. My mother and I fought breast to breast. Sometimes it felt like a fight to the death. Sometimes like an embrace. We had calm moments, too, in which I felt my mother's sweetness. I adored her as well as fought with her.

After months of hating my clerical job at LAN, feeling tormented and desperate because I was so bored, I finally gathered up my courage and gave in my notice. The women I worked with were relieved, because I'd become careless, and they'd had to tell me off. I felt ashamed of having let boredom and frustration affect me to the extent that I was letting them down and not pulling my weight. Eventually, realising how angry I felt at having so little time to write, I did the sensible thing and decided to look for another way of earning a living. As a farewell present my colleagues gave me a big stack of self-carboning typing paper (to use with the little Olivetti Lettera 22 typewriter Dina, my sister-communard in Camberwell, had rescued from a dustbin and given to me) and a twisty-necked bottle of Limoncello.

In 1979 (I think), Stephanie, managing director at The Women's Press, hired me briefly, for a few hours every week. I did her filing (she often worked at home in her smart little house in Bow) and grilled her lamb chops for lunch. I was grateful to her for publishing me but not grateful at all for her high-handed ways when encountered at close quarters. Stephanie did the sensible thing, finding another assistant. She did the supportive thing too, applying for a grant for me from the Arts Council. Her second application succeeded, and with what seemed the enormous sum of £1000 I retired to my (very comfortable) garret in Holland Park to get on with writing.

The room was wide and low-ceilinged. I arranged my books in wooden fruit boxes scavenged from the market, pinned up, around my double bed, postcard reproductions of saints, virgins, sibyls, poets and novelists. Alex lent me his big old armchair, covered in blue and green chintz. I would wheel this over to the window and curl up in it to write, pad of paper resting on the wide, fat arm. High up, I could watch the sky, the light changing as dusk began, dissolving from rose to lemon and pale green and indigo. Sometimes I wrote in pubs, liking my little pool of silence and concentration in the midst of the hubbub.

My thousand pounds bought me time to write, but eventually ran out. In 1981, thanks to Mandy Merck, whom I knew from Lesbian Left, I was lucky enough to be offered temp work at *Time Out*, where Mandy worked. Mandy, very clever and witty, was a priceless intellectual resource. If I wanted the low-down on Foucault, or Lacan, or Cixous, but didn't have time to read them properly, I'd phone her up. You want the ten-minute version or the five-minute version? she would ask in her Brooklyn accent. The five-minute one, I would reply, and then Mandy would give me a rapid distillation of the relevant theory.

I became replacement clerk to the editor's assistant Diana Simmonds. Di was a tall, handsome lesbian goddess, cool and humorous, with a wicked turn of phrase. She bounced on strong toes, seemed very athletic. Nonetheless her health was not always good. If she fell ill or took time off, I stepped in. I sat and typed in a little fifth-floor cubby-hole I shared with John Fordham, the editor. He had a proper desk, facing the door, and I perched at a sort of side counter. Our two glass walls gave on to Covent Garden market, which still, in those days, sold fruit and veg, though the big wholesale market had gone. At 10 a.m., when I arrived for work, the cream-coloured cobbles looked freshly washed. If I looked down Southampton Street, I could see beyond the Strand, flowing with traffic, down a little alleyway on its far side, to the river, which seemed to flow between buildings, between streets, sparkling and glit-tering in the sun, a street turned to liquid silver. Dr Johnson had walked along here. So had Virginia Woolf, thinking of Johnson, of his night strolls with Boswell, of the prostitutes accosting them there.

Now I too could stroll these streets. I was a *flâneur*, a *flâneuse*. However, lots of men assumed that as I was wandering the streets by myself I must be touting for business. Only men were *flâneurs*. A lone woman walking along the street was a

185

street walker. Similarly, if you stood outside a pub, waiting for a friend, you'd be accosted non-stop. How much? the men would murmur, sidling up: how much? Most of them were repulsive-looking. I felt deep sympathy for the prostitutes who had to service them. George Sand, in order to wander freely, unaccompanied, through Paris (as well as save money on elaborate toilettes), to run home by herself from the theatre at two in the morning, unaccosted, had resorted to male dress. My version was a big overcoat, flat shoes. How angry I felt with the men who curtailed my freedom to wander obliviously! I had no sympathy for them whatsoever.

I could talk to Fordham about all this. A shy man, tremendously droll, he was also patient, tolerant and kind. Nothing seemed to faze him. He loved women and women loved him. On my second day at *Time Out*, his lover Ros Asquith, who wrote theatre reviews for the magazine, drifted in to say hello. She was skinny and long-legged, with enormous dark blue eyes, a thick mane of chestnut hair, and a sense of humour to match John's. She was tall and John was short and they got on very well because they were equally eccentric as well as loving each other so much. She and Di introduced me to all their close mates in the office, including Penny Valentine, the rock journalist, habituée of Dusty Springfield, the Beatles, Rolling Stones and Elton John, who now wrote for the TV section, and Sally Bradbery, who wrote for the food section. Sally did café as well as restaurant reviews and awarded chips rather than stars. She loved cricket and opera and was very well read. She was a good friend of Val Wilmer, the photographer, famous for her portraits of black musicians, who also did work for the magazine.

Eventually Ros, Di, Penny, Sally and I formed a women's consciousness-raising group, meeting in each other's homes to discuss our lives. After Penny gave birth to her son Dan, we met at her house most of the time. We would have supper together. PV, as we all called her, the descendant of Jewish-Italian immigrants who had worked as waiters near Russell Square, was an excellent cook. I remember her sliced courgettes dipped in rosemary-sprinkled batter then fried in olive oil. Sometimes we brought in fish and chips, to spare PV the work. Consciousness-raising also involved wine, general chitchat. When the formal part of the evening began, we went round the table, listening to each other in turn. We had twenty minutes each in which to talk, and then people asked questions. The meetings were confidential, so that we could say what we really meant. Working in an office staffed by clever, ambitious journalists, you watched your back to some extent. In the women's group, you were equals who tried to help each other. We called it giving support. This was, of course, a crucial plank of the feminist raft. *Time Out* was ostensibly liberal and groovy but in some ways an old-fashioned and sexist institution. Although many of the male journalists were individually brotherly and sweet, women in the office as a group still had to struggle to be heard and properly valued, given responsible jobs. The NUJ chapel was strong, however, and as a result we earned decent money.

Working at *Time Out* I learned invaluable lessons about office politics, the intricacies of commissioning, editing and paying contributors, the processes of typesetting and printing. Matt Hoffman, the literary editor, encouraged me to write occasional book reviews. Two hundred words max: a good training. I also did quite a bit of walking up and down the corridor outside the newsroom, peeping adoringly through the open door at Duncan Campbell, the news editor. What a peach! Cool, handsome, funny. He was well out of reach, because he was Julie Christie's steady. Julie came to our parties and benefits. She was radical, very intelligent, extremely shy. She never sought the limelight but just mixed in with everybody. At one party at a lesbian commune in Gloucester Drive, Finsbury Park, attended by many *Time Out* friends, Judith Williamson, a film critic, always very hot on cultural theory, started discoursing about film and the camera's gaze and how it created beauty. That woman over there, for example, she said, pointing: that blonde, she'd look great on film. It was Julie of course.

I enjoyed dressing up for parties and to go into work. I bought most of my clothes from the second-hand stalls at the top of Portobello Road, where the market overflowed into Golborne Road. I remember a black, polka-dotted 1950s dress, with pleated skirt and three-quarter-length sleeves, which I wore with a wide plastic apple-green belt showing off my small waist. I had a severely cut black 1950s suit I adored, nipped in at the waist, the back of the shoulders yoked in curves of overlapping black ribbon, with tiny curved pockets outlined in black ribbon, buttoned in jet. I had a Victorian lace-edged shirt, and a long red rubberised 1950s mac to whose collar I pinned bunches of violets. I had a grey poplin nurse's dress, a French-blue overall. I enjoyed parading these outfits. I liked men looking at me and having to decode me. Just as much as I also liked sitting invisibly at home writing and being the voyeur in my imagination. I liked to look and I liked being looked at. But I dressed according to how I felt. On days when I wanted to be invisible I slung on old jeans and raced cheerfully along and no one noticed me and that was great.

My intermittent temp work brought me new friends but not enough to live on. In 1980, I applied for and got the job of writer-in-residence to Labour-run Lambeth Council, ruled over by Red Ted Knight, thorn in the flesh to the Labour Party and *bête noire* of the right-wing press. Down to Brixton I whizzed on my bicycle, to have a look around. I sat in a café, to get my breath back, drinking a mug of tea and relishing the décor. Open shelves, painted alternately in dark red and pale green, formed boxes holding ornaments: a soda siphon, three tins of peaches with navy and yellow labels, a bunch of multicoloured plastic flowers stuck in a jug, a plaster-of-Paris Alsatian. I ate sausage and chips and chatted to the café's Italian owners while a grubby white cat, attracted by the smell of frying bacon, scratched itself against the lintel.

I was given office space in Brixton library, which I did not use, as I was keener on the outreach aspect of the job. The idea was to take poetry to the people, if they wanted it, and to urge them to have a go even if they did not; to run writing work-shops in day centres and youth clubs. Wherever The People were to be found there would The Poet be also. I was ready. I was willing.

I toured all the Lambeth libraries, meeting my new col-leagues. I remember disliking the librarian at West Norwood, a smoothie in tasteful grey slacks, grey and blue tweed jacket, who referred comfortably to the badly behaved disturbed girls in the local hostels, the low-achieving truant children in the truancy centre, as though they were just fixed points, objects not human beings, in an unchanging land-scape. He obviously disliked me too: in his terms I presumably seemed over-idealistic, just a scruffy girl, unap-preciative of his incisive introductory speech. He pointed out the statue of a nude Oedipus, tucked away in the library's back yard. It's got, that statue's got, an obscene nickname, he told me with a smirk. I put on my cheerfullest voice: Oh really? What's that then? Do tell me. He looked sideways, and then down at his tasteful, well-polished shoes. We call it Oedipus, he said stiffly.

Sometimes I travelled from Holland Park to Brixton and points further south by tube. One day on the platform at Victoria I chatted to a woman doubling as train guard and cleaner. She straightened up from her mop and bucket and waved to the driver to press the button to close the doors. Another guard wandered up and joined us. Above the roar of trains they explained to me about fluffers. All the fluff from people's clothes flies off down the tunnel, you see, and then every night we have to go after it, and roll it into a big ball, and then we set fire to it. Afterwards, I wrote in my diary, 'I couldn't believe that last bit; were they having me on?'

Sometimes I got off the tube at odd stops just to explore. One night I walked along the Embankment from Fulham and Chelsea to Pimlico, looking into lighted windows, having fantasies out of *The Woman in White*. I imagined kidnappings and murders being committed in that lonely darkness. I peered through a pair of lodge gates at a circular drive, and beyond that, far away, a huge old house with gables and wings and yellow lights winking in its black façade. I felt back in the eighteenth century; I was a small boy creeping through the grass.

One of the Lambeth jobs I enjoyed most was Girls' Night at a youth club near the Oval. Lots of sports and other activities got laid on for boys, but practically nothing for girls; they weren't supposed to need to be kept out of trouble. Girls' Night had therefore been set up and was run by energetic Teresa, very proud of her London accent which a professor of linguistics had recently recorded on tape for a project at his university. All the girls who attended were black. I just sat about at first, getting to know them. Then, to those who wanted them, I offered writing tutorials. Sometimes the girls made crafts. We did a lot of dancing. They tried to teach me to dance to soul music. I was pretty hopeless; kept swinging my hips too much (the way we had danced in the late sixties). The girls were fabulous and didn't give up on me; they kept me tapping and shrugging. Afterwards I would sit in the pub with Teresa, and Hilary and Gordon, artists painting a sternly socialist-realist street mural, featuring portraits of the multicultural community, for a local council estate. The locals I talked to found the mural ugly and dreamed of something more poetic and fanciful, featuring waterfalls, unicorns and forests. Teresa was brisk, tough, unsentimental, full of curiosity. On the night the Brixton riots broke out in April 1981 she jumped into her car and drove over there to take a look.

Towards Christmas 1980, I had been, accompanied by a librarian called Fiona, to visit the women doing a thirteen-week fresh-start course at Brixton College of Further Education. They had already visited Brixton library with me, so we weren't strangers to one another. Rob, their teacher, had organised a film showing of *Double Day*, a film about women's lives in Mexico, Bolivia and Argentina. It was strong and moving and I kept weeping at the women's courage and endurance. The woman sitting next to me was writing her Christmas cards to the class while she watched. She obviously concluded I was a poor creature. She nudged me, told me to cheer up, and passed me a boiled sweet.

When the lights came up my neighbour on the other side described the trouble she was having with her boiler and how she'd wiped the floor with the man who fitted the thermostat wrongly. Both women told me briskly that they had enjoyed Rob's class, but that its equal opportunities aspect didn't mean much to them, what with the economic situation and the unemployment crisis. Then they sprang up and tugged me into the classroom next door for the Christmas party. Within five minutes the group had decorated the room with coloured paper streamers, fixed up a sound system belting out reggae (scorning me because I didn't recognise the band), and set up a bar dishing out drinks and food. They gave me a half-pint of sweet sherry and we drank to their future.

I zoomed off, pursued by Fiona, who preferred to move slowly, and got the bus to the women's carpentry collective in West Norwood. All the passengers on the bus were entertained, during the ride, by a woman loudly describing her sister's operation. She was slit open and all her innards pulled out and the tumour, when it was found, was as big as THIS. We all turned round to look.

The carpentry workshop was sited in a former factory. Eight women stood at their benches busily sawing and planing wood to make stools. The week before they had made bookshelves and after Christmas they'd make bathroom cabinets. The room in which they worked was vast and airy, with one wall, practically all window, giving on to a graveyard littered with Victorian monuments toppled about like pulled teeth. Mrs Beeton, the carpentry teacher told me, was buried there. This was the last day of term, and also a student's birthday, so at one o'clock everyone downed tools and we had a party. More bumpers of sweet wine and some excellent pâté. One of the women told me all about her mother, who'd had to send her off to a council boarding-school when she was four, and never told her when her birthday was, and forgot to turn up for her wedding as well. This week her mother had said: make me a Christmas cake and I'll come and collect it on Tuesday night. So this woman had stayed up half Monday night icing the cake and then her mother turned up a day late for it and decided it was too heavy, anyway, to take back to Ramsgate on the bus.

This woman would have been the star of the writing group I'd have liked to start, but the carpentry teacher wasn't keen. In any case, it wasn't the moment for serious discussion, since everyone was drinking hard, intent on merriment. So Fiona and I departed. We plodded through the backstreets to the station in the winter sunshine, passing derelict cars, their rusty flanks surreally decorated by an itinerant artist with painted pigs and flowers. We leapt on to the train and rocked away to Streatham Hill. We were going to attend the Lime Trees Christmas party.

I'd been coming regularly to Lime Trees for three months. This was a council-funded day-care centre, in a large, detached Victorian house, for people with mental illnesses who had been released from psychiatric wards back into the community, for what was called rehabilitation. This meant sitting all day in a workshop making crafts, which sold cheaply in local markets. I thought that the clients (as they were called) got ripped off, but they valued the company, and being able to get out. When they got too bored making little toys and fancy what-nots, they attended my Friday poetry workshop in the dark, gloomy sitting-room. Proclaiming your love of poetry ensured a leisurely hour in which to snooze, do the crossword puzzle in the newspaper, or chat. The poetry-lovers were pretty glum much of the time, their suffering dulled by drugs, usually Largactil. We groped our way through the fogs towards each other.

At the beginning, facing a roomful of silent, remote-looking people, I felt clumsy and shy, blurting out my enthusiasms. They didn't mind. They were shy too. I soon felt at home with them. They didn't, most of them, want to write poetry, heaven forfend, but they quite enjoyed sitting back in their armchairs while I read it to them. They told me what they wanted to hear and I brought it along the following week. Kipling's 'If' was a great favourite. They wanted to live up to its message. They liked Dylan Thomas too: his raciness, pace, swing, dark undertow.

They called me the poetry lady. There were about a dozen of us. I especially liked Kathy, a woman of about fifty with a sorrowful, harshly lined face. She loved classical music, Beethoven in particular, but could not bear listening to it for long as it made her feel too emotional; if she put a record on all her anguish erupted. You read poetry quite nicely, she told me. On the other hand, Gloria, a glamorous, heavily made-up blonde, didn't think much of my efforts. I disliked her, because she interrupted all the time, warned me never to say anything upsetting in case it caused her to have a fit, and wrote copious amounts of bad poetry, very fast, tossing off verses about kittens and clouds with silver linings, which we all had to admire. Gloria, in her sixties, dressed in flamboyant and sexy costumes, which seemed like disguises: short slit skirts, sheer black stockings, stiletto heels. I assume, looking back, that her sentimental poetry was her way of wiping out unpleasant feelings, but at the time I just felt secretly intolerant. Grace, another poetry amateur, a childlike, sweet person in her seventies, didn't like Gloria's sexiness one bit. She didn't like the mention of love or sex because if she thought about these subjects she might explode. Jack, a quiet fifty-year-old, suddenly one day burst out and recited a poem he'd written about a man alone in a room feeling afraid of the ticking of the clock. I praised it. Then Jack retreated into his silence again.

On this occasion, the Christmas party had so far involved a Nativity play and a magic show. Fiona and I had arrived in time for the singsong. Christine, the ebullient, powerful matron, a middle-aged blonde with an alarmingly jolly manner, had a penchant for theatricals. When Prince Charles married Lady Di, six months later, Christine got dressed up as the blooming bride, complete with tiara and bouquet, and processed around the craft workshop with two social workers holding her train, to everybody's bewilderment. Today she was busy shepherding three tightly corseted actors in Victorian music-hall outfits towards the piano. I assumed we were witnessing chaps doing a sort of mock Hinge and Bracket performance, then realised that these three ecstatic sopranos, clad in evening gowns and large feathered hats, were not drag artistes at all but Real Women. They clasped their hands in the air and led us in bosom-swelling renderings of 'The Lambeth Walk', 'Maybe It's Because I'm a Londoner', and other songs I didn't know though everyone else did. Even Grace whispered along with the chorus of 'Three Old Ladies Stuck in the Lavatory'. We had all been dished out spoons, cymbals and tambourines so that we could play accompaniments. At 4 p.m. the bell for tea rang and the clients rose as one, dropped their percussion instruments, and surged to the door, rather to the astonishment of the three Dame Ednas at the piano. I was then introduced to the Mayor, who fingered his gold chain, glanced at my weird clothes, and delicately enquired about my mental health. The clients returned to dance the hokey-cokey. I got home that night pretty tipsy.

I was also invited to join in some sessions with an adult literacy class, learning from these students and their tutor the lengths to which they went in everyday life to conceal their lack of knowledge; their fear of being found out. Grown men admitted their vulnerability, willingly submitted to the discipline of the classroom. Desire was the key: encouraged by their tutor to write their life stories, realising that someone wanted to read them, considered them compelling, they learned fast.

On a couple of occasions I went to the hostel for homeless people near Waterloo. The men could come in to shower and shave and wash their clothes. First of all, as preparation, I had to attend the social workers' morning meeting. Young university graduates spouted highfalutin long-winded theoretical sociological claptrap. Then they pushed me out 'on the floor' without a word of guidance. Thrust towards a large group of strangers, I felt scared. I was an intruder. The men crowded up to introduce themselves and to talk to me. They were kind and friendly, much more sensitive than the theory-babbling social workers. They all wanted to tell me their stories but we did not manage to set up a writers' group.

Lambeth, the home of 'mad' radicals, was often in the media firing-line. The *Daily Telegraph* got hold of me by phone and asked to do a phone interview. Flattered, I suppose, and not understanding that I was being stitched up, I cooperated, politely answering all the female journalist's questions. She asked me what I looked like. Curly-haired, I replied. Then, having sent a photographer round to snap me, she wrote a snide little piece implying we had met and talked intimately. 'Michèle Roberts, a chatty girl with curly hair . . .' As I remember, as it seemed to me, the article managed simultaneously to suggest that I was a lesbian paedophile preying on innocent black girls in the sanctuary of their youth clubs and also that I was Ken Livingstone's puppet and heterosexual sidekick (Ken Livingstone led the left-wing Labour group running the Greater London Council, which partly funded my Lambeth residency). The *Evening Standard* picked up the story and ran their version of it. Nobody at Lambeth Council was willing to defend the job I was doing. The Greater London Arts Council, when I asked them to help, suggested I write my own letter of self-defence. Lambeth had been going to employ me for a second year but dropped the idea. That was that.

On my last day in the job I stood near the churchyard in Streatham where I used to buy earrings from the market stalls, and waited for the bus to take me back over the river. The old woman standing next to me burst out laughing and pointed to the shop window behind us: see those knickers? I swivelled and looked at stands of underwear. The knickers were made of lace and frilled satin, two minuscule triangles tied at the side with silk strings. The woman said: when I was young, you could buy a pair of knickers for one and elevenpence. Change from two shillings in those days. Look at those things! Five pounds for a pair of knickers! They'd hardly keep you warm! Her face was brown and wrinkled as a walnut, and she looked straight into my face and laughed out loud and made me laugh too.

I struggled with rejection on a second literary front. I had written my second novel, 'The Heavenly Twins', too fast, over-confidently, and The Women's Press had rejected it. The reader's report (by Hannah Kanter, a friend of Sarah LeFanu's) said there wasn't enough childhood, mother-and-daughter stuff in it. I was upset: I'd done that in my first novel, for heaven's sake. Now all that was dealt with; I didn't have to create another heroine with an unconscious, with conflicts. Wrong again, apparently. I did. Stephanie said contemptuously: it's so childish. It was too intro-spective, as well, apparently. I felt completely anguished. Did I feel angry, too? I must have done, but I couldn't articulate it. Anger turned inwards, against myself: I felt so despairing I fan-tasised throwing myself off Westminster Bridge. Lisa Alther, a good friend of Stephanie's, consoled me: she had drawers stuffed full of unpublished novels before finally getting *Kinflicks*, her blockbusting bestseller, accepted.

After six months' gloom and block, I set to and began rewriting the novel. Sandra-the-therapist helped me, reading the typescript and commenting that I'd left out something crucial. What was it? I had to explore that gap. Dive not into the river Thames but back down into the unconscious. The rewritten novel turned into *The Visitation*, finally published in 1983. It dramatised questions about sexual love between men and women and tried to answer them.

All my novels enact problem-solving, pose questions of content and form then try to answer them. You have to invent the form that best expresses the content. They're integrated; part of each other. After many false starts I discovered that I was rewriting the myth of the Fall from paradise, tracking from paradise lost to paradise regained. I was disagreeing with Milton and D.H. Lawrence, though, in the conclusions I reached. I used the figure of a pair of twins, a boy and a girl, to explore gender difference. Sara Maitland suggested including an opening paragraph describing the twins pre-birth; she was absolutely right. Writing the novel, I discovered that what had scared me so much was the thought of sibling incest. I also discovered that the Fall meant, to me, the loss of the mother, the loss of the nurturing maternal body. We're pushed out into the world, mourning, and just have to get on with it.

I split up with the man I'd been seeing. He had begun to get involved with someone else. He told me that I frightened him: I was too emotionally intense, too sensitive, with too strong responses. I knew he was right: we did not really suit. Next day I wandered around Hyde Park, then sat unhappily in the ICA café. Sad as I was, I could not stop observing other people. A man at the neighbouring table was telling his companions how his father got rid of his mother: he put hair-remover cream in her shampoo bottles. The man added: my mother had a real slave mentality: she loved looking after him.

I treated myself to a taxi home. With the driver I discussed sex and feminism. He asked: but who'll be the blade and who'll be the handle? You have to decide, girl. When a man and a woman get together, it's a ball of fire. Then he added: and they should be companions. I'm married. My wife has the children and I drive the cab. I see my boy at the weekends, my pride and joy.

I wasn't my parents' pride and joy, though things between us were slowly beginning to mend, thanks to my sessions with Sandra-the-therapist, to the support given me by women friends going through similar struggles themselves (men friends were good fun but didn't want to know about so-called heavy stuff), and to my parents beginning to realise that I was adamant about continuing to write, whatever the cost. Once, Dad confided on the phone that he understood I'd had to fight him so ferociously in order to become independent. He had deliberately never offered me a penny of financial help after I left university, wanting me to stand on my own two feet, and I thought that that was absolutely right. I felt proud of managing all by myself, and when I didn't manage too well, I certainly did not tell Mum and Dad and nor did I ever ask them for money. Of course I asked not for money but for love. They couldn't always understand the language with which I asked but stuck it out in long, passionate conversations. I don't want to be an old patriarch, Dad said on the phone that day. I remember how I overflowed with love for him when he said that.

He had been one of three brothers: Reg, Arthur and Mick. Grandpa had called them Veg, Arpic (Harpic) and Micky Drip (short for dripping). Reg, my father, knew he wasn't his mother's favourite. He cared for Nana now and had done for years, ever since she moved in to live with us when I was ten years old. Grandpa was dead, and so were Arpic and Micky Drip. At Uncle Mick's funeral wake Dad told me in a furious whisper to cross the room and stop Nana crying. I didn't. While Nana, aged ninety-nine, weakened and died, Dad got furious with her all over again. He just couldn't bear it. He couldn't bear the thought of losing her and he couldn't bear his grief. I witnessed his pain and could not comfort him. After the funeral, sitting alone in the house, Dad heard her walking to and fro upstairs. He told me this. When I reminded him of it, a few years later, he vehemently denied it. He wanted to believe only in reason and logic. They shored him up against the dangers of emotion. Tears might start to flow and never stop.

That day on the phone Dad reminded me of Grandpa's favourite toast: a guinea-pig and a cat! And Grandpa's word-twists: birds were dribs and monkeys were yeknoms. Dad still vanquished me in discussions, each of us storming at the other, but I began to realise that now he loved me not just as his child, the would-be-nice little girl, but as the person I had become. I knew Nana had loved me. Her love was my template. Her linguistic inventiveness too: her original turns of phrase, the plays she had written as a young woman, the rude rhyming epics she extemporised when she babysat, the plays she had written for us as children to perform at Christmas. (One of these melodramas starred my parents, Dad as villain hissing at my mother: what, girl, you dare to thwart me thus?) When Nana died I drank a lot of whisky and rushed around *Time Out* telling everyone my darling grandmother was dead. Inappropriate behaviour, said Sandra-the-therapist.

I wished I'd heard Nana walking up and down after her death. Other people saw ghosts; I didn't. I didn't see Nana's ghost, but went on relying on the memory of her love. I had coaxed her to write her memoirs. She'd written four pages before she died; I have them still. I have all her letters. No one will ever again write to me: well dear, look after that cold. Have a basin of onion gruel at night. Or some rum. I hope your lodgings are not cold and full of draughts. In her late nineties Nana had read *A Piece of the Night*. She didn't quite get it, she wrote to me, so she was going to reread it. Who were these Elizabethans? She meant lesbians. I still call sapphists Elizabethans.

I had lost Nana but still had my lovely women friends, trusty and true. Sarah LeFanu rang me one night: she and Chris had just returned from Mozambique. I zoomed over to see her and we spent the evening together. I listened to hours of stories about Mozambique. Sarah was thinner, much more elegantly dressed than previously, and seemed older. Well, she was. She had been away for two years. Next day I wrote in my diary: 'I woke up this morning happiness everywhere, like being a child, simple, pure. Sarah is back.'

She and Chris bought the Fleetwood Street (Stoke Newington) house from James (who moved to a flat in Notting Hill), and moved in. I bicycled up to see them; my old stamping-ground. Sarah had begun work as an editor at The Women's Press. So far she hadn't seen through Stephanie, whereas, I wrote sourly in my diary: 'I know from my own and other women's experience how brutally she can treat her authors.' Sarah, Chris and I got back into our rhythm of going out together, to Sissinghurst for picnics, to pubs on the banks of the river Lea, to pubs in Stoke Newington Church Street; sitting talking and smoking on pavement kerbs as we'd always done, feet in the gutter, swallowing golden beer. On one such occasion I recorded that Sarah looked like an apricot, with her pink and brown skin, golden-red hair, flushed cheeks. She took off her black cotton Chinese sandals and wriggled her toes among dead matches and cigarette stubs. Such pretty feet she had: small and firm, flowering with toes like a sea-anemone.

Sarah, before going away, had introduced me to her old friend Julian Turton, a solicitor in the music business, who had a flat in Westbourne Grove. Jules, black-haired and plumpish, a kind and cheerful sybarite and gourmet, often invited me to supper. Sometimes his girlfriend Cassandra Jardine joined us, sometimes his flatmate Artemis Cooper. All Jules's friends were posh. He was an Old Etonian himself, but just about the only one I had ever met (Oxford had been full of them) who was warm and unpretentious. Jules was excellent at friendship: merry and inclusive. One night he cooked me sausages and filled me with wine, and then swept me off first to the Electric Cinema to see a glum Fassbinder movie, and then to visit his pal Ivo Dawnay, another Old Etonian, who needed cheering up, apparently, because he had just got married. The wedding had been small and simple: only one archbishop and only one telegram from Royalty, from the Queen Mother, Ivo's god-mother, accompanying the gift of some glasses. Ivo did not look cheerless at all (nor did his bride Chantal) but nonetheless we caroused half the night and finished up all the red wine in the house. (Ivo later introduced me to his sister Caroline, who worked as a literary agent for Peters, Fraser & Dunlop, and she took me on.)

The Electric, lit by elegant side lights in shaded pastel glass lamps, was a favourite haunt. I often went there to watch old movies. I'd stuff my pockets full of joints and get stoned while watching *films noirs* or 1940s classic women's weepies. Jules did get married in the end. He met a radio producer called Olivia. That was it: love at first sight. Clearing out his flat, preparing to move, he presented me with a wheel-back kitchen chair, which I have still, and a fabulous pair of 1950s black silk very high-heeled shoes, left by a passing girlfriend. I adored Jules. He was so funny and so generous, whether he was making vats of mayonnaise to accompany mountains of shrimps for a lunch party or whisking me off to music gigs (Echo and the Bunnymen and others) and never letting me pay for my ticket.

He was a good liberal but not, of course, a leftie. At *Time Out*, we acted out our left-wing idealism by striking. We had always had equal pay. Now Tony Elliott and his management team were trying to change that and introduce pay differentiation and hierarchical pay scales. After months of negotiations, the chapel finally decided to go on strike. We picketed the building for several weeks. Sim and the Resisters played benefit gigs. The strike broke; people couldn't afford to stay out of work too long. A group of us went off and formed the rival listings magazine *City Limits*, working from premises in Upper Street, Islington. John Fordham and Nigel Fountain became the new editors, with PV (Penny Valentine) working alongside them as chief sub. We all had equal pay, including the cleaning staff. I applied for and got the job of Poetry Editor.

My first interview involved going up to Bradford and interviewing Joolz and her fellow punk rock poets. We sat in their big communal kitchen and drank many cups of tea. Through Duncan Campbell, who knew him, I commissioned the poet Heathcote Williams to write us a poem. It contained the immortal lines: 'the people who run Tesco's must be Buddhists/ there is nothing there that you could possibly want.' Or words to that effect; I can't precisely remember. On our lawyer's advice, I had to get Heathcote to tone it down a bit and of course he felt fed up. When Lady Di was about to marry Prince Charles, Heathcote created a shrine to her in a local phone box in Notting Hill, complete with square of carpet covering the stained concrete floor.

I began to feel restless in the Holland Park house. I dreamed, increasingly, of finding my own place. Some of my friends, on regular incomes, had managed to get mortgages. Sarah and Chris, for example, were happily ensconced at Fleetwood Street. Roy and Pascale had moved to Paris where Roy had got a job as office manager at *Le Monde*. I visited them a couple of times in their spacious flat on one floor of an old building on the Rue St-Honoré near Les Halles, much admiring the block's grey-blue walls and wide, shallow staircase with its bare wooden treads. Ali, like me, could never have afforded her own place. She was still living in Lynne Segal's communal household in Highbury. Lynne was increasingly making her name as a writer on gender. She had curly red hair, a merry and mischievous freckled face, always just about to tremble into a smile. Sometimes, in summer, we held writers' groups meetings in the tangled, overgrown garden. My old friend Sian, from Oxford days, whom I still regularly saw, now co-owned a house in Leeds with friends.

My own existence felt precarious, in terms of earning so little, but also stuck. I couldn't see a way forward. I was through with communes; through with living always in someone else's house, as a guest or at best a housemate but with no power. Fond as I was of Polly, Sim and Alex, I wanted to live on my own.

A while back, one summer, Polly, who had a cottage in the grounds of her mother's country house, had taken us all down there for the weekend. The thatched cottage, Arts and Crafts style, perched in its own little garden at the edge of woods jostling with tall cow-parsley. We spotted the cuckoo we heard calling, and at night listened to the nightingale. The cottage, with its witch's-hat roof and veranda on two sides, evoked the most enchanting of doll's-houses. We spent a fine weekend, unusually happy in each other's company, cooking and gardening. I weeded the rockery, pulled up nettles, enjoyed forking these up and heaving them over the fence into the woodland of larches beyond. Rabbits frolicked about. We sat in the sun. We ate outside at a small table just big enough to hold four white plates with blue rims, four wineglasses, the tiny jug full of wild flowers I had picked. One evening feast involved Alex serving us roast lamb, new potatoes, carrots and cabbage, followed by rhubarb and egg custard. In the hay-scented darkness we lolled around the table by lamplight, very relaxed, chatting easily, no one feeling obliged to race off to get on with some work. Sim cooked another good meal next day: celery soup, *carottes rapées vinaigrette*, followed by brown bread, Stilton and oranges. That night I made a risotto with lamb stock and leftover lamb. I think we'd all decided that Polly, as hostess, didn't have to cook.

I wrote in my diary: 'I was shot through with terrible sharp darts of envy. Seeing the cottage, and all the pretty things Polly can just go out and buy for it without having to worry about the cost, I was filled with envy, and that made me realise how much I desire, how passionately I long for, my own home, just a little place, which I could do up & paint & decorate & arrange & fill with things I chose. Oh God it hurt.' I concluded: 'the desire for my own home just has to simmer.'

That weekend, Polly introduced me to her mother, a keen gardener, who was currently busy developing the production of wild flower seeds. Polly took us into her mother's house for drinks. I just remember a blandly formal drawing-room as background. Her mother showed me around her greenhouses in which she kept her tame owls, and then into a long string of greenhouses joined together by interconnecting doors.

Standing in the last one and looking back, you could see down all of them. The first one contained flowering sweet peas (some particularly lovely dark red ones called Beaujolais), the second one geraniums, and the third poppies in a great raised stone trough. I don't remember what Polly's mother looked like. I remember those poppies: yellow and orange and amber and pink. The sun was shining on to the dusty greenhouse panes and on to the flaking pale paint of the wooden struts propping the glass panels, and the sun rocked and swung in the flowers, making them more transparent and their colours more brilliant. Their hard, thin stems, fringed with green hairs, were very long, slightly bent and waving under the weight of the flower-heads. And at the top of each stem a burst of colour, a large, delicate flower, wide open, with its petals catching the sun and letting it through. Like fruits, I wrote; like butterflies; like humming-birds.

The weekend proved an oasis in an arid time. Gradually, life in the shared house had become more and more difficult and strained for all of us. Polly was moving away emotionally from Sim. She had a separate room now. Alex and I were uncomfortable witnesses of our hosts' pain, fraught discussions, confusion.

My own problem was feeling unable to write in the house, with Alex typing away overhead and Polly typing away just underneath in her new bedroom-cum-study. When you write you need to let go and flow out, losing your boundaries, so that language can dance up and change itself about, but if other people are nearby you can't let go. It doesn't feel 'safe' enough. You are pushed back inside your ego. At first, before they moved to Paris, I had rented a room from Roy and Pascale, in their communal house in Queen's Park, to use as a daytime office. The room was bare, quiet and impersonal. I saw no one all day long. When I felt tired, at midday, I lay on the floor on cushions and slept. Then in the late afternoon I bicycled back down Westbourne Grove. But that arrangement could not last.

Alex was potentially on his way out, having fallen in love. One night, a young art historian had arrived for supper. Small and slender, she had silky black hair, dark blue eyes, wore a turban, was altogether stylish and chic. Very feminine, too, with a wistful air, a plaintive voice. Alex cooked. Later on, as usual, we all drifted off to bed. In the morning Polly and I gawped at Alex, bare-legged and slippered, clad in a dressing-gown, making a tray of breakfast for two. Never before had he appeared in a dressing-gown in public. That meant he was serious. His visitor, indeed, was the woman whom he would marry and with whom he would buy a house in north London. He and I parted good friends. Before he left, he took me sailing one weekend: magical dawn sorties, catching the tide, along Essex creeks. He also taught me some carpentry: how to make a picture frame out of a cupboard door. He presented me with a little canvas roll containing some basic carpentry tools.

Increasingly, I felt that I should leave. Increasingly, I hid in my room. I did love it: the fat blue and green armchair which had supported me through so much reading (though now I had to give it back to Alex), the potted palm under the window which cast sharp and distinct fan-patterned shadows, the green-ery waving outside, the softness of the carpet under my bare soles.

Leaving would be difficult. My problem was financial, as usual. On my low income from bits of freelance work I could not afford commercial rents. I had no savings. I tried to get on the local housing list, but, as a single woman with no children, I was not a priority. The council worker explained to me, when

I visited the housing office, that a sudden influx of Spanish workers, in urgent need of accommodation, had to go to the top of the list. I had lived in the area for three years but had no rights. Part of me respected the Spaniards' plight, and its solution, but another part felt their being prioritised was deeply unfair. I experienced a surge of racist rage. I felt depressed and despairing. I knew I was not prepared to take a 'straight' job. Writing still came first. I hung on to knowing that.

1979. The Tories were now in power, led by Margaret Thatcher. On election night, the communal garden behind our house had been loud with the popping of champagne corks as the results came in, the whoops and cheers of jubilant right-wing neighbours. Fraught and desperate, I went on searching. The Notting Hill Housing Association had closed its waiting list long ago. There were too many people in my position; it could not help all of us. I did manage to get on to the list of a housing association based in Earls Court which looked after single women, whom it provided with bedsits. If I waited long enough, three or four years, they would eventually find me something.

I felt completely stuck, very miserable. Polly had been so generous to me, letting me live in her house. Now I felt trapped in it. I couldn't leave because I had nowhere to go. Increasingly I longed to live by myself, to have not just a room of my own but a home of my own. I found myself buying a couple of threadbare rugs at Portobello Road for a few pounds each. I also bought some French white porcelain serving-dishes. I joked to myself: oh, I'm preparing a trousseau. But where would I live?

Rescue: Frieda, a woman I had met through Centerprise, the arts centre in Hackney, rang me up, having heard through joint friends of my need to find a place. She was the tenant of a Notting Hill Housing Trust flat locally, just one street over from the market, but had just moved into a commune in Belsize Park. While she worked out whether or not she wanted to stay there, would I like to take over her flat? This subletting was illegal, of course. In effect, I would be squatting. If discovered I'd be evicted and she'd lose her tenancy. I said yes immediately.

Chapter Eight

NOTTING HILL GATE

Holiday times with
Duncan Campbell,
Penny Valentine
and Ros Asquith

My new flat occupied the second floor of a turreted building at a crossroads to the east of Portobello Road, tucking itself into the corner of Powys Terrace, lined with shabby Victorian houses, and Talbot Road, which at this end jostled with little local shops. Through Powys Square you walked to the market, just a hop, skip and jump away past the Anglican church and the Tabernacle community centre. Close by, to the north, in All Saints Road, the Mangrove café functioned as a popular centre for the local black community, particularly the young men. Lots of cool Rastafarians hung about in there or mooched on the pavement. The local police seemed threatened by this, and by Frank the owner's radical politics. They harassed him. Their pretext: his alleged drug-dealing. This let them raid the café regularly and cause everybody a lot of bother.

My compact little flat had two rooms, plus a tiny, doorless kitchen in an alcove with a curved outer wall, and a tiny bathroom. Having painted the back room white, and put all my books into it, stacking them in dry-stone-wall effect as I had no bookcases, I then discovered how damp it was. Impossible to use it. The books stayed there, as I had nowhere else to put them, and many of them grew mould on their covers.

I lived in the room at the front, which I also painted white. In one corner I put a low double bed (scrounged from a skip) covered with a pink and green paisley Indian bedspread. I painted the floorboards pink – I always liked pink floorboards – displayed my French plates and green house-plants on my little dresser, laid my two Turkish rugs. Robert, my new lover, got me a second-hand square pine table from a junk shop. I stood it under the window and flanked it with Jules's wheel-back kitchen chair on one side, a wicker chair from Oxfam on the other. I wrote at that table, ate off it, chopped vegetables on it, put the washing-up to dry on it. Penny Valentine gave me a 1940s desk lamp: a willowy metal nymph supporting a pale pink glass shade in the shape of a sphere. I put my white enamelled dishes on the single shelf in the kitchen, hung up my single saucepan, my frying-pan. Here a deep old sink, with no draining-board, nudged an ancient gas cooker. I bought a small second-hand fridge. I could stand in the middle of the cramped space and reach everything I needed: carrots, knife, cold-water tap, gas ring.

Making and arranging my own interior gave me great pleasure and satisfaction. My makeshift arrangements charmed me. Rather like playing doll's-houses when young. My little hinged plywood box was as real, as temporary, as I wanted it to be; when I got tired of it I could shut it up, fasten the latch, and scarper. I didn't mind the shabbiness, even though, as well as being damp, the flat was icy: the gas fire gave minimal heat, draughts whistled up through the bare floorboards, the big window had loose sashes, and for a while I had no curtains. At night I shuddered with cold and found it hard to get to sleep. I bought a hot water bottle, and dressed for bed in a Victorian nightdress, a cardigan, and a pair of thick socks. Sometimes I donned my second-hand fur coat as well. I had no hot water, because both the kitchen and bathroom Ascots broke shortly after I moved in. The bathroom, with its dirty, broken lino floor and peeling ceiling, was not a room in which to spend much time. I bathed at friends' houses. When my friend the scrupulously neat and chic Harriett Gilbert (the novelist and journalist) came to visit she teased me about the veil of dust on the cracked mirror propped above the cracked wash-basin. She reported amusedly that no sooner had she begun padlocking her bicycle to the lamp-post outside than a drug dealer leapt out from behind a skip and offered her dope and cocaine. I felt my street cred shoot up. Harriett was blonde, elfin-faced, boyishly slender. I liked to flirt with her. When we met our treat was to talk about books, books, books.

That first night after moving in, I lay awake for a long time; alert; listening. The curtainless flat seemed part of the street. Only a thin membrane separated me from the city outside. Inside and outside overlapped with each other. The noises seemed like burglars: they broke and entered the flat, and me too, as though my skin were plasterboard. The windows rattled in the wind. Light streamed in from the street lamps. Shadows swung and leapt across the walls as cars drove past. Voices close by yelled and cursed. Glass smashed. A siren wailed far away. Upstairs, a woman cried out and a man responded angrily, cursing and thumping. His violence punched my ceiling.

The couple upstairs, I discovered a few days later, were elderly. She was feeble, almost housebound, and he could not cope with having to help her. He drank too much, lost his temper, threatened her with upraised fists. They screamed and shouted most nights. Sometimes I went in to visit her but only when he was out. Fiercely independent, she accepted visits and conversation but refused state help. When her husband fell ill and got taken into hospital I did her shopping. Eventually, the Social Services removed her to hospital too. A new tenant took over the flat: a young woman, Mary, with a tiny baby. I didn't get to know her; she kept herself to herself. One night I unexpectedly dreamed of her, and the next morning read in the paper that she had been killed in a traffic accident in France.

The little shops, close by, were ordinary, varied, and completely agreeable. A furniture restorer displayed an array of lame chairs and sofas in need of healing. Next door a picture restorer showed off an array of broken frames. Down the street the Scottish grocer sold his Brillo pads and dusters. Opposite, the stitcher of men's suits advertised her services with a large framed photo of herself, Kathleen Jones, Tailoress, wreathed in plastic roses, and a still-life/sculptural composition of buttons, reels of thread, and lengths of rumpled pinstripe suiting outlined with chalk marks.

I liked to start the day with coffee in bed. Still in my nightdress, I would run down to fetch a newspaper, throwing on wellingtons, buttoning my big tweed overcoat over my nightdress. Once or twice I locked myself out and had to dash into the shoe-repair shop, which doubled as a locksmith's, and the kindly men would come out and pick my lock for me.

Sometimes I breakfasted with Robert, having stayed the night at his flat. I met Robert at a Women's Press party to which I'd been invited by Sarah LeFanu. He knew one of the Women's Press authors, through his mentor Doris Lessing. I liked the look of him as soon as I spotted him. He was short, wiry, a coil of energy. Close-cropped black hair, dark almond-shaped eyes, a very intelligent, creased brown face. Cool clothes, too: second-hand jacket of pale linen over jeans and a T-shirt. We got chatting. Long before the party finished, he suggested leaving. I took him home and we went to bed straight away. Sarah rang me the following morning: had I been kidnapped? No, we'd kidnapped each other. Next day Robert sent me a postcard, a reproduction of a miniature painting depicting a couple in a garden, whose legend read 'An Indian mystic and his wife'. He was telling me about himself but I did not realise that.

For a while we saw each other regularly. I got to know his small daughter Cleo, who, living with her mother Janey during the week, spent weekends with him.

Janey, Robert's ex-wife, with whom he was on good terms,

summoned me to dinner at her nearby flat, I imagine to check me out, make sure her daughter would be OK in my company. She cooked us roast guinea-fowl, which impressed me. An anthropologist by training, she had a sharp intelligence, a clever face, wore interesting clothes. I didn't think that we were necessarily on opposing sides just because we both had relationships with Robert: women did not have to be separated by men. Janey and I did not meet through feminism, however. And I did, eventually, realise that I was indeed jealous of her: she was more enduringly part of Robert's life than I would ever be. She, like Robert, was a close friend of Doris Lessing's. In the 1970s she and Robert had run a free school which, I thought, perhaps inspired the vision of the wild children in Doris's novel *The Memoirs of a Survivor*.

Although I felt so strongly sexually attracted to Robert, finding him so lovable, so good to talk to, I didn't manage to create a lasting and equal relationship with him. He was ambivalent about being loved, often needed to push me away, constantly tried to dominate me.

Much of my powerful self-assertion, my appetite for life and experience, converted itself into energy for writing, struggling with language, repeatedly diving into the unconscious to find new forms, new stories, new meanings for words. I didn't see writing as a substitute for living (I wanted perfection of the life *and* of the work) but somehow it made living possible. I lived freely in reading and writing. I fell in love with Robert because he seemed a real soulmate, then found he wanted our relationship to be conducted completely on his terms. No commitment. I discovered after a while he was having a sexual relationship with another woman besides myself. Well, we didn't believe in monogamy, did we? No babies, he said. Not too much emotion or intimacy. If we became close, afterwards he would not want to see me for a week. He refused to look after birth control; that was my job. He had a good warm heart, but it was for his family of Janey and Cleo, and for causes: the boys he taught at the comprehensive in Holloway; his search for spiritual meaning. Not much left over for me. Every time I thought of leaving him his sweetness tugged me back; then he'd be cool and distant next day. He liked being with me because in my company he could let out his deep thoughts and emotions; then he would abruptly withdraw. He was a tempest tossing me about.

Nowadays self-help books tell women that we must accept that men, being from Mars, need to retreat into their caves or pull away like stretchy rubber bands. Robert was from a planet further away than Mars and I circled him in my little space-ship, annoying him with my bleeped messages.

Sometimes I accompanied him to visit Doris. He acted as her handyman, fixing shelves, putting down lino, cutting the grass. Doris's domestic life, in some ways, was as unconventional as her fiction. One day I spotted a row of blue willow-pattern plates, all filled with water, neatly arranged in a row on top of the stone balustrade surrounding the little terrace giving on to the garden at the back. I asked what they were doing there. Doris explained that the plates, being new, were too bright. She was busy fading them in the sunshine.

Doris was very involved with the Sufi movement under the leadership of Idries Shah. I turned over Shah's books at Robert's flat. They suggested that Sufism was the oldest religion of all; the source of all subsequent spiritual disciplines and spiritual practices. Doris once mentioned to me how useful it had been that in the beginning of her Sufi studies she had been required to say what she believed and why. Now she believed in the need to save mankind. The cold war threatened. The Sufi response to this, Robert let slip, was to build underground shelters. The

Sufis would survive even if ordinary mortals were too stupid to see the light. Once or twice I accompanied Robert and Doris to Sufi conferences on science or philosophy. I found the speakers cold and boring. Nor was feminism remotely on their agenda. Sufis seemed very middle-class to me, and smugly filled with certainty. I remember meeting a young Sufi woman called Angela for the first time at Doris's house one day. Angela is only eighteen but she is very wise, Robert had said. I happened to notice Doris's pretty French butter-dish, from Quimper. Since I liked Quimper ware, I spoke my admiration strongly. Angela ticked me off: you shouldn't want things the way you do; if you didn't want things then you wouldn't suffer from not being able to possess them.

But I wanted everything, I wanted to embrace and enjoy the whole world. Reading Marion Milner, the psychoanalytical writer who discussed creativity, I was discovering that you could want passionately, and then you could accept not having, and make a gesture of being empty, letting go, and then the world would give itself to you, pour itself into you, all its fruits, beauty, harvest, joy. Wretched, priggish Angela. I disagreed with her then and I still do. The moment stood for all my differences with Robert. He belonged to this group of young people around Doris whereas I did not. He was her disciple whereas I was not. His search for meaning was taking him in a different direction, away from mine.

We did have some good times. We went to Ireland, to stay with some hippy farmer friends of his, inland from Bantry Bay. The farm perched on a mountain. We left the car halfway up and continued the journey by pony and trap. Warm hospitality met us, included a certain austerity. These hippies disdained lavatories: we had to go out, up the mountain, and squat. No bath or shower, either; a cold-water tap sufficed. I found a mountain stream and slunk off to lie in it. We spent time helping our hosts Jen and Dave clear a field of rocks and stones. It was very hot. I borrowed a pair of Jen's hot-pants and wore them self-consciously but with pleasure: first time I'd worn hot-pants. (Not really a garment seen at feminist conferences.) We drank poteen. Robert spent a lot of time lying under the car, fixing it, while I looked after Cleo.

Jen was a saintly, gentle person from a rich family, who had given up bourgeois comfort in order to live in this extreme simplicity. I certainly couldn't have done it and was relieved no one was asking me to. Jen cooked good meals culled from her vegetable patch. We helped her pick peas and look after the sheep. To check for foot rot we had to catch the sheep first, as they nipped ever higher up the stony slopes of the mountain. I developed a fast run, a flying tackle, clasping the sheep around their hind legs and hanging grimly on. You couldn't do that to male lovers; they kicked and fled.

We left Jen and Dave's house to have a weekend away with Cleo, camping on the rocky beaches of the Atlantic coast. We collected mussels which I cooked *à la marinière* for supper. Then we returned to Bantry Bay, visiting other hippy friends of Robert's en route. At one farm the men were forking over the silage on top of a big lorry. Automatically I jumped up alongside them and began to help. I was the only woman wielding a pitchfork; all the others stayed in the kitchen, making the tea. Hippy men liked their women to be earth mothers in long skirts, not to enjoy themselves outdoors in the sunshine heaving silage with pitchforks. From that group of people I remember above all a five-year-old child called Naomi, one of the most remarkable I have ever met. Dark-haired, sturdy, with a level gaze, she pottered about, playing, enjoying herself. She didn't require adult attention; she seemed utterly serene;

richly sustained by her inner life; complete in herself. She was happily absorbed in whatever she was doing, propelled by her imagination.

I noticed children more, perhaps, because my friends were beginning to have them, and because I had come to love Cleo as the original, creative child she was, leaping about to the *Cats* soundtrack in her pink leotard, telling her wild stories. Sarah LeFanu wanted children. She and Chris were going to get married. Penny Valentine had given birth to her son Danny. Robert and I went on holiday with them and with John and Ros, my friends from *City Limits*, renting another of those houses in Provence. We drank a lot of local rosé, ambled about reading and chatting, and Robert and I went on long walks, climbing up steep hillsides. I was skinny and nimble. Robert complimented me: you climb as well as a man. My friends told me later they whooped with laughter at the extravagant moans and groans coming from the bedroom, next to the kitchen, which I shared with Robert. I was trying to persuade myself this was a grand passion which would last, while Ros and PV stuffed tea-towels into their mouths to throttle their giggles.

Work sustained me. Two days a week I went in to the *City Limits* office in Upper Street to edit the poetry page. I loved the job. Low pay but high satisfaction. I enjoyed the power I had. We believed we were making a difference to the culture we lived in. We were reshaping it. These lofty ideas coincided with pretty basic working conditions. Our office space was cramped. I shared my plywood counter with the Film section. First of all, on arrival, you had to find a typewriter to use, then a chair, then the key to the book cupboard. You rummaged for review copies. You collected your post, all the flyers about forthcoming poetry events. Then you had to go and have a fight with Fordham and Fountain, the co-editors, about column space.

They always wanted to give some of mine away to advertising, and I wanted to run poems. I would lecture them on the enormous importance of poetry to the world, to world affairs, to the psyche, to the revolution, and they would look rueful and make wry quips.

I learned that common sense ruled office life. The first time Fountain subbed my copy, an intense, poetic piece I'd written on commission about a walk through Peckham and Camberwell, I felt he had destroyed it and me as well. I went into the Ladies' and wept. After that I toughened up and realised that producing journalism was not like writing a novel and that you did best if you could joke with the blokes and just get on with things. PV, to her credit, did not behave like this. If she felt like it, she stormed, shouted, wept, made them take the time to listen.

Besides poetry listings, my half-page contained reviews, a graphic or photo, a poem when there was sufficient space. Hundreds of poems thumped in every week. Review copies started arriving by the bagful. I scooped up armfuls of books to take home and read. I went to readings and met other poets. Michael Horowitz, the founder of Poetry Olympics, was one of these. I got to know him after giving one of his anthologies a cool review, criticising him for including so few women poets. Why should that be? I demanded. Answers on a postcard to M. Horowitz, I suggested. Michael rang me up in a rage. Didn't I realise I was using a *Private Eye* code-word and instructing readers to send him turds? We made up the row and made friends. He decided to do his homework and borrowed books by women poets from me: I listed fifteen of them in my diary. He did indeed start putting women on at his gigs; myself too. He was a jazz-playing imp. One day when I went to visit him in his Notting Hill flat he was still getting dressed. He pranced before me in his scarlet underpants. Then he donned a bright floral shirt, a pair of flared loons (retro-chic). He was devoted to the memory of his dead wife, the poet Frances Horowitz, but made space for other women. His current lover, Inge, a very intense, sensitive, poetic German woman, provided all the practical support for Michael's Poetry Olympics performances and publishing. Her devotion to Michael kept his shows on the road.

I went on meeting with the women writers' groups I was involved in. We went on publishing poetry pamphlets and we gave our own readings also. The audience for live poetry was hungry, intense, large. I did solo gigs too, making the rounds of the weekend pub circuit. Sandwiched in between one stand-up comic and another I often felt nervous. I just had to stride on stage, grab the mike and get on with my performance. But it often felt nerve-racking reciting passionate metaphor-filled poems about female desire to a horde of drinkers waving their beer-glasses and shouting for the band to come on. One woman said to me afterwards: I always wear a long skirt then no one will see my knees knocking. My knees didn't knock but my heart did.

Poetry could sometimes move people to rage. At one gig I did at the Theatre Royal in Stratford some women erupted in the middle of my performance, yelling I was a vicious anti-Christian. They stormed out. I felt rather pleased with myself.

I started teaching a few hours a week at the City Literary Institute in Holborn. This, similar to the Workers' Educational Association, provided all kinds of further education courses. Politics was part of the agenda. Philip, my head of department, taught the history of revolutions. Feminist ideas had not yet been hived off into the universities and called Women's Studies. They were still accessible to anyone who wanted to study them.

Accordingly, I gave a course on Doris Lessing's novels, then one on sexual politics which I taught with my friend Sarah Benton (who was now working as Deputy Editor for the *New Statesman*), and then I began to teach creative writing too.

I also taught briefly in primary schools from time to time as one of the poets on the W.H. Smith scheme 'Poets in Schools'. I remember one small Turkish girl in an East End primary school saying to me: I'm going to become a poet, miss. Well, stick at it then, I said to her. I will miss, she said.

Over the course of two years, 1981–3, I was one of the writers-in-residence for Bromley schools. Genteeller than the East End. I toured four of them. With my co-writer Paddy Burt, I had good talks and arguments. I liked Paddy, because, although she was older than I and had written a lot more books, she treated me as an equal. At lunchtime, at one particular school, she would beckon to me and we would slink away, beyond the playground, into the neighbouring woods, and sit down on a log, well screened from snoopers by trees. Paddy would produce cans of red wine from her handbag and offer me one. Then we would dive into conversation about books and writing. That way we escaped having to hobnob with the middle-aged women teachers in the staffroom, who, nibbling their Ryvita and cottage cheese, talked about little but dieting. I loathed these women unreservedly.

Looking back, I think they scared me; I didn't want to end up like them. Their gossipy staffroom circle felt repressed and claustrophobic: I much preferred Paddy's company. She was middle-aged, too, but she was unconventional, open-minded, ardent, funny, original. She didn't bother with shop-talk. One just did not think about her age when in her company.

Another way of earning bits of money was to teach creative writing in community venues, such as Battersea Arts Centre, where I taught a lunchtime class of young women, most of whom were mothers of toddlers attending the Centre's crèche. I took it all very seriously. I encouraged them to commit themselves utterly to writing, to struggle to invent new forms, I mentioned the vocation of the artist. One of them burst out: oh fuck off for heaven's sake don't be so ridiculous, we don't want to be artists! I felt I'd been patronising and was ashamed of myself. I also felt angry: I hadn't realised I had been hired to teach a nice hobby.

I taught also at Oval House in Kennington. I read slush-pile typescripts for publishers. I wrote occasional reviews for *Gay News*, the *New Statesman*, *City Limits*. To save money I bicycled everywhere. Occasionally I took the tube, especially when going to see Robert late at night. One evening I was accosted by a rat. It shot up to me like a battery-operated grey hairbrush and then shot away again into the darkness of the tunnel out of the rain. I grubbed around like that rat. I foraged. We recognised each other.

I worked hard, dashing from one freelance job to another, but didn't make enough money. I couldn't afford to get my shoes mended or to join friends in the pub for a drink. A half of cider now and again and that was it. New clothes were out of the question. I lived on brown bread and peanut butter and cabbage. A healthy enough diet, tartly pointed out my new friend Sarah Maguire. I had met her in a poetry class I taught briefly when Judith Kazantzis, who ran it, became temporarily ill and I replaced her. I warmed to clever, independent Sarah, with her fine poems, her very short hair, her 1940s crêpe frocks. She lived in a Notting Hill Housing Trust flat at the top of Powys Terrace, on the far side of Westbourne Grove. We liked to think we could lean out of our respective kitchen windows and wave tea-towels at each other. (I was much taken, at this time, with the punning title of the French feminist rag *Le Torchon Brûle*, The Burning Tea-towel/Torch.) Sarah was as poor as I. A vegetarian, she had the knack of cooking well on little money. She taught me how to cook with spices and I taught her how to make risotto. I spent many evenings in her tall shoebox of a kitchen, which boasted a large statue of Ste Thérèse of Lisieux donated by her photographer friend Crispin. Superintended by Ste Thérèse, we squeezed into chairs at the table nudging the cooker, and talked furiously.

Friendships were the oxygen and fuel in my life. Work was harder going. I felt I had little time to sit and think about writing, let alone do it. My romanticism about the new flat had worn off after the first winter. I felt depressed by the cold and damp, the lack of greenery beyond the window, the racket inside and outside the building. Bags of refuse piled up on the pavement by the entry door. The pavements were heaped with an urban compost of old prams, cider bottles, broken ironing-boards, gashed sinks, black plastic sacks of discarded clothes. The rubbish vans did not come round often enough and the dustbins got stolen and the hills of rubbish grew.

I fought my depression when I could. I bought myself a bunch of chrysanthemums I could not afford, or a fifty-pence bottle of red wine from García's. Sometimes at night I just lay in bed and cried. I felt full of doubts about my book, worried it would be rejected again, that it was self-indulgent and boring (that Mother Superior still sneaked up on me). I felt lonely too; cut loose; rattling in the void. I felt whirled about with terrific anxiety and insecurity, plus a feeling that the hard time would never end. I scrabbled at the bottom of a black pit, slowly starving to death, and no one could hear my shouts for help, and I would die here, alone, and no one would know.

I wasn't good at admitting to friends, apart from Sarah

LeFanu, how hard life felt. I tried to be brave and repress mentioning my struggles. A chosen poverty, after all, oppressed less
than an imposed one. I was a privileged middle-class woman
who could always get a job as a librarian. I wasn't really
oppressed. I had a way out. I just didn't want to take it, that was
all. To my family I was resolutely cheerful, determined not to
give them the chance to say I told you so. James and Jules were
both very kind, buying me supper from time to time. When
Jules cooked for me, the occasion turned into theatre. Holding
aloft a mushroom, he would read aloud from the recipe book:
listen to this, Miche, it's just like Shakespeare! Visiting Sarah
and Chris, I admired their baby, Alexander, and admired the
lawn that Chris had nonchalantly laid one afternoon for the
baby to play on. Sometimes I babysat. Alexander became an
observant and communicative toddler, who, spoken to a great
deal by his father and mother – when he cried, Chris would say
to him: what's your beef? – began to talk at eighteen months.
One day I wheeled him to the little zoo in Clissold Park, and
pointed out the nice birdies to him. Alexander reproved me:
African starlings. When I carried him into the back garden one
night to look at the crescent moon, he quoted the Angela
Carter children's alphabet he'd had read to him: moon; banana;
letter C. Sometimes at New Year I stayed with Chris and Sarah
at Chris's family cottage in the Lake District. Highlights
included drinking red wine and then sledging down the steep
side of Tarn Hows to skim at top speed across the frozen surface
of the lake, or proving Pythagoras's theorem with foot-print
diagrams in the snow. By day we sat in a huddle around the
coal fire, reading, and by night we drank beer with whisky
chasers in the local pub and played darts.

I did manage to leave Robert eventually, after a comi-tragic
night featuring gross misunderstandings. He had just read my

essay on spirituality, which I'd been commissioned to write for a forthcoming Virago book edited by Sara Maitland. I'd tried to trace the development of my thoughts on the subject. This isn't about spirituality, he protested: this is just autobiography. I felt completely put down, unable to protest. Then we went to bed. In the morning I rushed away back to my flat. I phoned him to tell him the relationship was over.

I had lots of energy suddenly, for going out and enjoying myself. Celebrating my freedom, I went to lots of parties. I went to a benefit gig raising money for the women's peace camp, protesting about cruise missiles, at Greenham Common: bands and cabaret acts. I had gone to Greenham several times, along with thousands of others, and joined in the protests, which were carnivalesque as well as serious, featuring music, art, theatre, song and dance, and also regular break-ins to the base, women dancing on top of the huge concrete bunkers before being arrested and dragged back outside the high barbed-wire fence.

Spring 1982 arrived tentatively. How long an English winter can seem. December and the solstice are the year's hinge; we swing around the corner into a belief that the darkness will dwindle, only to plunge into January and February glumness and raw cold. Now, plodding through March, I relished occasional bursts of sunshine, warmth, a haze of summer almost, the smell of newly mown grass, the chemical yellow of daffodils. It was impossible not to be happy some of the time, despite my weariness because I took on too much freelance work. On one occasion when I blurted out my troubles, Sara Maitland was sweet to me, feeding me soup and artichokes. We talked about writing.

Spring retreated. The cold weather still occupied my flat. My feet were ice lumps. Dear Jules gave me some of his old clothes:

a grey pinstriped suit and a black dress jacket. I wore the suit, plus pearls and diamante earrings, to the Poetry Olympics party at the Landesmans' house. Fran Landesman was a jazz poet who performed regularly on the cabaret circuit. She did a very good turn on sweetie-pie little girls adoring daddies. That night, slinky in a long beaded frock, she was weaving around offering drinks, smouldering one minute and cracking jokes the next. Jay Landesman, stately in his armchair, complimented me on my suit, which was very like his. We discussed tailoring and labels. His pinstripe had been specially made for him by a tailor in New York City. It incorporated different aspects of suits worn by *film noir* heroes. He flipped back the jacket's lapel and showed me the big personalised label embroidered in silk inside. Wearing my suit I felt worldly and flirtatious and cheerful. I raced off to have supper in Stoke Newington with Chris and Sarah. Chris cooked *moules à la marinière*. James, who ate with us, gave me a lift home in his ramshackle car. He became convinced the gearbox was about to give way, so we abandoned the car outside his parents' chic Regency cottage in Barnsbury and took a taxi the rest of the way. It must have cost a fortune. Who paid? James, I suspect. He came in to try and mend the dripping overflow in my lavatory cistern for me. He ended up controlling the erratic ballcock by wedging it with a china plate and a packet of tampons, then raced away again. 'Friends are stalwart sources of pleasure,' I declared to my diary: 'I want a companion not an intermittent hasty dark Lawrentian passion, I want a lover who's a friend.'

Similarly, I wanted a father who was not a distant Byronic hero, not an angry authority-figure. My thoughts about my father were changing, as I came increasingly to understand him. Now my love for him was based on greater knowledge. When Ursula Owen, Virago co-founder and editor, invited me to write a piece for her book *Fathers: Reflections by Daughters*, I felt able to write about Dad by tracking the heroes of various novels that had mattered to me. Sara Maitland wrote a piece for the same collection. She helped me find my form by writing about her split vision of her father. That encouraged me to explore how much my view of my father had been filtered through literature; how much my father had been veiled from me. He had not been around, because he was out at work all day, and in his absence I had made him up. The 'real' person was far more interesting and far more lovable. I had become stronger. Accordingly he stopped shouting at me and bullying me. He began to respect me and tell me things. He delighted me by reading and enjoying my piece in the *Fathers* book.

An immediate practical problem was, yet again, needing to find somewhere to live. Frieda, who had remained the official tenant of my flat, wanted to stay in her commune in Belsize Park and give up her tenancy in Notting Hill. I could not, of course, take over her flat, because I was renting illegally. In any case, Frieda told me, the Notting Hill Housing Trust was about to evict the tenants in our block in order to do up the property.

I would be homeless again. Back I went to the housing search. I felt stuck and despairing. I would never earn enough from writing books to live on. Earning the money to live on left little time for writing books. I can remember sitting on a deserted tube platform one night at this time, the wind from the tunnel whistling past, feeling utterly wretched, just managing not to cry. People say sternly: you must not be self-pitying. To hell with that. I do feel sorry for that younger self. She was plummeting towards rock-bottom. Why on earth shouldn't I pity her? I couldn't do it then. I would berate myself: come on! Get up! Cope! Probably just as well. I did keep going.

I tried to present a brave face in public. Around this time I became involved with the group of poets working to produce the radical poetry festival Angels of Fire. Jay Ramsay, the most energetic young poet I'd ever met, a cross between a whirlwind and a whirling dervish, got us all together. Jay was very ambitious, intense, tall and thin, with a huge need to talk for hours to any woman willing to listen. Like his lover Sylvia Paskin (who taught Film Studies at the City Lit), I did listen. Stepping into his inner universe I felt tossed up and down. Quite daffy I thought him, in one way; highly organised and practical in another; that's to say like many of the poets I knew at that time, including myself. Jay was fascinated by esoteric systems of knowledge. He told me about chakras, the points of energy along the human spine, and the rainbow chakra body, praised my 'Artemis fire'. I didn't mind at all being compared to Artemis.

I liked hearing Sylvia's tales, too. One concerned visiting the Venice carnival with the artist Michael Rothenstein. They shared a room to save money. Sylvia would return late to the hotel to find Michael already asleep. He went to sleep with a different-coloured handkerchief spread over his face each night: red, blue, yellow, green. Was this his version of the rainbow chakra body? No, he was just besotted with colour.

The Angels of Fire festival ran over several days, at the Drill Hall off the Tottenham Court Road, with a different line-up of poets each night. All sorts of poetry: political, concrete, abstract, experimental, stand-up, fall-down. Attila the Stockbroker, the self-appointed Poet Laureate of Slough, Benjamin Zephaniah, Joolz, James Berry, Allen Fisher, David Gascoigne, Maureen Duffy, Ali (Fell), were just a few of our stars. We had a bold poster designed by Michael Rothenstein, featuring a fiery rooster, and printed our own magazine. Jay, of course, was able to present his one-man poetic monologue

'Knife in the Light'. That, I realised, was a major *raison d'être* for running the festival. And why not? We had all sorts of music, too, and one ballet spectacular performed to no music at all by an alternative ballerina, a young woman in heavy boots. I could not see that her clattering bounds and leaps counted as ballet but kept this to myself.

I enjoyed getting all dressed up as compère night after night. For my own performance my costume consisted of my black Biba zip-up short fitted blouson with long, tightly buttoned cuffs, worn over a pink *Sylphides* frock with very full pink net skirts, from Portobello (an outfit which doubtless dramatised my ambivalence towards classical ballet and ballerinas). I read poems inspired by my love affair with Robert: a sequence about Persephone plunging into the underworld with her lover Pluto.

Afterwards, in the interval, a man with an ugly, interesting face, a big nose, an eager look, approached me in the mêlée of people making for the bar and complimented me on my poems. He had been making a drawing while listening to them and asked permission to send it to me. I felt flattered, even though he looked so straight, wearing a suit, and although he seemed old. I gave him my address. A small painting, finely drawn in ink and overwashed in indigo watercolour, duly arrived, depicting Persephone as a tiny figure dwarfed by the Piranesi-style architecture of the underworld.

I wrote back to say thank you. When William wrote to me again, I accepted his invitation and went to have lunch with him at his flat in Leinster Square, Bayswater. Rather severe, his décor seemed to me. Grey and white striped curtains and grey carpet. Uncomfortable-looking, bucket-like sofa: canvas slung on bamboo poles. Chairs draped in white. Although William was dressed in a grey suit and tie, he himself seemed less severe than shy and formal. He sat me in the sitting-room, with a copy of the *TLS*, while he cooked. We ate rice and drank white wine. He was so overexcited, he told me later, that he forgot to offer me the tomato salad he had prepared and put in the fridge. We talked about poetry and art. William was an historian of Renaissance architecture, specialising in Palladio. I knew what Palladian architecture was, from novels, but was ignorant of Palladio. William, expounding his life's passion, brought him alive. He made a translation for me: a villa is actually a farmhouse. He was preparing a catalogue of all Palladio's drawings, was in the process of writing the script of a short film about him, and had just written a short exhibition catalogue on him.

I felt I had entered a new world. Light years away from life down among the poets. Different codes. Different behaviour. Yet, at the same time, I knew this world and could feel at home in it: I'd been snatched up by a space-ship and whirled back to an Oxford college. I could, if I admitted it to myself, speak William's language. I was intrigued by the old-fashioned formality of his manners, charmed by his comic turns of phrase, flattered by the way he listened attentively to everything I said. He walked me home because, he explained, he thought me slightly inebriated. What an absurd and pompous expression! My friends and I all said 'pissed'. Sarah LeFanu rang me up that afternoon: he could have been an axe-murderer and you went to his flat without knowing anything about him!

I went on seeing William. With him I could unapologetically express the side of me that had gone to Oxford, read Virgil in Latin, *Beowulf* in Old English, had, to sum up, learned about Western culture of the past. When I was working with people who had had a different style of education, I shut up about what I knew, not out of shame or denial, but because people could feel left out or snubbed if you carried on talking about things they'd never heard of and using language they couldn't understand. Was that being patronising? It felt like a form of manners. I felt distressed when in company upper-middle-class people used incomprehensible code-words or slang which excluded other people we were with. People got put in their place. There was indeed an invisible club called Oxbridge (as James once explained to me) which couldn't help but look down on outsiders. I hated that attitude, but knew that when I chose to I could speak the Oxbridge language. I was a multilingual chameleon. I could alter my conversation, my vocabulary, subtly shift my accent, according to whom I was with. Adapt and survive.

My father had been a would-be master of disguise. He had adopted what he must have hoped was the poshest of posh accents. To hear him on the phone, rapping out old boy and old chap, you'd think he was straight out of a novel by Evelyn Waugh. Well, so he was. Evelyn Waugh and Dornford Yates were his mentors, his protocols, his self-help books. Did he recognise Waugh's cruelty? I don't know.

My father had climbed from one class into another. I had certainly dreamed of doing so as an adolescent. My fantasies had centred on living in an ancient manor house (small but perfectly formed) with a walled garden, in the intervals of pursuing perversion and poetry in Paris. Living in Polly's house in Holland Park, I had briefly put that dream of luxurious living into practice. Now, about to be homeless yet again, feeling trapped in writerly poverty, I let those fantasies stir once more. William's world seemed such a glamorous one. He had actually known E.M. Forster at King's. He had been a friend of Anthony Blunt, the scholar turned spy. He knew Anita Brookner too, and took me to a cocktail party she gave (Anita, exquisitely dressed, bandbox-crisp, did not actually attend it – she spent her entire time outside in the hall, welcoming her guests). His friends all seemed comfortably off, witty and learned to boot. My role was that of intelligent ingénue. I played it well. Some of his friends saw through it and some didn't. One of them said to me a few years later: we all thought you were just a pretty little thing.

William and I went to the Murillo exhibition at the National Gallery together. Luscious Madonnas whichever way you looked. I was entranced. Suddenly I could see the point of having been Catholic: I could understand Western art. When William took me with him on his two-week trip to Italy to shoot his Palladio film, I was knocked out a second time, this time by Italian worldliness, nothing to do at all with Catholic spirituality. We stayed in Florence, Venice and Rome. William gave me a whistle-stop tour of Renaissance art and architecture. Italy exploded at me: gorgeous and pagan, witty and cruel. Voluptuous nymphs and goddesses and satyrs tumbled about. On my own, after the visitors had gone, while William talked to the Director, I explored the gardens of the Medici villa in Rome, happily getting lost in a maze of green rooms. Raphael's frescos in the Farnesina, mixing images of godly and earthly pleasures, a kaleidoscope of breasts and artichokes and wings and tails, felled me.

I fell in love with Italy, as a result of that visit, and therefore assumed I had fallen in love with William as well. I certainly admired him. He was clever, funny, sophisticated. He liked women. He was due to go to Italy for six months on sabbatical. He proposed to me: I'd be willing to marry you, if that would be of use. Did he get his grammar of love quite right? A small strong voice inside me said clearly: don't marry him. On the other hand, I felt flattered that such a distinguished scholarly person wanted to marry me. No one had ever proposed to me. In my libertarian circle, nobody got married.

Sarah LeFanu had got married, wearing cloth-of-gold. She was Sarah, who had a mind of her own, who did as she thought fit and as she chose. I had been Sarah's unofficial bridesmaid. Arriving at Fleetwood Street, to accompany her and Chris to the registry office at Hackney Town Hall in Mare Street, I discovered they had no flowers and promptly raced off to the local florist to buy them both buttonholes. The taxi arrived. Boarding it, Sarah paused, looking back at me. Well, old girl, she said: this is it.

I took William to Fleetwood Street to have supper with Sarah and Chris. Their attitude: do what makes you happy.

I realise, now, that my homelessness, my desperation to escape my rut of poverty, my despair, thinking nothing would ever change, must have had something to do with my saying yes. Marriage would take me not only to Italy but into security. My parents would be pleased and relieved. I was tired of struggling. I wanted to give up the struggle and escape.

One of my women friends, a dedicated, serious feminist, summoned me to her house and upbraided me: you have a duty to women to set an example and not get married. I felt cross with her. I also remembered her great kindness to me when Lin (of the street theatre group) died of cancer: she had held me in her arms all night while I wept, and comforted me. But now I ignored both my inner voice and my friend's voice and went ahead.

Chapter Nine

BAYSWATER

Performing at Angels of Fire

William and I got married at Kensington and Chelsea registry office in December 1983. On the morning of the wedding he woke me up at seven o'clock, crying: there's still time to escape! I pretended not to hear.

I had met his family briefly in the preceding months. My introduction to his parents happened in the street outside his Bayswater flat. Dr Binns, his father, would not come in because he feared contamination by germs. He had survived bowel cancer some years previously and now maintained constant surveillance against dirt. William's mother, on that occasion, handed us as a present some pillow-cases she had inherited from an aunt. She couldn't use them, because the aunt's ear-wax might have leaked on to the candy-striped cotton and left indelible, if invisible stains, but they would do for us. One Sunday we went to visit William's sister in her big, hotel-like, late-nineteenth-century house in the Kent countryside, which functioned as a conference centre. She lived there with the wealthy man, older than her father, whom she had married, and was very happy, running his business for him. Dr Binns, heavily gloved, carried with him a wad of newspapers, which he shoved at his daughter's Dalmatians as they fawned around us, for them to bite on, in case the slobber from their mouths should infect his hands.

The husband showed us his collection of silver miniatures and trinkets, kept inside a secret compartment behind a false wardrobe door in his bedroom. Glancing at my red shoes and red fishnet stockings, and quickly realising I hung out with thieves and vagabonds, he said with a meaningful stare: please don't tell anyone about the whereabouts of this cupboard. I promised not to. Later, Mrs Binns, a fat woman, soft as a freshly baked scone, with puffy ankles, gave us tea in her spotless bungalow, having first sent us straight upstairs to wash our hands. The sitting-room bristled with cleanliness. There were no pictures for the germs to hang on to and all the food was wrapped in cling-film.

Mrs Binns sewed all her own clothes. She gave me, on this occasion, a collection of her old hand-made cocktail frocks and jackets from the 1960s. They are upstairs in the spare room, she said: why don't you go and try them on? Grey brocade and flesh-coloured brocade, all exquisitely stitched, and all a bit dull. They fitted but did not feel right. I took the clothes back to Leinster Square but never wore them. I hung them up in the cupboard in the little back room and there they stayed. We did not see William's parents again until the wedding.

Wedding bells rang. Warning bells rang even louder. Pride would not let me back off. I could not stand the ensuing loss of face if I admitted, at this late stage, that I had made a mistake. Having survived certain feminist friends' disapprobation, I could not now turn round and tell them they were right after all. I thought, optimistically, that things would improve. And I was desperate to escape into the golden Italian world William had shown me. I was very fond of him. We would work it out. That's what I told myself.

I went shopping for a wedding dress, and bought two. One warm long-sleeved blue and green one to get married in and one dark blue backless one to wear at the subsequent party. Sim kindly offered me the big drawing-room in his house at Lansdowne Road in Holland Park, where he still lived, for the reception. William and I slept in my old double bed upstairs for a couple of nights beforehand and I spent the days cleaning the house, sticky with dirt, with the help of my mother and sister. Sim had let everything slide. Mould sprouted in the kitchen. Paint flaked from the walls. Cat fleas were jumping in the carpets and had to be ruthlessly exterminated. On our wedding morning William spotted a dog turd just outside the front door. Having removed it, he then felt obliged to go out, wearing rubber gloves, and scrub the pavement with disinfectant; otherwise his sensitive father, having become aware of the turd's aura, would not feel able to enter the house.

My women friends all loyally attended the party. Lesbian goddess Diana Simmonds even wore the Gloucester Drive frock, blue 1940s crêpe sprigged with flowers, the communal garment the sapphists (from the eponymous commune) passed around for straight occasions. My father made a lengthy speech about the auld alliance between Scotland and France. Stef Pixner, from my poetry group, jumped up and made an impromptu short speech about my being a writer and a feminist.

The wedding night consisted of a trip to Piccadilly to visit William's old friend Patricia, a rich widow living in Albany amid much splendour of crystal and gilt-framed looking-glasses. Patricia, dressed in a bobble-edged blanket, had attended our wedding that morning, and had taken off her wedding ring and pressed it upon us: go on, darlings, you must have a ring and gorblimey I don't need the wretched thing any more. Patricia and William watched TV, Roger Corman's horror film *Piranha*, his spoof of *Jaws*, and I fell asleep on the divan behind a screen in the hall.

William's lofty-ceilinged flat in Bayswater, its floor-length windows overlooking Leinster Square, was ideal for a single person. He lived in what had been the big drawing-room of the Georgian terraced house. The uncomfortable canvas sofa and chairs formed a sitting space at one end. A desk toppled with books and papers. A platform, reached by a wobbly ladder, bore his bed, and his collection of scholarly and antiquarian books filled the space underneath it. Large rubber plants stood about in pots. This décor had been composed by his ex-lover Peri, who now lived just along the road in a Notting Hill Housing Trust bedsit. Bulging black plastic bags of her things lined one wall of the little back room, where her old clothes took up most of the cupboard space, for she considered the flat just as much her domain as William's. It held her overspill. The little back room was supposed to be my study, but it was impossible to work there. Peri had furnished it, and it seemed to me that her spirit occupied it, along with her bags of old jewellery, her bales of material, her weird pictures, her collections of feathers and coins and ribbons and bits of felt. She had arranged the tall-ceilinged, narrow shoebox of a kitchen, too. And in the tiny bathroom, high up, she had wedged an enormous dead branch which I dared not throw away. She loved dead things. She loved suspending them on strings: bits of old animal bones, bird bones.

Straight after the wedding we went to Rome, where William was working on the exhibition *Raffaello Architetto* (Raphael as Architect). We stayed at the top of the Spanish Steps in the Herziana, the German Institute, which rented us two massive sunny rooms, very bare but full of light, with gleaming parquet floors, a single bed in each one, and some massive Victorian wardrobes and chairs (plus an inventory, in case we walked off with the wardrobes). William was out working all day, and worked in the evenings too, after I had made us supper in the tiny kitchenette. Dorothea's marriage to Casaubon, and their wedding trip to Rome, recurred frequently to my mind.

I went sightseeing by myself day after day. I sat in cafés. I wandered along the Corso looking at the dress shops and the ugly scarlet and black clothes displayed: tubular shapes, huge padded shoulders. Such clothes did not suit me at all. The Roman women parading past in super-smart outfits seemed aggressively feminine, with their red mouths, lacquered hairstyles, high stiletto heels. They scared me. Luckily I had Serena, James's ex-lover, to talk to, still his good friend, now a junior lecturer at Rome University. She taught English literature and enjoyed speaking English. An ardent feminist, Communist and Freudian, she engaged me in passionate discussions about novels, poetry, love and sex. Political commitment didn't mean scruffiness, however. Serena, from a well-to-do intellectual family, had a *signora* come in once a week to iron her flowered cotton blouses. Another *signora* came in to clean. I didn't consider myself scruffy, but I didn't iron. I had discovered that if you hung things up carefully when they came out of the wash, they dried without wrinkling. Good: more time for reading. I clothes-shopped in the market near the railway station, browsing along the stalls, and found things there I liked: a long, narrow, striped black and white skirt buttoned all the way up at the back with big cloth-covered buttons, a pale blue linen top with lace inserts, a sleeveless red silk dress with a tulip skirt. Italian femininity had its positive side: politics and clothes could coexist without problem.

Since I did not yet speak Italian I could not talk to William's colleagues. When we went out to supper with them, I couldn't utter a word. I spent innumerable nights listening to interminable Italian conversations on art history, unable to understand or to join in, desperate to speak and to communicate but unable to. My version of Hell. Without language, I felt completely invisible and that I did not exist (and anyway who was this Signora Binns? I did not know her). Also, I became cut off from politics. Uprooted from the old structures back home,

I could not plant myself into new Italian ones. I discussed politics with anyone I met who talked English. I went to see Dario Fo act in his political comedies. I went to the Communist Festa dell' Unità. But it was all at one remove.

Of course, I should have gone off and taken Italian classes. This would have been difficult, because we moved around a lot, up and down between Florence and Rome, with forays elsewhere as well, but I think I must also have been unconsciously resisting getting involved. Part of me was hanging back, scared to plunge in too fully. I began to speak basic Italian quite quickly, because I did the food shopping, and needed to ask for what I wanted. The shopkeepers in the little streets webbing the foot of the Spanish Steps began to feel like friends. While they served me they talked to me as a matter of course. Hunger drew language out of me.

I discovered I could speak conversational Italian about a year later, when we were temporarily living in Venice in an attic flat at Santa Maria del Giglio. William went off somewhere to do research and stayed away about a week. I felt lonely. So I invited Manuela, a young art historian friend of William's, to supper. She spoke to me and I found I could understand and reply. Listening to Italian flowing over and around me, all those months, had let it soak in. Manuela spoke to me honestly, directly, affectionately, with humour, telling me the story of her life and of her affair with her much older lover. I courted him for months, she crowed: and in the end I got him! For the first time since my arrival in Italy I felt I was able to express myself fully to a new friend and not be just William's nice, smiling wife.

Wife! The word didn't suit me at all. I tried hard to carry out my side of what seemed a bargain, to behave appropriately, to appear a grown-up *signora*, but inside I was still a wild girl, a hooligan, a messy boy, an amazon. In disguise. What on earth had I gone and got myself into? Sometimes we would be ushered into yet another lecture hall, to meet some English or American academics, and someone would say: ah, here are the Binnses, and I would feel angry and terrified, my self slipping away; lost. As William's wife I was treated with special courtesy by the boss art historians, the elderly male ones in silk suits who ran the conferences. They would kiss my hand and dish out a compliment or two. Then ignore me. To the young female art historians they were much ruder, interrupting their presentations to criticise. They threw their weight about and expected to be treated with deference at all times. I observed them closely, the comedies they enacted, and recorded their doings in my notebook.

Not all the Italian women I met were deferential, however. I recorded a lunch with Frommel, one of the directors of the Herziana. After sherry in the barrel-vaulted frescoed salon, we processed to the equally impressive, antiques-furnished dining-room. Here, Frommel's aged, mustachioed maid, Augusta, dressed in a dirty overall, served us lunch, unfolding and refolding Frommel's napkin and criticising his table manners. However highfalutin the conversation on pediments and pilasters became, she flapped in and interrupted it, clucking, pulling things straight, slapping down dishes, telling Frommel to hurry up and eat before the roast veal got cold.

William was very charming to women and had many women friends. Not so much a woman friend in every port as a woman in every provincial capital: there was always someone eager to put us up in her comfortable house, to drive us about, to show us around. These women, often unhappily married, trapped, fretting to get away but not daring to break free, poured out their hearts to William, and he listened, his head on one side, his fingertips tilted together. Changing their lives did not seem an option for them. They preferred to complain bitterly and stay where they were and have a kindly man flatter them and make them feel special. I recognised their dilemmas, dimly, because I was unhappy myself, but I did not always feel sisterly to rich women swishing about in this season's fur coats and deprecating my lack of elegant handbags.

Maura, for example, a fashionably dressed Roman matron who put us up after we had to leave the Herziana, not only had His and Her bathrooms in her big flat but tubes of a special brand of His and Her toothpaste too. Middle-class Italy in the early 1980s seemed to take gender division to a near-hysterical extreme. In the company of some of William's lady admirers I felt uncouthly masculine. I particularly disliked the more snobbish of these women, obsessed as they were with *bella figura*.

I trotted about after William, finding out about him. He liked to tease, play, make learned jokes. He loved drawing people out, though he gave very little away in return. Men liked him too, because he played a 'feminine' role: not threatening, not overtly competitive. He was proud of having brought out the 'feminine' side of himself. When he wanted, he could be coquettish, childish, good fun. When he had time, he could be an enchanting companion with whom to visit churches, palazzi, villas, exhibitions. I remember his taking me to visit, for the first time, one Sunday morning, the Villa Borghese, and promising me treasures and treats. We walked through empty streets full of light, washed in a clarity and purity that made me feel like flying into them; edges and colours both hard and transparent. He introduced me to the statue, reclining, of the hermaphrodite, joyful and erotic; to Raphael's *Deposition*; and to Bernini's *Apollo and Daphne*. I shivered all over looking at this sculpture. Perhaps it enacted my own unspoken conflict

246

between being with a man and doing my own work; it did not feel simple to do both at once. Fulfilling the man's needs left less time for writing. As you walked around the two linked figures you saw new surprising relationships between them: there was flight and there was following and there was a kinship, Apollo's eyes straining beyond Daphne and she seeming as though the laurel tree had caught her, not just that she willed her transformation into it. An extraordinary statue: you saw a whole narrative blurting out of it and simultaneously constantly creating it; one of the loveliest and most troubling things I had ever seen.

Haunted for days by this sculpture, I ended up writing a poem about it. I came back to look at it on my own, and was snared by a well-meaning museum attendant who walked me around and told me tales of his life. Then I strolled through the Borghese Gardens. I ended up sitting on a bench on the Belvedere, at the side of the Villa Medici, where I scribbled in my notebook. Hot sunshine; eau de cologne wafting in the cold air from the elegantly dressed woman seated nearby; cooking smells and the clatter of dishes and cutlery and the murmur of voices from the restaurant behind the privet hedge. Under foot, pebbles were white and smooth as little eggs. I was trying to understand the effect of the Roman light: 'sun deep and glistening in the heart of umbrella pines, shining on gravel and earth and leaves, transforming them. Light *in* things. Their being. What animates them. The quality of the light is staggering. It is a great pure emptiness, it is as golden and solid as stone, it sings like a vessel of music, it vibrates and spins.'

At other times during our Rome sojourn I sat in libraries and read (finding relevant texts in French and English), taking copious notes for the novel about Mary Magdalene which I was finishing writing, which would be published in 1984 as *The*

Wild Girl. The novel had been sparked off by my transition from being single to getting married. The Catholic Church taught that a single woman could not be both holy and sexual. Why not? Why did a woman have to be split in two? I began to re-imagine Christianity, to imagine a Christ who loved and listened to women. Finally I found my form: a secret Gospel written by Mary Magdalene and subsequently suppressed as heretical. I made Mary a visionary, a mystic, a sexual being, a lover, a mother. I wrote in the first person, the first time I had done so, and (like Patrick Brontë's children) discovered the freedom of holding up a mask and speaking through it.

Researching the novel's background was intensely enjoyable. The research fed the story directly, although of course I made up a lot; I was a good heretic in my turn. I studied the Gnostic Gospels via Elaine Pagels's work on them. I drew on all the myths and apocryphal stories that I could discover about the saints of the early Church. I connected these to earlier Greek and pagan myths. I read theology and ancient history and studies of symbolism and everything in between, dashed down thoughts about life, death, sex, religion, politics, the unconscious, gods and goddesses, art, time, the universe. Writing poetry alongside my novel, I reaffirmed my belief in metaphor: that it expressed a deep truth; was never merely decorative. It had a profound religious sense: it reached towards the interconnectedness of all things – the truth I discovered in the mystical experiences I had from time to time, which I recorded in poems – by asserting: this is that. It incorporated something numinous. The gods lived in metaphor. Words were impregnated with spirit. When you created metaphors you summoned the gods. I saw metaphors as symbols, with one foot hidden in an invisible, mysterious world. You accessed that world through the word.

Twenty years later, a student said to me: you are always

seeking ecstasy. I found it, then, through writing. Looking back, I see that although marriage might not have made me happy it opened me up to engagement with the intellectual world, into grappling with masses of new ideas. In that respect Italy and William were very good for me. Lost in books, I lost my ego, stopped fretting, flew free, felt happier because I was trying to make something. Reading, thinking, writing. Creating: that was what mattered. (Oh child, Nana would say, exasperated, when I stormed about unhappily: stop creating. Creating a drama, she meant.)

Maura (very kind and hospitable despite her floor-length mink coats and gendered toothpaste) could no longer put us up. Serena lent us her flat, on the sixth floor of a nineteenth-century apartment block near the railway station. Coming back from the market, laden with shopping-bags of food, I would take a deep breath, entering the hallway, then slowly climb the six spiralling flights. At the top I would look back down at the deep well of steps. These smelled like a church, of incense and soap and flowers. Perhaps someone wearing perfume washed the steps every morning, carried freesias up them. Serena's flat floated between rooftops. Long windows let in tall oblongs of light. It spilled into the tiny kitchen crammed with green plants. The bedroom had a little balcony whence I looked down at the organ grinder's green music-machine far below as it pumped out sentimental tunes.

I envied Serena: a single woman living alone in her own flat (still fairly unusual in Italy at that time); what bliss. The sharp pain of envy made me see how much I wanted that for myself. Instead, I was a wanderer, perching precariously in other people's rooms to write during their absences, necessarily tidying myself away as soon as they came back. I couldn't imagine how I could ever own my own flat. I was too poor. I was a migrant. I hopped from place to place and did not belong any-where. On the other hand I was surviving, with enough to eat, a roof over my head, living in one of the most beautiful cities on earth, and had time to think my own thoughts. So in that sense I knew I was very privileged, very blessed, and felt I should not complain. Mustn't grumble! That's what the old ladies in London said to each other at bus-stops. I grumbled in secret. My diary was my room of my own in which I could speak and act as I liked. Reading created me a temporary house, spun a cocoon around me. My diaries for the 1980s repeatedly note that the act of writing means inhabiting a paper tent. You carry the tent, your paper house, with you, scrunched up in your pocket, and then put it up when you need it and it magically inflates.

The weather in December 1983 in Rome was as different as could be from that of an English winter. One day in the Campidoglio (art museum) library, for which William had pro-vided me with a reader's ticket, the female librarian dashed across the sombre, barrel-vaulted reading room, walled with ancient calf-bound volumes, pulled aside the flounced linen curtain screening one of the tall windows, yanked open the window and let in fresh air and golden light and warmth and blossomy scent. She cried out: '*e come la primavera!*' ('it's like the spring!').

The exhibition on *Raffaello Architetto* having duly opened, and the men in silk suits having delivered their lengthy speeches, we returned to Florence by train. Our hot, crowded compartment brimmed with black-clad nuns. The one sitting next to me prayed and looked holy all the way, glancing severely down her long nose at her companions who chatted gaily and did not keep their eyes lowered as she did. When they got out, she pulled from her bag a fine white silk scarf which she wrapped around her throat, looking discreetly pleased with herself. I spent the journey taking in all the colours beyond the window: khaki earth, yellow-brown earth, scarlet and black vines tied on to turquoise stakes, pink- and lavender-tipped trees on green hills, gold sunlight, a gold cockerel, yellow houses with green shutters and orange-patched plaster, blue sky, pale green rivers, orange beeches. You could name the forms in words but the scene seemed near-abstract at the same time: the forms carried the colours; were colours. I wanted to take these landscapes into my arms; embrace them; squeeze and pummel them; lick them. I was all hungry eyes and mouth. How amazing to be Italian and to be able to take all this ravishing beauty for granted.

William's flat in Florence occupied the top two floors of a building in Borgo la Croce, which ran from the little piazza just inside one of the city gates towards the heart of town. A quiet backstreet, it saw no tourists. The local church of Sant' Egidio, its interior all gilded curlicues and twirly bits, was ordinary, by Florentine standards, and the local shops similarly nice and workaday. Twice a day, in the morning, and after the siesta, there came a loud rattle down below us in the street as the shops' metal shutters clattered up. The sign that the city was waking up out of its slumber. That noise means Italy to me; that and the throaty cooing of pigeons. We had a nearby café, and wine shop, and a hardware shop. In this delectable place I bought a little tin grille for making toast on top of the stove, and pieces of the blue-speckled, blue-spattered local china; pleasing, well designed and cheap.

The market of Sant' Egidio was soberly everyday and workmanlike: concrete-floored, surrounded by warehouses, sheds, parked lorries. To me a paradise: fruit and veg stalls spilling cornucopias of produce, the frosty air scented with garbage, loud with the hoarse cries of traders advertising the season's specialities. In winter these included walnuts, long *radicchio rosso*, striped and frilled like tulips, artichokes, blood oranges and pomegranates. I bought bouquets of tiny violet artichokes and watched the traders preparing mountains of them at top speed, knives flashing as they stripped off the outer leaves which they cast upon the ground. In the covered part of the market I learned to keep my place in the queue of thrusting, jostling women, to call out what I wanted, to distinguish between different sorts of oil, ham and cheese, to become choosy and shrewd. A little further along towards the city centre was the *latteria* (dairy), the launderette, a bank. On the far side of this, a double row of antique stalls, where I bought old silver ex-votos in the shapes of hearts, stomachs, backs, legs. The narrow side streets of the district brimmed with furniture-repair shops, shoe-repair shops, paper-making shops, bookbinding shops; all kinds of craftsmen lived and worked here beyond these dark little doorways.

What a difficult place Florence was to walk through! No pavements. Plenty of dog turds. Cars and scooters and motorbikes whizzing past as you flattened yourself against the wall. The winter turned surprisingly cold. Icy winds howled along the streets and the Florentine matrons burst forth in fur coats and fur hats and the markets sold great swags of red-berried holly.

In the summer, I would discover, the city stagnated in heat, which scorched you like flat-irons; turned into a humid swamp. Mosquitoes roamed at night, scenting their prey. William would not let me use a mosquito spiral, nor mosquito repellent, because they emitted poisonous fumes, so I got bitten a lot and flaunted ugly red bumps and scars. He taught me his technique for killing the fanged beasts: once they had bitten you, and were perching on the wall, glutted, you could squish them with a paper handkerchief, carefully wetted so as not to mark the plaster. Then you could observe the red patches on the tissue: your blood which the mosquito had sucked. Then you could itch and scratch and lie sleepless, fretting.

Why didn't I stand up to William and insist on my right not to be bitten? I treated his needs as more important than mine. Other people's needs were automatically more important than your own. The lessons of Catholic childhood still haunted me. Not to be negotiated with. That was that. As a feminist I knew I ought to assert myself, and struggle for what I needed, but when it came to it I couldn't always do it. I felt too vulnerable. This was William's place. He controlled it.

I put all my anger into my diary; my paper house; my paper cupboard. Writing contained and shaped unacceptable feelings. Anger felt like a red imp jumping up and down and growling and wanting to bite. A cross red baby-imp. From time to time I opened the cupboard and the red baby-imp burst out. The cross red-faced baby was myself. Writing the baby meant gingerly picking her up, learning how to rock her, comfort her. When I looked at frescos in Florentine churches and saw devils and demons portrayed as little red imps I used to grimace in recognition. If I had angels inside me I certainly had devils too. Being human meant balancing between the two but of course it is much easier just to recognise the angel side. Anger is an abstract word for intense physical pain; a red fire burning inside.

William's dark little flat had thick stone walls which kept in the cold in winter and the heat in summer. With its red-tiled floor and old wooden shutters it was a charming place, in its way, though not comfortable. Again, furnished and arranged by Peri, who had lived here for several years. In 1976, the year of the great floods, she had walked around the district high up, hopping from roof to roof. William had a tiny loggia on his roof, clogged with pigeon shit, with a view of roofs and TV aerials and more pigeon shit. I never went up there. The stairs up to it were blocked with boxes of Peri's things.

The main room held a sink and cooker in one corner, a dining-table, a red-cushioned basket chair where William sat in the evenings to read, a bookshelf, an antique glass-fronted cupboard in which the china, pots and crockery were kept. I liked laying the table with the indigo porcelain plates. They gleamed in the shuttered lunchtime darkness of the flat. Wherever you go, wherever you live, I think you pick out your favourite things from what you find there; you discriminate; and choose to use them. I did, anyway. I learned to discriminate in Italy. That's what Italians did: picked out, exactly and precisely, what to eat, drink, wear. While I found living up to Italian sartorial standards exhausting, I enjoyed selecting this herb and not that one, this wine and not that one, this spoon and not that one. I liked those dark blue plates and I liked William's wineglasses, heavy in the hand, tiny bubbles of pale green caught in their translucent thickness. Off the kitchen was a tiny slit of a bathroom, tiled in blue, and to the other side was William's small study and his small bedroom, an almost-double bed crammed in alongside a trunk and wicker hampers, most of them full of Peri's clothes. Downstairs was an extra room, which William had recently bought, but not yet decorated. Peri's stuff was in there too.

For a while there was a great charm to living in Florence. I met more of William's women friends. Carla, a teacher, drove us to a New Year's Eve party at a villa in the countryside. She whizzed us along narrow walled roads between fields and olive groves and up into the hills. We entered the house (still a working farm) through a ground-floor loggia and climbed a staircase to the upper floor. Carla's friends, the sons of the house, showed us around the four bare rooms, the big kitchen with its wide fireplace and ancient stove. About twenty of us sat down and feasted and then we cleared away the table and chairs and began dancing. William enjoyed dancing; he whirled me about in an invented dance. He whispered to me: Carla looks like Hamlet; and indeed she did. She was a very slender figure dressed all in black, black tight sweater and short black tight skirt, black tights, white lace ruffles at wrists and throat. Her hair was cut in a bob, her chin and nose thrust forward as she wandered about aloofly inspecting the guests and the food, observing everything but remaining detached and of course melancholy (many Italians seemed melancholy and Carla especially so). After dancing with me William danced with all the other women and was a great hit. Within five minutes of our arrival at the party Carla pointed him out to me deep in conversation with a very pretty girl in a red frock. She laughed: he's always like that, he was the same about you too, you were the one he forsook others for and now it's your turn to be forsaken. Then she went all Danish and melancholy again.

As a writer, I felt homeless in Florence. The flat, like the one back in London, was set up for a single person. I could write if William went out to the archive, but not if he was working at home. I did not have my own space. There wasn't any. I should have insisted on clearing all Peri's junk out of the downstairs room and using that as my study. But to remove her stuff felt too aggressive. I didn't dare. There was nowhere to put it.

Another reason I felt powerless was because in Italy I had no outside job and earned no money. When we were in the UK again, as we were regularly, I picked up bits of teaching and journalism, and so managed to pay my way, to pay for my flights to Italy, my flight to Boston when I accompanied William there on a brief visit to give lectures, and to save for my tax bills.

However, much of the time in Italy William had to support me. Accordingly, I did all the cleaning, shopping, cooking and washing-up, ran errands, acted as hostess when his friends came to dinner. So I can see, looking back, that I worked hard and made a substantial contribution, but at the time I felt powerless and unable to ask for anything (no Wages for Housework in this world – Selma James would not have approved). Most of the time I couldn't afford clothes or books.

I did have some good times in Florence. I would visit Santa Croce and gaze at the fresco narrating the life and adventures of Mary Magdalene, brave, sexy heroine with flowing blonde curls and a red cloak; just like a comic strip. I would wander the streets and deliberately get lost just to see where I ended up. I sat and read in the university library, drinking up history, theology and hagiography, taking yet more notes for *The Wild Girl*, wrestling with final drafts, musing on literary form. Sometimes William went up to the Harvard University villa, I Tatti (formerly owned by the connoisseur and scholar Bernard Berenson), in the hills outside Florence, to use the library, and sometimes I took the bus up there to meet him for lunch. All the resident and visiting scholars gathered on the terrace, or inside the *salone*, depending on the season and the weather, for *aperitivi*, and then, after we had seated ourselves at the long refectory table, the female cooks served us delicious Florentine food and good local wine.

Afterwards, when the academics dispersed back to their books, I would wander in the landscaped garden then settle under a cypress to read. I remember going into the I Tatti orangery in winter, standing in the half-dark between the big rosy terracotta pots bearing the orange and lemon trees, seeing the yellow fruit gleam, stroking the waxy green leaves, smelling them. I remember, in summer, the white glare of sunlight on the stone shoulders of classical statues, the contrast of the dazzling white stone against the dark evergreens behind them, the crunch of gravel, the smell of box hedges in the heat. I remember taking off my sandals and walking barefoot, my eyes shut, among the sweet-scented flowering shrubs, feeling the dry cropped turf tickle my soles. The gardener, a bent old man in blue overalls, talked to me as he watered the pots of evergreens on the edge of the terrace. He showed me his mid-morning snack: a thick slice of rough bread dipped into olive oil and salt. He taught me his gardening aesthetic; what mattered was form, materials, textures. Privet and box, cut into severe shapes, suggested coolness. Colour came not from bright flowers but from terracotta; the ubiquitous dark-green plants.

How fortunate I was, knowing all these scholars interested in Renaissance gardens. Off we whizzed by car, a young art historian at the wheel, to visit them. In the course of the four years of the marriage I travelled all over Italy, usually by train but sometimes by car, visiting a host of cities and seeing sumptuous things, often being given privileged access to parts of palaces and villas closed to the public. What riches! The images lodged themselves deep inside me, and then surfaced later in novels, short stories, poems. On the other hand, sometimes, forced to gaze for hours in scorching heat at Renaissance fortifications or church façades, while the boss art historians droned on, I grew bored and irritable and couldn't have given a damn for scholarship and just wanted to lie down in the shade.

Working on Palladio, William needed to spend time in the archive in Vicenza, in the Veneto, packed with the maestro's buildings. Here, we stayed in a Palladian palazzo in the centre of town, thanks to the count who owned it, who was one of William's patrons. He put us up in a room on the mezzanine, formerly the granary floor, just behind one of the enormous pilasters on the façade. The taps in the tiny bathroom emitted just a drip, so I collected water for washing in a bucket. I bought a little camping table from the supermarket and wedged it under the window, between the bed and the wall, so that I had somewhere to write. I had to wait until William left for the archive in the morning, and then stop before noon in order to race out and buy food for lunch. There was no cooker, so I didn't have to cook as such. William insisted on returning home for lunch, like a good Italian husband. We had no fridge and fresh food went off quickly, so I had to shop every day. At night we ate spaghetti in a canteen-style restaurant, then sat in our room and read. Sometimes I just took myself off to one of the cafés at the edge of the piazza and tried to write under a sunshade. Easier just to smoke and drink coffee and watch the parade of sumptuously dressed locals.

One night in Vicenza we dined with a new friend William had made: Tommaso. Recently divorced, fiftyish, he lived (unhappily) with his widowed mother in a seventeenth-century villa, formerly an Augustinian convent, just outside the city, opposite a slightly older villa, La Malcontenta, with stone figures of dwarfs topping its walls. We ate outside, in the walled garden, under an enormous cedar, by candlelight.

Tommaso was a count, from a rich family (counts seemed two a lira in the Veneto). As well as this villa near Vicenza, as well as a palazzo and a couple of apartments in town, he owned a country house up in the nearby mountains at Lavarone. I was still at the stage of being impressed by the omnipresence of counts, and how many of them William knew, because their sixteenth-century houses were so architecturally remarkable, and by the sad fact that most of the counts were not like characters in opera but dull and super-correct. Many of them wore silk suits and silk ties all day long, even when lunching informally at home with friends at the height of summer. Tommaso did not bother with such nonsense, such disguise. He was big and burly, with short, curly black hair, a creased face, intelligent eyes. He dressed very well, in old, comfortable-looking linen jackets and trousers, everything of course beautifully cut.

Tommaso wrote poetry, so we bonded over writing. Tommaso's writing rather than mine. I listened to him a great deal. He expounded his theories of aesthetics and read me his latest works.

I put up with his lengthy discourses because he knew how to charm me, make me feel special. I found him a glamorous, sexy figure. Snobbery, I realise now, came in too – I liked being friends with a wealthy Italian aristo. No accident, I am sure, that I wrote an essay on romance while sitting in the garden of Tommaso's house in Lavarone. He'd said: oh, come and stay in my little place in the mountains. The house was of course huge, furnished with carefully chosen old pieces of furniture and nineteenth-century folk art, encrusted with cellars and attics. Staying in a place straight out of a gothic novel let the romantic dream swim up for analysis. I knew I wanted such a house for myself, but not the sort of marriage and class system that gave it to you. But I liked staying chez Tommaso and trying to imagine that life. I don't remember feeling explicitly envious of his wealth, partly because he was so generous towards me and partly because I could see that wealth had not made him happy. He was a very lonely person.

I liked exploring Tommaso's dark, mysterious dwellings, stuffed with ancient pictures, porcelain and furniture. I liked looking at all his things, his treasures, which he showed me carefully, one by one. I liked the shabbiness and the great age of his houses, the feeling that you could get lost in these puzzling structures layered with corridors, laced up and down with several staircases. These entrancing buildings acted as symbols of the imagination, the unconscious; they enshrined memory. Tiptoeing through them, I felt I could touch the past; touch ghosts.

Tommaso, on the other hand, seemed very alive. I liked cooking with him. A precise and rigorous chef, he taught me to make a proper *ragù* (meat sauce), to make *pastasciutta* cushions, fried and swollen, to make risotto with sausage, risotto with blue cheese. I would sit in the kitchen and watch him as he worked, and we would chat, and smoke cigarettes and sip red wine in the intervals of chopping and rolling, and this comfortable domesticity made me feel normal and acceptable. Sometimes after supper he sang, loudly and passionately, and sometimes I would join in. Then we would drink grappa or *amaro*.

William was also very sympathetic to Tommaso, and did his share of listening too. In return, Tommaso was most generous to us, taking us out to little *trattorie* high in the hills to eat good local food. The first time I tasted truffles and squid ink was in his company. He would read us his poems and ask us for our opinion. He wanted us to sing for our supper and so we duly did. He took us for long walks in the forests, which he loved, and in which he felt truly at home. He taught us to recognise different kinds of wild mushrooms and berries. He showed me his studio in the city, in his palazzo, and some of the works of art he kept there, and he showed me the small flat to which he took prostitutes. I was startled when he disclosed this side of his life: he sounded so cold and hostile towards these women. By trade he was an antiques dealer, specialising in pre-eighteenth-century objects and paintings. Once, when he and I met up in

London, he took me with him as he trawled the dealers of Mayfair, and I saw a completely different London from the one I knew: wealthy, soft-carpeted, glittering, expensive, hushed.

On another occasion Tommaso took me to Bologna for the day. While he conducted his business with another antique dealer, I went sightseeing. Over lunch (I ate *garganelle* for the first time – ribbed squares of *pastasciutta* rolled up diagonally then dressed with meat *ragù*) Tommaso expostulated: why had I wasted time looking at inferior churches in backstreets? I loved church furniture, that was why, and had enjoyed admiring hectically baroque statues of Madonnas, saints and angels, a wax baby, lace-wrapped and spikily-haloed, posed in a glass and gilt box. (The Baroque was of course the Wrong Period.)

Similarly I loved going crib-crawling, from one church to another, around Christmas-time, and studying the elaborately decorated and peopled Nativities. The best cribs, such as the one I saw in the church of the Sancti XII Apostoli in Rome on my 'honeymoon', had streams and ponds with real water in them, plastic swans bobbing on top. That Roman one was peopled with working models: a shepherd boiled a pot of water over a tripod with a fire beneath, that had flames and smoke issuing from it; a boy fishing for a fish that fluttered to and fro; ships sailing across a bright blue sea past a flashing lighthouse. When you put 100 lire in the slot Baby Jesus jerked his arm up and down in blessing, while a magic-lantern star looped endlessly, flashing on and off, across the backcloth, a luminous blue veil of night sky against which an angel appeared then disappeared, like a ghost.

Tommaso, like William, had austere tastes. They both necessarily scorned the elaborately decorated confessionals, the writhingly ecstatic Virgins, the elaborate reliquaries which so fascinated me, in favour of gazing raptly (Tommaso with a lit cigarette cupped discreetly in his palm) at Renaissance pilasters and columns and architraves. I gazed at these too, but not as a scholar does, for hours. Sometimes, when William was in off-duty mode, he would come and look at reliquaries, and be funny and playful about them. But most of the time he was busy making important new discoveries. Palladio must have designed this tomb! Palladio must have designed this window! While they looked and looked, with utter concentration, at shapes in stone, I dithered about in markets, picking up the exquisite printed paper orange-wrappers that littered the paving-stones, collecting enchantingly designed brown paper bags and greaseproof-paper cheese and salami wrappers. I made my own small space: I became a connoisseur of *objets trouvés*, of *art brut*. I named and listed my treasures and put these words into my writing.

Thanks to Tommaso I met my dear friend Giuliana Schiavi. Her lover Umberto had been at school with Tommaso and the two men were still good friends. Giuliana's attic flat overlooking the Corso in Vicenza – from her balcony one stared across the narrow street at the huge capitals, looming very close, at eye level, of the house opposite – was furnished with a witty eclecticism, raffia masks dangling from the gold-painted lavatory cistern, strings of beads hanging from door handles, big wicker trays holding things in the kitchen. Well-designed cheap modern cutlery mixed in with Japanese lacquer trays and Chinese enamel plates, and a huge wooden chest, called a *madia*, formerly used to store flour, in which Giuliana now kept packets of pasta. She kept her clothes in a green and white striped wooden beach hut in the flat's hallway. Together we cooked, smoked, ate, talked, played music, sunbathed, bought cheap clothes in the market, strolled in the piazza, sat in bars, and talked some more. We told each other our life stories;

recognised each other's struggles. We had a lot of fun. One of my fondest memories of Giuliana is helping her cook 'just a simple vegetable lasagne' during an August heatwave. Dressed in a skimpy black bikini she waved a cigarette in one hand and stirred three separate sauces with the other. We chopped three sorts of vegetables and sautéd them. The kitchen sweltered. I sweltered. Giuliana remained her unsweaty, olive-skinned, beautiful self, laughing and expostulating.

When William and I lived in Venice for a while, so that he could consult the archives there, Giuliana and I would meet. She would come to Venice or I would go to Vicenza, by train, or we would meet halfway, in Padua. We looked at art and architecture, but we looked at the ferociously chic clothes shops too. In St Anthony's Basilica I admired the public lavatories, which were signalled 'Gabinetti di Dicenza'. In Venice Giuliana and I would walk about and hop from bar to bar for coffee and cigarettes. The flat William had rented in Santa Maria del Giglio was at the top of an old house in a narrow *calle* (alley) near the boat-stop, just round the corner from San Marco. The small bedroom had an antique dressing-table squashed in under the window, and here I wrote. Pushing open the shutters, leaning out, peering across a mass of roofs, I saw the tops of masts go by, as ships steered towards San Marco. They seemed like church spires, the churches slipping their moorings and making for the lagoon, the open sea.

After three years of this peripatetic life, following William around, living part-time in Rome, Florence, Vicenza and Venice, I would know that I too wanted to slip my moorings and make off. Wonderful as it was to look at blue Tiepolo ceilings in the Gesuati Church then embark from the nearby Zattere on Tiepolo-blue waters under a Tiepolo-blue sky, towards the Giudecca, to eat seafood risotto in the little outdoor restaurant, window-boxes full of little Tiepolo-blue irises, near the Redentore, to sit on high-up balconies above the Canal Grande in the shimmering golden dusk eating fried squid and drinking icy Pinot Grigio, to wander *piazze* and backstreets and discover new churches, new galleries, new exhibitions, I couldn't be a tourist for ever. I didn't want to be a wife any more, either. I was fed up having to do all the domestic chores: William simply refused to share them, so that was that.

Spring 1986: Simone de Beauvoir died. America was at war with Libya, and American F111 fighter planes took off from British bases. I felt disgusted and angry. We were no more than an extra state of the USA; a colony. I witnessed this from a distance, did not get involved in any Italian-based protests about anything.

With my women friends, for example Sarah LeFanu and Giuliana, I talked about politics on the telephone. On the level of personal politics, we went on giving each other support. That helped me feel less isolated. The fact that they listened to me and talked to me helped me feel braver about admitting what I felt. I wanted to commit myself full-time to my writing and return to Britain, where, increasingly, I had a presence as a writer. *The Wild Girl* had been published. Cross Tories, and cross Christians, who disliked the idea of Jesus having a lover and enjoying rapturous sex with her, tried to get my publishers, Methuen, prosecuted for blasphemous libel. That didn't happen, but the novel received a lot of publicity, which of course helped sales. I was, perhaps naïvely, surprised by the amount of hate-mail I received, threatening me with hellfire. An ex-nun I knew told me that I would burn in Hell. She really meant it: I felt punched by her aggression.

I did get fan-mail too, from radical Christians of both sexes. My mother hated the novel, and felt personally attacked by it, which was very painful for both of us. With one part of myself I felt terrible for causing her pain, and with another part I felt I had to go on writing against authority, against authority's canonical books. I had learned that if you write against authority you can't expect the authorities to turn round and thank you. Anyway, having rewritten the New Testament, I then turned my attention to the Old, and began writing a novel about the goings-on aboard the Ark. I called it *The Book of Mrs Noah*. It featured the Ark as an archive, with a crew of sibyls, joined by God the Father, telling each other stories. The Gaffer, as I called God, was suffering from writer's block. He'd written one bestseller but couldn't think how to start another.

At the same time, on my trips back to the UK, I began to take part in mainstream literary life as well as in radical activities around books. I gave talks and readings, hosted a TV series on up-and-coming young poets, sat on the literature committee of the Greater London Arts Association, taught at the Arvon Foundation, interviewed authors such as Kathy Acker and Dora Russell for *City Limits*, wrote book reviews. I went to the States, too, on a solo trip, and did readings at universities around New England.

My life had changed and I had changed, too. I was more open about my drive to write and to publish my writing. I had become, in that sense, less communally minded and more what we called 'individualistic'. I fell out with three women I knew at this point. They denounced me for bad behaviour: kowtowing to William, to the literary establishment, abandoning the struggle. I felt stabbed by each woman in turn. I felt angry as well as hurt. I still found it almost impossible to be openly angry with people I was fond of; to their faces.

I think, now, that perhaps these three women envied me my bit of success. Envy was difficult for feminists to admit, let alone discuss, at that time. We believed in sisterhood and equality and supporting each other and indeed put those ideals into practice. Feminism had been my life-support; my chosen family. It was hugely important not only in private life but as a public identity. It still required courage to say you were a feminist, since feminism was ridiculed non-stop in the media and by everybody who hung on to the status quo. So for feminists to admit our shortcomings, our difficulties, put us on the defensive and felt very painful. We felt we opened ourselves to additional attacks. The three women currently angry with me coped with their feelings by translating them into moralism, expressing loud disapproval of my bourgeois literary ambitions and lifestyle. I was a Bad Girl who should behave better. I felt devastated, but I just had to become more independent and cope.

In summer 1986 William accepted a job in Harvard. I was supposed, of course, to accompany him, but we agreed that I would stay behind in Italy for a few weeks to supervise the renovation works on his flat in Florence. These had been scheduled for months but delayed because of bureaucratic problems at the local Soprintendenza, the office that oversaw the restoration of historic buildings. Permission was finally given. The works were suddenly now about to begin.

William flew to Boston in July. I nervously interviewed the architect, Gian-Pietro Nicola. He assured me that he would act as supervisor of the works and instruct the workmen day to day. Everything was fine. Perhaps I would like to pack up the flat? First of all they were going to take the roof off, in order to check and repair the beams and rafters. After that, they would enclose the room on the lower floor into the main body of the flat.

In came four workmen, all old friends who had grown up together in Calabria. I just had time to put small things into boxes, and drape the furniture in plastic sheets, before they knocked all the plaster off the ceiling of the main room. First they revealed a woven cane layer, like basketry, and then the beams. Tides of rubble flowed across the floor; clouds of plaster dust settled thickly on to everything, including me. I had a white wig.

Antonio, the foreman, chatted to me over a cigarette. One of seven children, he had come up north and become a builder. Impossible to get decently paid work in Calabria, he said, because of the Mafia. He hated priests, who were borne along on the shoulders of ordinary people. Friendship was the most important thing in life. He used to keep a diary. Once he had been loved by an older woman in Rome who had wanted him to stay with her for ever. But now he sent money home to his wife and children every week. He and his three workmates all did this. I pictured the women, waiting for letters, for phone calls.

White veils swathed everything in the flat, the gleaming plastic sheets wrapping the furniture now themselves sheeted in white dust. Clothes swung like ghosts in the wardrobe and I too was a ghost, creeping from room to room. Masonry fell, a rubble of bricks and stones. The workmen brought in scaffolding, via a rope and tackle fixed at the front window, and erected it at the back of the house. They passed bucket after bucket of debris over the back windowsill, the rope rattling over the creaking pulley; the house emptied itself out of the window, a body throwing up; no stomach left; no heart.

Every night I cleaned up, sweeping rubble into corners, taking up the filthy newspapers protecting the red tiles and washing the floor, unveiling the cooker and fridge and swabbing off the layer of grit and grime that had seeped through, re-washing the dirty, dusty lavatory and sink and bath. Finally I would wash myself. Then I would cook, and eat supper on a corner of the study table, pushing aside the covering sheet of plastic. I would set my place with a candle, a jug of flowers, a glass of wine. I would smoke a cigarette. Then I would fall into bed and dream all night about mending the house, before jumping up at six to let the workmen in.

I tried to keep up. I tried to keep the house up. I couldn't. It was crumbling like my marriage and I felt like Humpty Dumpty as the main room tumbled, vanished, its walls pulled down. The roof lifted off like a lid, replaced with a canvas. I felt I was collapsing too. I was the house falling down. The builders stopped being charming and made sexist jokes. The architect treated me like a silly woman, when he did bother to come round to check, and the official at the Questura (police station) shouted at me when I went to collect my *permesso di soggiorno* (temporary residence permit) because I'd filled the form in wrongly. I swore to myself I was going to be strong and that I would cope.

I moved out, as the bath and lavatory were now full of rubble and the builders were working in the bedroom and study as well as the main room. I escaped to stay with Maggie, an American art historian friend of William's, who had a flat on the far side of the Duomo, near the railway station. With enormous kindness, she put me up. I slept on her study floor. William did not write and did not telephone. Nor did he send me money to pay the builders and buy materials. I left urgent messages for him, to which he did not respond. So I paid the workmen out of my savings. Then the Vigili Urbani turned up, told the builders they hadn't got proper planning permission, threatened them with jail, stopped the works. They slapped a suspension notice on the front door. Nicola the architect, when

I finally ran him down after days of fruitless telephoning, airily admitted he'd forgotten to obtain a certain *permesso*, told me patronisingly not to fret, that he'd get it from the Comune (the local council) the following day. I tried to console the workmen, who were scared they would lose the job and get no money.

Weeks passed, which I spent phoning officials, bureaucrats, builders, husband, to no effect. The late summer turned to autumn. I visited the flat every day, to check on its state. I wandered the backstreets near Maggie's flat, exploring, peeping into dark little shops selling bedsteads, junk, groceries. I had no warm clothes, and started to shiver in the chilly mornings and evenings. I bought myself a huge old Irish tweed man's overcoat, with raglan sleeves and big leather buttons, for £40 in the Mercato Centrale of San Lorenzo near Maggie's street. Shopping for food here cheered me up: the marble façades, inlaid with marquetry, lettered with gold, of the butchers' stalls. I admired the premises of Annibale Carrocci, tripe merchant (his name so close to that of Annibale Carracci, the painter), who sold his wares from what looked like a pulpit, a mahogany frame set with cast-iron rails and hooks, and his counter like an altar inlaid with coloured marbles. Nearby, sides of beef flopped like red coats on barrows. I found a second-hand book-exchange shop, with a range of paperbacks in English, so at last was able to get hold of enough novels to read. At night I read for escapism, to allow myself to fall asleep. I read the complete works of Dick Francis, and related strongly to the male heroes enduring testing, terrible times. I managed to finish revising *The Book of Mrs Noah*, writing on Maggie's kitchen table. I shouted at the architect over the phone, incoherently, because I lacked good abusive words in Italian.

Eventually the men from the Comune arrived, dressed in smart jeans and leather jackets, bearing slide-rules, and discussed the problem with Nicola. They ignored me completely. They at last issued the *permesso*. The works began again. William still did not write or phone. Not one single letter or postcard! I felt he had completely abandoned me. I used to go into a hotel to ring him (for which you paid enormous sums) and he would talk about how busy and fraught he was. He accused me of dragging my feet and not getting on with the works fast enough. He promised to send me money to pay the workmen, then did not.

Occasionally I escaped by train up to Vicenza, and spent weekends with dear Giuliana. Leaving her to return to Florence, I would feel utterly bereft. One Sunday the trains went wrong and it took me nine hours to get back. I sat shivering and miserable on the cold platform at Bologna and clenched my jaws so that I could not cry and told myself: well, this is all experience.

It poured with rain. The flat became a sea of mud. Rain dripped through the open roof, through the floor into the flat below, and fell on the sleeping baby of the tenants down there. They harangued me for a long time, with justifiable fury. The workmen harangued me. They went on strike in order to get paid. I paid them. Nothing else to be done.

Finally the roof came back on. The architect promised to oversee the rest of the works. I thanked Maggie for her great kindness and got on a plane to England.

Chapter Ten

CAMBRIDGE, MASSACHUSETTS

Displacement

I stayed in England over Christmas, wanting to spend time with my friends and family. I remember locking myself into my parents' bathroom, in between bouts of festivity, and burying my head in the bath towels and weeping.

I had decided that I ought to see William through what remained of his first academic year. It seemed too mean not to go out to North America at all. He needed his wife to show up and prove she existed. So despite hardly being able to walk because of bad back pain (a psychosomatic injury I was sure, designed to prevent myself from having to leave) I got myself on to a plane for Boston.

As soon as I arrived in Harvard, William departed to give some lectures elsewhere. Columbia University? Yale? I can't remember. I had to cope on my own with getting used to this new place. As I knew nobody, I felt lonely. I lay on the floor and willed my back to get better. Snow fell. The streets and sidewalks sheeted with ice. Harvard Yard disappeared under whiteness. William had been given an apartment in Lowell House, one of the colleges, to tide him over until he bought somewhere to live. Once I could walk again, I rattled about between the dark sitting-room, with its armchairs covered in apricot velveteen, and the dark kitchen, bedroom and bathroom. No one to speak to. I jumped at the sound of my own footsteps, my own indrawn breaths. I took up too much space; I disturbed the air.

An obscene phone-caller harassed me a couple of times. I was feeling vulnerable, not in control of anything. His aggression punched me all over. His slimy delight was equally repulsive. The second time I talked back furiously to him, taunting him with his sexual inadequacy, and he shut up quickly and did not ring again. I wrote down what he had said, chopping it up and twisting it about, and made found poetry out of it.

The central heating roared, encouraging insects to come out and play. Cockroaches bounced out of drawers and cupboards when I opened them. Their leaps and their wavy feelers scared me. I bought, in the local shabby, run-down supermarket (the only one in walking distance), a black plastic device, pierced with holes, called the Roach Motel, which I parked on the floor behind the kitchen door. The label showed three roaches dressed as spivs, in dark glasses, wearing slouch hats and trench-coats with upturned collars, going into a Hitchcock-style gothic house. The black-lettered legend read: 'the roaches check in – but they don't check out.'

I had checked in and now longed to check out. Harvard did not suit me and I did not suit it. I didn't give it a chance. I didn't want to. I could see, once he returned from lecturing, that William was enjoying his new job. He felt valued and respected for his learning and scholarship. He was important: people hung on to his words. I trailed about after him, a faculty wife, duti-fully attending stuffy formal parties, receptions and dinners, smiling nicely and chatting nicely and inwardly seething with boredom and rage. I felt muffled by the flat. I tried to cheer up its dull, anonymous décor, buying Italian soup-plates, white with blue spots, and Italian indigo and white checked tea-towels, buying bunches of flowers. The bookshelves rattled with emptiness. The walls remained bare. Most of William's col-leagues lived in graceful white clapboard houses in tree-shaded avenues around Cambridge. They urged us to house-hunt. William informed me he had decided not to buy a house, but to spend his money on antiquarian books. All right, I said.

I regularly asked people to supper. That gave me a focus. At least I could create something, even if I couldn't write much. At least I could now cook proper Italian food. Being bored by academic chitchat *chez moi* was preferable to eating in the noisy college dining-room and having to talk to loud, cheery students I didn't want to have to be nice to. I loathed living in an institution. I loathed having to be polite all the time. I loathed the way most of the male academics did not bother speaking to me. I felt contemptuous of the prevailing genteel liberalism that masked right-wing attitudes and practices. Harvard University was still investing heavily in white-ruled South Africa. Nobody I met seemed to care, though the students demonstrated from time to time.

Left-wingers surfaced occasionally at the Graduate School of Design amidst the visiting European architects who flew in for brief fellowship visits. I remember Rafael, a charming, clever Spaniard who visited, and whom I asked to supper with his wife Belén. She was warm, lively, well dressed, intelligent. Rafael obviously liked women very much, liked talking to women, and didn't have a problem with femininity plus brains. Unlike one academic who said to me loudly at dinner one night: writing's your little hobby, isn't it? Have you ever published anything? Oh, via vanity presses, of course. He treated his wife as his dogsbody, and, once his sons left home, lamented that he had nobody intelligent left to talk to.

Sometimes at dinner I got drunk and made impassioned long-winded speeches about feminism and embarrassed my guests. One night I told a bunch of delicate-minded academics the tale I'd just read, in a book by Judith Brown, of some seventeenth-century nuns who'd been heretical lesbians. The Inquisition measured their clitorises: a big clitoris meant you were a mini-man and would get punished extra-ferociously. I quickly realised that the word clitoris was not normally bandied about in Harvard dining-rooms. Everyone lowered their heads over their *spaghetti alle vongole* and pretended I had not spoken. People in New England were kindly but puritanical. Women dieted and stayed in control of themselves: at lunchtime they ate only salad and only drank mineral water. Defiantly I smoked too much and drank too much and slept away the afternoons and generally felt myself turning into a Mad Housewife.

Of course I met some delightful, eccentric, original people whose company I enjoyed. They tended to be outsiders or part-time outsiders: black artists, gay writers, émigrés of all sorts. I got to know Irit, a radical, theory-loving, Israeli art historian, who took me to a couple of political meetings and introduced me to Jewish anti-Zionism. I admired Larry, who by day worked as assistant to the Dean and by night became a soul singer. He took me to clubs in Boston to listen to jazz. William and I went to his gigs, witnessed his transformation into red-robed shaman urging us towards ecstasy. His girlfriend Bella, who worked as an administrator, always looked beautifully dressed: shimmery silks, turquoise and silver jewellery. Even her raincoats shimmered, thin silvery-blue fabric blew about her like the pale petals of flowers. She showed me the good, cheap clothes shops around, the bargain basements in Boston. Like a lot of the women I met, she was trying to write, and showed me her novel and asked for my advice.

The black middle class seemed strongly established in the States; much more visible than in Britain. Larry and Bella moved in a world of young professionals, all very ambitious and hardworking. They encouraged me to seek out experiences of my own away from the campus. I went to a Black Poetry con-ference in Boston, for example, and spent three days listening enraptured. William and I made a quick trip to New York, meeting up with the writer Irving Weinman (the lover of my poet friend Judith Kazantzis) and going to the Blue Note jazz club with him. I lunched regularly with Jehane Kuhn, William's first wife, now married to historian of science Thomas Kuhn, and Emily, an architect friend of Alex's (Alex from my Holland Park days), who'd moved back to the States with her husband: an agreeable threesome. Jehane was kind to me, but it was impossible for us to become close: too many husbands in the way. Clever, witty, beautiful Emily I liked very much, and wanted to get to know better.

William and I had stayed with the Kuhns in their big house on Beacon Hill in Boston on a previous trip. They had not one but two black maids who came in to wash and iron. Supper chez Kuhn meant good food (Tom cooked osso bucco one night, marrow bones and all) and passionate conversation. Tom was a big, vital, handsome man in his late fifties. I could talk to him, even if we disagreed about feminism. When I got drunk one night and harangued him about men's ways of categorising and controlling women I felt he understood that I was unhappy and forgave me my tipsiness. He was a kind man, as well as a brilliant one, and I liked him a lot. After that heated debate, which I lost because as usual I became too emotional, I dreamed I was a heretic dressed in red, who left a gruff book-seller (Tom) and dived into the grate, went through the fire, up through a dark chimney-like tunnel, and finally emerged into the open air.

This dream went into *The Book of Mrs Noah*, which I was redrafting for the final time, and showed me how much I still split intellect from feeling in a way I characterised as bourgeois and masculine. I had to go away from that world of categories, into the freer space of poetry and art, with their capacity for subversion of established categories, in order to discover my own language and vision, try to integrate body, mind, creativity. Abstract words separated things; I wanted to make art that recombined them. Tom had (famously) developed the concept of the paradigm shift. He recognised the force of history in shaping science but not that of gender. He was aware of the discrimination towards black people practised all around us (how much did his two black maids get paid?) but could not see that women (black or white) suffered in any particular way. His white male academic friends were well off. Their wives benefited (as long as they toed the line). I tried to argue that becoming a feminist could make one aware of other sorts of oppression, such as racism. Tom exclaimed to me he thought it repulsive to compare the suffering of middle-class white women to that of black people. That was that.

I was reading Evelyn Keller on gender and science. I was reading about women and philosophy. I learned that I was still a traditional woman, apparently: I trusted abstract reasoning less than thoughts that came out of my own experience in the world and from my own inner life. Poetry and novels arose from very deep down inside. They struggled up out of darkness and broke into the light. I trusted this process. I knew that language existed 'outside' in the world, made by human beings, embodied in oral and written stories and poems, and that of course these fed me as a writer, but in order properly to value a perception I needed to experience it as coming out of my deep self. I knew that the imagination was in the belly; cooking slowly; a sort of compost heap. A hay oven!

I can see now that my idea of writing and thinking owed a lot to the medieval and Renaissance mystical writers I had read and been inspired by. A mystic, having read (or having had read to her) the Bible, trusted not only the sacred Book but her own

vision of God, even if that meant disagreeing with the authorities' version. A mystic did not need the (male) authorities to
mediate God to her. She encountered God directly. Obviously,
an unlearned and illiterate woman would need to claim her
own experience as authoritative if she had not been able to read
the sacred texts.

Modern mystics may not use the word God at all, of course.
Atheists can have mystical visions, and do. Plenty of people
have mystical experiences but do not talk about them for fear of
ridicule. Freud labelled these rapturous encounters with the
universe oceanic feelings, the bliss of the baby at the breast, the
baby not a separate self but simply part of, dissolving into, a
great flow of pleasure. I thought Freud wrote off mystical
experiences too briskly. When I had them (for example rocking
by bus through the bleak industrial landscape of New Jersey)
they were certainly triggered (I think now) by regular, hypnotic
motion (the jogging of a maternal lap, I suppose), by my own
resulting dreamy state. At the same time, however, they seemed
not only to incorporate a regression to pre-linguistic infantile
bliss but also to embody a valuable truth an adult could cherish, try to put into words, not the words of conventional
grammar which separated things but the words of poetry which
recombined them. *Je es une autre.* My version in one poem was:
the one body is both of us. At these moments of ecstatic dissolving (which of course happens with sex too) we are not
separate from the world but part of the world's body. Painters
know that. Bonnard painted the radiant body of the world; the
body illuminated from within. To know that body you have to
plunge into it, let it plunge into you. Look at his last painting –
that cherry tree in white blossom, painted on his deathbed. The
tree is itself and the tree is him and he is the tree.

I had my first mystical experience at the age of ten, wandering into the Quaker graveyard in Harrow-on-the-Hill (was it connected to Grandpa's death? I wonder now – perhaps). Bees buzzed. Peace took hold of me, saturated me. I felt the presence of God (those were the only words for it I had at that time). Mystical experiences went on happening, often when I gave up cigarettes (yet again) and the world rushed into me because I had no barriers against it. I had more blissful moments in Bali, when I tripped on magic mushrooms, or on those occasions when I dropped acid or took opium, but I trusted more the experiences not provoked by drugs but just by dreaminess, contemplation, letting go without realising it. Nothing to do with being a Good Person or believing in God. Not a reward for virtue. Just a gift given to you by the world: the felt knowledge that we are all deeply connected to one another and to all forms of creation. Becoming aware of that in a moment of illumination means loss of self and simultaneous great joy.

My image of creativity, I saw some years ago, was a dark (dead) body becoming illuminated, becoming golden (alive). I discovered, when I looked back at them, that many of my novels open with an image of a dead body, an image of death (speechlessness) and finish on an image of life, of creativity (spoken language). Writing the novel means that the dead body sits up on the bier and speaks. I don't plan this. It's the arc the novels wish to describe. I can see that the gold body image probably derives from alchemical symbols of transformation but I don't need to explain it to myself while I'm actually writing. While I'm writing, the act needs to remain in some way mysterious, and does, because the thinking ego dwindles away. I can think about the process afterwards, if I want to. Creating happens in a kind of dreamy darkness, in which one is, paradoxically, as alert and focused as possible. Creating means a particular sort of thinking. Editing and criticising come afterwards.

The Protestant idea of conscience, which I learned from Charlotte Brontë's writings, linked, for me, to the independence of mystical thought: conscience dwelled inside you and you did not need to consult a priest in order to listen to it. Catholics, of course, were supposed to need (male) confessors to keep them on the right lines. I was done with all that. But I still needed to wrestle with male authority-figures from time to time, to test myself out, to test out my strength, even if that implied continuing to accept their view of the world. The carnival happens on the church steps, as Juliet Mitchell once remarked. At the same time, gradually, I was coming to see that I had to go on making, and relying on, my own view of the world, and keep on letting it evolve and change. The Harvard I encountered was not the best place in which to do that.

I needed to thrash things out with friends. I did meet some fascinating women, particularly at the Center for Cultural Studies, with whom I struck up astonishing instant friendships. But the friendships were like one-night stands: intimacy that could not endure; people moved on so fast. I would meet a woman at a lecture on Gertrude Stein, or H.D., or the figure of the mother in contemporary fiction, talk to her over drinks afterwards as though we'd known each other for years, and then discover the following week that she'd flown off to a new job in California.

What intrigued me about Americans was that when you scratched their surface you discovered the European, the Asian, the Indian, below. 'American' seemed a smooth white coat of sameness and glibness; I liked the more complicated identity underneath. This did spring out. Once, on one of my many long solitary walks, roaming the suburbs of Cambridge, I chanced on the Portuguese district. All the little white houses had large plaster statues of the Virgin in their front yards. Since it was raining that day all the statues wore plastic rainhoods tied on over their veils.

We got through the scouringly cold winter and spring, the sudden thaw, the melting of the dirty yellowish ice that lay in rumpled heaps on the sidewalks, the onslaught of rain and slush. The air warmed. Green buds showed. I bought a long narrow linen skirt, in French blue, and wore it with my frilly Victorian blouse, and roamed about the streets in it, feeling hope return, feeling sexy, wanting to make love. I exchanged letters with a male poet I'd recently met and fancied, who had sent me his latest book. Flirting with him by mail kept me going.

In May we flew to London. William went straight on to Florence and I followed him after a few days. I felt I had to tell him face to face that I was leaving him; that was more honest than just not showing up and then telling him by phone. We spent a harrowing afternoon. We both cried. Then I threw some clothes into a bag and ran away. I jumped on a train and went to stay with Giuliana and Umberto in Vicenza. I stayed with them for a month, grieving, in hiding, licking my wounds. Then I returned to England in time for the publication of *The Book of Mrs Noah*. I'd jumped into my own Ark, hauled up the anchor and cast off, was making for the open sea.

Chapter Eleven

WIVENHOE

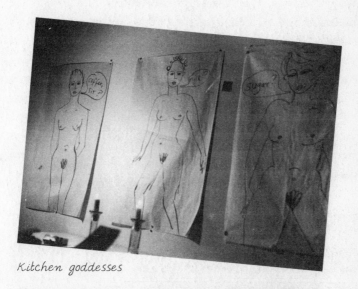

Kitchen goddesses

Teaching writing to City Lit students

I left behind one collection of books in Florence, and a smaller one in Harvard. More libraries lost. But I couldn't have carried them with me. I left behind in Lowell House my cherished Italian soup-plates, but I packed my indigo tea-towels. William would not have noticed their loss. I also left behind a self-portrait I'd painted in Vicenza, my face represented reflected in three window-panes. Splits. I'm sad I lost that picture. But William had encouraged me to paint and draw and I am grateful to him for that.

William had let the London flat for six months to a young Italian chemist called Henrietta. She occupied the platform bed in the big room at the front, and I camped in the little back room. I liked Henrietta, with her long flowing streams of golden hair and her long flowing streams of consciousness over breakfast. I took her out for long, weaving walks, showing her Bayswater's shabby streets and squares, its delis and cafés, serving food for all nationalities. I introduced her to Khan's, the huge, canteen-like restaurant on Westbourne Grove, to the splendidly ornate décor of the local swimming baths. We gazed at the women in long black robes and veils, their faces concealed by black and gold masks carved stiff as birds' wings, who strolled Queensway. We went to poetry readings and book launches at Saqi Books on Westbourne Grove.

I cooked for us both at night, since I didn't like the meals of stewed vegetable gloop she offered me, and we made each other laugh with our stories of our lives, the particular vocabularies we used. Henrietta always referred to her lovers as her fiancés. She felt that was more decorous, however many of them she had at once. On the kitchen wall I had pinned up three of my black and white drawings: large, almost life-size cartoons of curvy, curly-haired nudes who offered the onlooker Tea, sir? Coffee, sir? Sugar, sir? They were my satires on my housewifely self, and they were also my little kitchen spirit helpers, like the invisible ones in the palace of Eros, who bring Psyche delicious food and drink. Henrietta fell in love with these plump, helpful nymphs and so she rolled them up and took them back to Italy with her, to put them up in her kitchen in Milan.

I had become obsessed with the story of Psyche and Eros, which I had read in *The Golden Ass* by Apuleius, and knew I wanted to write something based on it. Psyche had darted out at me from many of the Renaissance frescos I had seen in Italy. She had jumped into a long poem I wrote about restoration work in Palazzo Te in Mantua. I discovered her in the Fitzwilliam Museum in Cambridge sporting elegant open sandals laced up with golden strings. Now she wanted to take centre stage in a play. Could I write one? I'd written street theatre fourteen years before, but that was very much in a group under Ali's guiding star. I reckoned I'd have a go.

I felt free, despite being homeless and penniless. I had no money and no savings. I had nowhere to live, since although I was still technically married I was only perching temporarily in William's flat in Bayswater; I certainly did not want to share a living space with my husband ever again. I needed a job of some sort, but it was summer and no teaching was available. I decided there was nothing else for it: I would have to pray for help. Oh God, I prayed: please help me. Er, that's it.

The next morning, flicking through the pages of the *Guardian*, I noticed an advertisement for the job of Theatre Writer in Residence at Essex University. I applied for it and was summoned for interview. I felt nervous at first, not being an established playwright, but as soon as I started discussing theatre with the panel of academics my nervousness diminished. Enthusiasm took over. To my delight I got the job.

I found digs in the waterside village of Wivenhoe, the old fishing/commercial port, near the university: a room rented to me by Lily, retired from an administrative job at the university, now a widow. She said she hoped I'd be company for her, someone to watch TV with in the evenings. She missed her daughters, grown up and moved away. I did not make friends with her, however. She was intelligent, decorous and pleasant. But I feared what felt like her neediness, presumably because I feared my own and sat on it firmly. I felt I was a widow too, but did not want to join Lily's particular company of widows. Nor to be a daughter-substitute. I was still battle-bruised, unable to discuss it, needed to stay aloof. I paid her my £40 rent each week (quite a lot for those days) and considered that was that.

Her little modern house seemed flimsy as pasteboard, cramped and claustrophobic after American bigness. I loathed its genteel tastefulness, the pastels and florals of the décor, the dainty china ornaments on the windowsills, the navy-blue polyester sheets on my single bed. The little bathroom, carpeted and scented, was so ferociously clean I hardly dared use it. I cleaned up anxiously after myself every morning and then heard Lily going in after me and scrubbing vigorously. Germaine Greer once said: a woman does not need to clean her lavatory every single day. Lily did. I wrote a poem about living in the wrong house, about my hands still hanging up an imaginary apron on imaginary hooks. At night I came in, cooked myself a swift bowl of pasta in the kitchen, ate it, said goodnight to Lily, popping my head around the door of her blue and green William-Morris-decorated sitting-room, then retired upstairs to my little cardboard bedroom.

I felt extremely lonely. I read books (lots of thrillers). I drank wine. I opened the window, leaned out as far as I could, smoked cigarettes. I wrote my play. I went to bed early. I heard Lily come upstairs. We breathed quietly on either side of the thin wall separating our rooms.

Night after night I lived like this, through the autumn and winter of 1987. I felt a dim pride in coping OK. I hadn't fallen apart. I was keeping everything together. I was managing. These homely expressions gave me strength. I was sustained by thoughts of Nana, heard her voice telling me she loved me and that I would come through. That's the ticket! Nana was a robust version of Psyche. When she saw what she called a pile of tack she set to and sorted it out. Very well. I would do the same.

Every morning I walked down the road the couple of miles to the university, and this walk alongside ploughed fields gave me great delight: the colours and textures of mud and sky. Walking induces rapture: the regular movement is a sort of self-hypnosis, I think; and then your ego dissolves and floats off and you are just a part of the startling beauty of the cold air, the light, the early morning. The end of the walk took me through Wivenhoe Park, and then up to the concrete towers, separated by the steps and *piazze* (the whole inspired by San Gimignano) of the university. Walking through Wivenhoe Park after the hurricane in 1987, looking at the giant trees felled by the wind, their roots heaved up out of great pits, I listened to the whine of chainsaws. One of the workmen, a man with a battered merry face, observing me dawdling past, cried out: if you've got nothing better to do all day why not help me move these trees? He shook his head over the corpses. They reminded me of the huge reclining Buddhas I had seen in Thailand.

My brief, as Theatre Writer in Residence, was to write a play, which would be performed by a professional cast at the

Mercury Theatre in Colchester, directed by Faynia Williams, the resident theatre director at the university. Alongside this activity, I was asked to work with the MA drama students. They were an international group: some British, some American, some Japanese, one Italian, one Moroccan. I was supposed to involve them in my writing. I took in drafts to show them, but it was hard for them to make head or tail of what I was on about. I was writing experimentally, non-realistically, messily, in bits and pieces, in visual images, in poetry. To find language I had to break down inherited forms of speech, destroy old grammars in order to construct new ones. I was being playful too, rewriting traditional nursery rhymes and chants. To the student onlookers, offered scrawled sheets of what resulted, my journeys into the underworld some-times seemed bafflingly chaotic. Dutifully, we persevered. With these MA students I attended seminars on theatre history, con-temporary drama: fascinating stuff. I loved being a student again, being given ideas and asked to wrestle with them. I loved learning about the-body-as-spectacle in seventeenth-century ritual and plays, about how to read Samuel Beckett texts, about Browning's manipulation of dramatic monologue in *My Last Duchess*.

I reconnected to the medieval plays I had studied at Oxford. I knew I wanted to write a play that did not reproduce illusion but challenged it. I hated plays where the audience was required to pretend it did not exist, hiding behind the sofa, as it were, while on stage people made speeches. I wanted the audience to be conscious and intimate witnesses of events that might be happening inside their own psyches as well as before them on stage. My models were the medieval mystery plays, where the audience follows the action that moves from travelling stage to travelling stage, and the Greek plays with their Chorus.

Attending rehearsals was huge fun: we leapt about playing games and doing all sorts of vocal and physical exercises. Also, witnessing Faynia's dynamic and inventive style of directing proved fruitful and inspiring for my writing. I quickly learned how much you could show through image and gesture, through non-linguistic language.

The Literature Department buzzed with intellectual energy. Colleagues were shy as people but generous as professionals, letting me attend their classes, organising open days in which we worked on writing in one big group. With one colleague, Roger Moss, I started a writers' group. Roger was funny, both warm and cool, friendly. He invited me to supper at his house in Wivenhoe. He had a quick mind and a quick tongue and we relished sparring and teasing. I also liked Jo Allard, an American, very much. In his office, next to mine, he had a harpsichord, and sometimes in the mornings I would hear it tinkling out eighteenth-century pieces. With Jo I sometimes went to the pub in Wivenhoe, down on the quay.

Elaine Jordan also formed part of that group. Red-haired and slender, she was quick as a fox. At a reception in the university she introduced me to Jim Latter, the artist who ran the gallery on campus, and he came to talk to me in my office about possible joint activities between literature students and gallery visitors. I took in how handsome he was, tall and sturdy with blue eyes and thick brown hair, but I was puzzled by his conformist clothes. Why did an artist working as an arts administrator have to wear dull, polyester-mix shirt and trousers? He made an off-the-cuff remark about women artists benefiting from positive discrimination, and I misinterpreted it, thinking he meant they received unfair advantages (as right-wing people often declared) and glared at him. He, in his turn (he told me later), didn't think much of the ankle socks I was wearing, fifties-style, with my high heels: too girly. Nonetheless, I took up his invitation and we organised a programme of poetry readings. Ali was one of the poets who came and read. One of Jim's exhibitions was of artists' books, borrowed for the occasion from the library at Chelsea School of Art. Also he put on ground-breaking young artists like Helen Chadwick and Laura Godfrey Isaacs. He told me about his time working at the Roundhouse in Camden Town in the seventies, co-founding the Sunday rock concerts there and also running the art gallery, putting on shows.

At weekends, when I dashed back to London, I saw my old friends. In February 1988 I put on a drinks party, at William's flat, to celebrate the launch of Sarah LeFanu's book on feminist science fiction, *In the Chinks of the World Machine*. Sarah's family all came, and many of our joint friends. Sarah Dunant turned up with her new baby, Zoë. Then some of the guests stayed to supper. We managed to seat twenty-five people, improvising tables from bookshelf planks set on trestles, and seating some of the guests on the sofa of poles and canvas. They sat gingerly and gamely on the extreme edge. I cooked 'sausages' of leeks, Caerphilly and breadcrumbs for the vegetarians, and for the carnivores an Italian dish of beef stewed in red wine. We had carrots in Marsala, green salad, cheese, and then the French cake of chocolate and chestnuts I always made for special occasions. We feasted and sang and toasted Sarah. I liked being in the flat when William wasn't in it.

In Colchester, at the Mercury Theatre, rehearsals began for my play, now called *The Journeywoman*. The actors let me sit in, but barred the MA students, much to the latter's disgruntlement. For a while I stayed in love with actors and acting and the theatre, then began to suffer when the actors disagreed with what I'd written and demanded that lines be cut. Oh, the agony of seeing my baby having its fingers and toes chopped off! In the end, I stayed away and just let them get on with it. The play was well received when it duly opened, though the reviewer from *Kaleidoscope*, the BBC Radio Four arts programme, didn't think it was feminist enough: she disliked the idea of Psyche searching for Eros, being drawn towards him. Silly woman! Feminists needed to explore women's desire, not deny it, and that's what my play was doing. I liked seeing the matrons of Colchester pile in, wrapped in furs, and drink up my scenes hinting at incestuous love between father and daughter (these were the days before incest became widely discussed). William came to see the play. He remarked how thin and fragile I was looking (all that walking to and fro between Wivenhoe and the university) and told me tales of friends' affairs.

I was about to start one myself. In early March Jim Latter had invited me to have a drink with him at the Chelsea Arts Club. Up Chelsea Old Church Street I strolled, admiring the pastel-pink houses and the pastel-pink blossom on the cherry trees. It was a very cold day but I pretended it was spring and dressed accordingly in my long blue linen skirt, a skimpy, tight-waisted jacket, my new Italian high-heeled shoes. Halfway along the King's Road I bought Jim a tiny bunch of violets from the flower stall there. I was early, so I weaved around some of the little squares off to the side. They frothed with graceful trees, fresh greenery. Walking down such pretty streets in pretty clothes and pretty shoes: an absurd but undeniable pleasure. Seeing Jim I got a shock. He had changed into his real self. He was wearing an old dark blue workman's shirt, old dark blue cords. His eyes were very blue, as though he'd unhooded them. We sat at a round wooden table, drank white wine, and began talking. Then we ran through the cold rain, Jim throwing his coat over my shoulders, and got into his Mini, which seemed to be held together by sticky tape. I took off my shoes and dried my wet feet on my handkerchief, and then off we drove across London in the sparkling dark, along the river, to Wapping, to Jim's former studio in a warehouse at New Crane Wharf overlooking the river, now a gallery, for a party launching a show by an American artist, whose name I have forgotten.

The paintings seemed to me like backcloths: fat stripes of silvery pale green, terracotta, cream. Why did I think that? I hadn't yet learned to look at modernist art and understand its self-referentiality. I didn't know that a painting of stripes could be about stripes. Jim would soon teach me! The artist wore a strapless evening gown in red brocade and was surrounded by hordes of black-clad Goths. Rich Goths, they seemed to me. Everybody was merry and tipsy. Two young men in the queue for the lavatory insisted I sing Schubert for them and were astonished when I complied. I sang 'To Wander Is the Miller's Joy'. I met people I knew from *Time Out* days: artist David Medalla, art critic Guy Brett. I was very pleased that some of 'my' people were there. Then Jim and I drove back to Islington to eat somewhere (I think we had fish and chips) and have another conversation which, I told my diary, was like 'wrestling and football and flower arranging all mixed up'. I felt as though I were sixteen, just out of the convent, kicking up my heels for the first time, and I felt worldly and womanly and sexually confident. Ooh la la ooh la la, as Colette observed on one occasion, telling her friend Marguerite Moreno about the start of her love affair with Maurice Goudeket. Maurice turned out to be one of Colette's true loves. I knew already Jim might turn out to be mine. He deposited me at Leinster Square and raced away.

The following day, flurries of snow alternating with bright sunshine, I strolled around South Kensington, ostensibly searching for the Moroccan Embassy, but also just wanting to be on the move, celebrating the joyful time of the night before, needing to explore new routes. I bought myself a pair of black lace stockings then walked back through streets I'd never walked along before. Sex makes the city fizz and spark. Sexual desire tugs you down unknown streets, breaks you apart, makes you want to jump and run. The city writes itself into you, around you, on to your skin.

I was looking for the Moroccan Embassy that day because I was trying to help my Moroccan student, Jamila, who had just had a baby and needed help with some documents. Jamila had arrived on the course five months pregnant. Her mother and husband were unable to visit and see her through the birth, so Pat, Faynia's assistant director, and I acted as Jamila's birthing companions, taking her into hospital in Colchester in the middle of the night and tending her as she laboured. I'd never witnessed anyone going through such pain for so long. Finally, early in the morning of the second day, her son shot into the world. Being involved with his birth was one of the most profound experiences of my life. It was a kind of knowledge. It increased knowledge.

Inside me, it connected with Easter and springtime and my own rebirth. Jim whisked me off up to the Lake District to go walking. We stopped on the M1 at the Services outside Birmingham, to refuel, and then sat on the wide green verge of the car park and had a picnic. Out of his rucksack Jim produced Gorgonzola, olives, red wine. I thought: this is the man for me. In the Lakes we tramped hills by day and then in the evenings found restaurants and pubs and then fell into bed and made love. When we came down late to breakfast, Mrs Cook, the landlady of our B and B, shook her head at us, remarking on our 'hectic nights'. We went on up to Scotland and did some more hill-walking there. On top of one mountain Jim rescued a lost dachshund, popping it into his rucksack and carrying it all the way down. It stuck its head out and licked his ear. I followed, adoring.

I had not wanted to fall in love, and felt scared, but it happened, despite my protestations to myself that I was a widow and wanted to wear black. After a month of being lovers, Jim and I were in love. I always compare starting writing a new novel to leaping off the cliff and hoping the angel will swoop down and bear me up on his strong wings, and I think falling in love is similar. You leap into the unknown. And yet you leap at the same time into the known. Your lover knows you, satisfies that deep desire you have to be truly known, and you do the same for him. You discover you are cut out of the same stuff.

We got close quickly. A strong telepathic communication developed between us. Driving along in the car between Wivenhoe and London, vaguely listening to the radio, my mind would unconsciously tune in to Radio Jim. I often knew what he was about to say just before he said it. Our minds flowed out and touched.

We chose each other. I felt that very deep down we were kin. We were alike. We were soulmates. We belonged together.

I began spending increasing amounts of time at Jim's house. Jim knew I was homeless. You can live here with me if you like, he said: why not move in properly? Come and live with me.

Chapter Twelve

TUFNELL PARK

Larking about with Jim

Jim lived at the northern, shabby end of Islington, in a district which straddled Tufnell Park (a green Victorian suburb now part of the inner city) and Holloway (tough and gritty – the mean streets), in an endearingly ramshackle house. The ceiling of his small attic bedroom was propped up by a plank. He slept in a bed on the floor, kept his clothes in a battered chest of drawers, and, like me, obviously did not do much dusting. When you stood on a chair in the kitchenette, which boasted the tiniest fridge I had ever seen, and put your head out of the skylight, you got an arching view of clouds, green tree-tops, pigeons strutting along the edges of chimney-pots, the hills and valleys of London roofs.

Number 21 Yerbury Road formed part of a Victorian terrace running parallel to Holloway Road. The original tiled front path, black and red diamonds, remained almost intact. The classical capitals of the stucco-clad columns at front door and windows showed sprays of acanthus. The front door held an opaque oblong of pearly glass. The date carved on a stone tablet above the porch read 1891. Jerry-built, all these houses, Jim said, thrown up in haste by their builders to make a profit. Nonetheless, the street was a pretty one, tree-lined, the houses' façades of grey-brown London brick fronted by small gardens full of flowers. One Polish neighbour grew tall arches of roses. Another displayed nothing but silvery-grey shrubs. Clematis montana wreathed the porches. Everything you needed was close by: shops and pubs. The local state primary school, at the end of the street, also functioned as a polling station at election time.

I had come back to familiar territory. Fairmead Road, the site of Ali's revolutionary commune in which I had lived fifteen years previously, ran off Jim's street at right angles. Jim and I had probably drunk in the same pubs, bought beer at the same off-licence, fetched home soapy cheese and white bloomer loaves from the same corner shop. I also discovered that his mother and father had worked for Kennedy's Butchers in south London, the old-fashioned meat and sausages shop with a 1920s sunburst window where I used to go when I lived in Camberwell in the mid-seventies. Jim's mother had probably served me at the till, while Jim's father had worked out the back. These seemed enchanting and meaningful coincidences.

Jim's parents, who died when he was still under twenty and just starting out at art school, had rented their flat in East Dulwich, squeezing themselves and their two children into three small rooms. With their death the flat had gone too; plus most of their furniture and possessions. Jim hung on to two boxes of black and white photographs, the spur from the horse his father had ridden in the war, his mother's tattered encyclopaedia of household management, *Enquire Within Upon Everything*. Because of his losses, Jim felt especially in need of the stability afforded by living in a house he owned, which could not be taken away from him. In fact Yerbury Road, it seemed to me, stood on shaky territory, the river Fleet (one of London's many secret rivers) flowing underground nearby, and (I fantasised) encouraging the houses to wobble and fall in on their foundations. Jim's house at the end of the row looked dramatically tumbledown, a wide crack in its stone porch evidence of its having survived bombing in the Second World War. Nonetheless it kept on standing up and it was home, sheltering his children, and he defended it. One night, late (a couple of years after I'd moved in), he went downstairs, wearing nothing but his skimpy dressing-gown, to answer the doorbell. Three drunks tumbled in and set about him. He fought them off single-handedly, threw them out and came nonchalantly back upstairs.

A large sycamore tree grew opposite the black dustbin in the tiny front garden full of bergenia, its green branches waving against the wooden sashes of the windows, and the back garden formed part of the double row of fenced greenery running between the back-to-back terraces, their yards, added-on kitchens, their old outhouses and privies and sheds. I loved those enclosed London gardens, those secret places; you saw them only from inside the house when you leaned out of the top window at the back and looked down. In May they erupted in froths of green and foam of blossom and the sweetness of spring nights crept in through the open windows and pop music drifted through the darkness like moths.

Jim had originally rented the house with friends, as an art student at Hornsey and then Chelsea, and had scraped together the £8000 necessary to buy it when it came on the market. (How? In Jim-language: a spot of wheeling and dealing; of ducking and diving.) He and his wife Linda (also an artist, whom he had met while studying typography at Maidstone before doing his Foundation course) had lived there with a turnover population of painter friends, whose influence could be seen in the interior décor: startling and pleasing juxtapositions of colour on the old enamelled fireplaces, on mirror surrounds.

Jim and Linda had split up when their second son, Leo, was still small, and their first son, Sam, was three. Linda had moved out with Leo, to live in a squat, and Jim had stayed in Yerbury Road, with Sam. Jim and Linda got divorced, but remained committed to being joint parents. They met every day, so that the boys could spend time with one another. Jim told me tales of bringing up Sam, cooking him the khaki vegetable purée he called Army Soup, taking him into the Roundhouse, going to coffee mornings with young mothers along the street who looked in surprise at a man being a hands-on father to a young child. Eventually, Linda and Jim decided that it would be better for the boys to have both parents under one roof, and that they should share the house again and legally co-own it. Accordingly, Linda moved back in and took over the ground floor, where she had the front and back rooms, the kitchen, and the use of the back garden. Sam had a bedroom at the back, on the first half-landing, near the bathroom, and Leo the room at the front another half-flight up. Jim had the two rooms on the second floor, knocked into one, divided by a heavy striped linen curtain, and above, in the attic, a small bedroom and a slit of a kitchen. He used the back half of his double room as a sitting-room and the front half as a studio.

I first met Linda in the middle of the night, when I crept down through the hushed house to the lavatory. Oh, you startled me! she gasped. She was a tiny, delicate, black-haired woman, with big dark eyes, wearing a pink silk 1930s nightdress under a flowered kimono. In the years to come Linda and I would go on meeting by chance in the middle of the night, and sometimes sat on the stairs, neutral territory, to chat. In the daytime, I met her when taking laundry down to wash, because she kindly allowed us to use the washing-machine in her kitchen, and to hang the wet things out in the back garden. Otherwise, Jim and I kept out of her way. When he needed to discuss the boys with her, he went downstairs. She hardly ever came into the top part of the house, except at Christmas, when we celebrated all together in Jim's big room, the curved 1950s cocktail bar set up with flashing fairy-lights and Jim, upstairs, wrapped in a big apron, flourishing a wooden spatula as he fried the rissoles – the family was vegetarian – made from a packet mix I surreptitiously tarted up with chopped walnuts and herbs. Over the years (unwilling to try to change the Latter traditions) I grew quite fond of these rissoles; there was even a certain cachet in not eating turkey like everybody else. I added other dishes to the classic menu: mushroom pâté, chestnut pâté *en croûte*. I made Christmas pudding according to a recipe provided by my mother, with grated apple and olive oil replacing the suet. Linda would also come upstairs to visit when she returned from her annual holiday in Greece with the boys, and they would all pile in, with presents of wine and pistachio nuts, with stories. She and Jim had created an unconventional and impressive set-up, a new style of family invented for the well-being of their two sons, which demanded tact, sacrifices, trust and goodwill on both sides.

One test of this trust, on the part of Linda and the boys, was that they were not formally consulted before I moved in. I had left it up to Jim to tell them but it must have been difficult for him to get the timing of the announcement right. I was spending increasing amounts of time at his place, half living there and half semi-squatting (it felt like) at Leinster Square. Jim's ex-wife and children accepted me, *le fait accompli*, with grace. They made me feel at home. I ended up living in that extended family for as long as the house lasted (when the boys were in their early and mid twenties Jim and Linda decided to live apart and sell the house). Linda had a lover, Barry, but he lived elsewhere. I rarely saw him. He didn't join us for Christmas lunch: the roast parsnips and spuds, the cracker-pulling and present-giving. He visited Linda on Christmas night, when she served him a big plate of the food she'd saved for him. This exclusion seemed tough on Barry, but that's how it was.

The boys did not need me to act as stepmother, of course;

they had their own adored mother downstairs who looked after them. They ate with her, did their homework in her kitchen. She took all the domestic responsibility for them. I got to know the boys gently, over time. They were as quick and slender as she, Sam fair and Leo dark. They were young teenagers, very involved with their own lives, their friends, going skateboarding, supporting Arsenal. They attended Acland Burghley, the local state comprehensive. I liked living with the boys, finding out about them, what they wore, the music they listened to. I enjoyed watching them tumble about with Jim on the studio floor, mock-wrestling, teasing and tickling, howling with laughter. I came to love them both. Sometimes they arrived upstairs to watch TV with us, or for supper. Sometimes they wandered out for walks with us, and we climbed trees together.

I liked and respected Linda. She was highly intelligent and sensitive, and gifted as an artist. She was now training to become a counsellor, as a surer way of earning a living. She was powerfully empathetic. She had a wild, funny streak, too, and when she grinned mischievously or laughed out loud she looked ten years old. Like many women then, she wore a lot of black, and quantities of silver bangles. She wore big silver hooped earrings. With her head cocked enquiringly on one side, she looked like a tiny black bird with silky, silver-tipped feathers. She was kind and generous towards me. In return, I tried hard to do the right thing. Since Jim did not give her any money for his sons, I began to pay her weekly maintenance for them, and when Jim remortgaged the house (with Linda's reluctant consent) in order to buy a second-hand MGB to replace the broken Mini, and to mend the big sash window on the top back landing, I took over responsibility for the mortgage repayments so that Linda (not involved in the mortgage but owner of half the house) would not have to worry. Jim adored his children, with an intensity I had never before seen a man display, and was proud of having been able to provide them with a home, but he was erratic with money. He shared it when he had it, cheerfully buying rounds in the pub, taking friends out to supper at the Chelsea Arts Club. He had certainly been very generous towards me, opening his house to me and inviting me in, sharing everything he had with me. He was happy that I came into his space. He teased me too. When I marched him off to Habitat to buy two breakfast coffee cups and saucers, he moaned that I was trying to reform him and turn him into a bourgeois.

The house had not been much tampered with, apart from that fashionable 1960s gesture of knocking two rooms into one. The wiring was ancient and the tiny bathroom rudimentary if intimate and cosy. The old gas mantles stuck out from the sides of the fireplaces. There was no central heating. We burned coal in the grates. At coal delivery time, Linda, or on one occasion I, seized a spade and rushed down into the cellar. Outside, on the front path, just in front of the step, the coalman lifted the silvery lid on the coalhole, tipped up his grimy sacks one after the other, and poured in coal at top speed. Down below you had to shovel for dear life as the smoky, dusty stream of knobbly coal poured in, swirled at your knees and threatened to drown you like a landslide. Since Jim often felt shy about intruding into Linda's space, I usually fetched the coal for our fireplace. The cellar door was just outside her kitchen. All through the year I would go down into the cellar, fill a big coal-scuttle and drag it upstairs, four flights. A bore. A chore. Just had to be done. My self-imposed task of carrying up heavy bags of shopping, brought home, dangling from my bicycle handlebars, from the supermarket on Holloway Road, sometimes felt arduous too. I often thought of the skivvy who might formerly have slept in the attic bedroom I shared with Jim. She would have carried up the coal just as I did. My parents had been the first owners of the modern suburban house in Edgware in which I grew up; I loved living in an old one whose past seemed tangible.

Yerbury Road was a house breathing history; seemed alive to me, like a body; agreeably rather than scarily haunted by its past, by its inhabitants of almost a hundred years ago. Some of that past I made up, inspired by the features in the house. For example, the little cupboard, concealed behind a small door in the eaves behind the bedhead in our attic, seemed to me a perfect symbol of the unconscious memory and got into the novel I was writing, *In the Red Kitchen*, filled with relics, lost diaries, treasures. The big window of pearled glass, with its oblongs of scarlet and blue at the corners, cast coloured shadows on the bare floor of the back landing, and let in the spirits to me, and therefore to my heroine, the nineteenth-century medium Flora Milk (inspired by the real-life Florence Cook), as I sat on the uncarpeted, dusty wooden stairs and daydreamed. When we redecorated we painted the steps cream but kept them bare. I liked sitting there, gazing out of the window at the sky: a transitional space, neither up nor down but in between. When Elton Bash, the builder (a friend of Jim's), came to take a look at the bashed-up interior walls before we mended and repainted them, I was enchanted to see the very skeleton of the house, the materials composing it: lath-and-plaster, the cavities stuffed with old horsehair. You could punch your fist into one of those walls and it would come straight out the other side.

We painted all the mended walls white. In my first months in the house I inexpertly wallpapered the lavatory, mindful that my family was coming to lunch on Boxing Day and might not approve of its newspaper-patched, scrawled-over walls, their palimpsest of grime. I pasted up strips of paper, sploshed fresh paint (salmon-pink – cheap – from the Chris Stevens decorating emporium just up Holloway Road) over them to blank out the uneven joins, scoured the ancient lavatory with bleach. Jim and Linda looked on wryly. Jim said later he understood what I was doing: marking the territory; laying claim to my right to affect the house. (Pretty cheeky of me; it wasn't my house.)

Not so much a right as a wish. I was reliving childhood fantasies: the house revived them in me. Unconsciously (I think now) I saw the middle part of the house as a damaged place, a bruised body, and wished to repair it. To make reparation. I wanted to rescue and cherish it. A child does that: gets in between her quarrelling parents and tries to mend their fight. That was the psychic space I occupied in this house: the space in between the alienated floors. A marriage had broken down, and the parents broken apart, and so their living space had broken apart too, and the linking, communal territory in the house, shabby and cracked, expressed that, glum as a depression. I wanted to hold up the house and with the force of gleaming white paint (the only colour that Jim would allow) I tried to do it.

My childish fantasy was an omnipotent one: the child blames herself for everything that goes wrong and decides that she has got to be the one to mend things. Eventually, the child realises that the damage is not her fault. She can let herself off trying to put everything right all the time. She accepts the broken house. She picks up the shattered bits and puts them together in patterns that please her. She's like an archaeologist remaking pots, an artist making mosaics. Out of the broken-up bits of language she picks up she makes books. She builds paper houses.

In reality of course I lived not in the middle of the house at all but very merrily with Jim up at the top. In reality of course Linda's quarters downstairs were neat and clean, well furnished and well cared for, as were the boys' rooms. Linda had carpets, pictures, hangings, embroideries, plants, shelves of books. It was just the part of the house between her space and Jim's that was shabby and neglected. Jim's flat was undeniably run-down. Holes in the lino and the walls and the ceiling. So we painted, fixed up new shelves, built a clothes rail and clothes cupboard on our tiny top half-landing. I scrubbed and scoured. We brought in plants in pots: camellias, azaleas and stephanotis. Jim had his pictures up everywhere, and I liked that. The flat was a studio at the same time; no real separation between the two functions. The house jumped about and was playful and changed shape and use.

I explored some of these ideas (the house as repaired body, as metamorphosing body) in *In the Red Kitchen*, which circled around hauntings, breakages and secrets. I had read Melanie Klein on love, hate and reparation a few years earlier, and was struck by how my ideas chimed with hers. Later on (in 2002) I read Bachelard's *The Poetics of Space*, in which he talks about the emotional shapes of the spaces inside houses and flats, and felt pleased that I'd got there independently. It always enraged me when Ph.D. students interviewing me (as they were beginning to do) assumed that novels were written to exemplify and flesh out theory. No, I would insist: it's the other way round. The theory depends on the novels. It is only made possible by them. Or, at least, a novelist, a psychoanalyst and a literary theorist might all be working on parallel tracks at the same time, making similar discoveries at the same time, in their own distinct languages. I refused to see the writer as a sort of babbling neurotic just waiting for the shrink–critic to make sense of the babble. But these were the eighties when the academic love affair with theory was at its height and novels were seen as poor things, really, poor relations of theory. The Author was dead and the Critic (not so much the Reader) took control and discovered all meanings. The pendulum had to swing that way, I suppose, to redress the balance, after the author had been seen for so long as heroic, lone, male genius, a god making the world all by himself, a colossus bestriding the globe, but I got very cross when the Ph.D. students failed to notice the huge amount of delicate, subtle hard work that went into shaping a novel. I still do!

The house was crucially an artists' house. I remember early on, one night, insisting that Jim show me his slides of his work. He had said to me the previous evening: let's have lots of food and wine and sex tomorrow. I cooked spinach roulade. I got dressed up in my new blue wrap-around top, like a dancer's cardigan. We ate and drank and talked about our work and our hopes and desires for it; excited, close, prodding and praising each other. Then I sat in the big 1940s armchair in the studio and Jim rained brilliant, brightly coloured images on me. The colours sang; electric. The paintings jerked and jabbed me; did not stay still; were in 2-D and 3-D both at once. They vibrated with colour and thought in colour. When we went to bed and made love I saw red crackling all round us. Afterwards, I was too charged with excitement to lie down quietly. The room didn't, either: the bed, the chest of drawers, my little desk in the alcove under the window, all touched each other and me and danced around me; abstract images leapt and transformed me. Nothing was separate any more. Everything joined up, tilted, swerved, I was a part of the room, a part of everything, I was all broken up into little bits and I was also all connected, enclosed in dusty blue space. I sat on the little rug at the foot of the bed and watched Jim sleep then got into bed, fitted myself into his arms.

Jim's being an artist was the core of who he was. I loved him for it. I loved his wildness, gaiety, ferocious commitment to art. Besides, he was the first man who had loved me as an artist and thought it was normal I should be one. Other men had shrugged, tolerated my being a writer, deprecated it, tried to ignore it. Jim took it for granted that making art was what you did. A vocation. A job. Hard work. You just got on with it. We were true partners, equals, egging each other on. I saw us (very romantically, I think now) as the two children in the Start-Rite shoes ad, hand in hand, walking towards the horizon. 'Children's shoes have far to go,' said the caption. So did Jim and I.

In a way the house was like Jim. Changeable, fragile as well as sturdy. That was part of its eccentricity and charm. When, from downstairs, eating my new invention of risotto with leeks and black olives, we heard the bedroom ceiling crash softly and voluptuously to the floor above us and ran upstairs to discover a blooming cloud of plaster dust, the floor vanished under a rubble of plaster chunks, we just laughed. When water dripped through holes in the roof, well, we could set buckets in place.

Jim could decorate very fast; not only could he stroke paint on to enormous canvases but he'd worked, in cash-strapped moments, as a painter and decorator. I spent a week laboriously stripping off old wallpaper in the bedroom, then (badly) painting the floorboards white, then stopped. The following night I came home tired from teaching at the City Lit. Jim handed me a bunch of pink tulips. Oh, I've done nothing while you were out, he said. I went upstairs and discovered he had put on two coats of paint in a few hours. We celebrated by nipping out to score some dope and then getting stoned. (The dealer was an old comrade from libertarian days. He did a bit of journalism, a bit of this and that, a bit of dealing to friends, and went to the Irish social club up the road to do line-dancing. I often bumped into him on Saturday mornings in Holloway Road, on my way to the car boot sale to prowl for bargains.)

Jim often gave me flowers. On occasion, when he was broke, he pinched sprays from neighbours' overgrown hedges, and once, having forgotten my birthday until after the shops were closed, robbed a roundabout of a few lilies. His boyhood experience working on Saturdays at his uncle's flower stall in Crystal Palace meant he was a quick, expert flower-arranger. He could twist wreaths and sort bouquets in a matter of moments. I loved watching his big hands move so deftly and fast between the stems. Once, for his birthday in April, we decided to eat in the studio. I set the table festively, covering it with my old lace and linen cloths, putting out two Quimper jugs full of the white freesias and blue anemones Jim had brought home. We perched on high stools, looking at the big canvas in progress on the wall in front of us, talking, drinking champagne. Jim produced a couple of loose floppy pink roses from somewhere and scattered the petals across the tablecloth. He was always doing things like that, on the spur of the moment. He would see what needed to be created and create it. Having to buy presents for Christmas and birthdays made him anxious, whereas on other days of the year he would arrive home with impromptu gifts: flowers, books of poems, little onyx boxes, a pair of bookends, a Victorian writing-desk. He gave me big and little paintings. He wrote me short funny notes, printing in capitals because he claimed his handwriting was so bad, and I kept the lot in the writing-case I'd had since I was ten.

Jim loved treats. He would roar off to Soho on his motorbike and bring home food from Lina's, the Italian deli in Brewer

Street just off Berwick Street market. Under William's tutelage I had gone to Fratelli Camisa round the corner, so enjoyed getting to know a different shop. Jim's previous girlfriend Anna, an Italian, had taught him to cook Italian dishes. He knew how to make proper tomato sauce, reduced right down to a paste. He would arrive back, beaming, carting in his bulging panniers, and produce with a flourish pots of olives, bottles of good olive oil, fresh pumpkin ravioli, dried *funghi porcini*. In those days you couldn't buy such things in the local supermarket. Sometimes he would cook while I was out, to surprise me, and I would arrive home to find him sitting up in bed, wearing his black woolly hat and his blue dressing-gown and brandishing a wooden spoon like a sceptre, to make me laugh, watching football on TV, and it would feel like a party and I would join in.

Sometimes at the weekends we would walk along the Regent's Canal and look at the boats. One evening we met a handsome young man in a silk waistcoat and helped him through a lock. He took his narrow-boat out at night wherever he chose, he told us, sometimes going as far as Bristol, sailing along through the night. How we wished, afterwards, we'd asked permission to jump on board. Or we would ride up on the motorbike to Hampstead Heath and walk there, or picnic in the rain under our green and white striped umbrella, then drink Bloody Marys at the Lord Palmerston on Dartmouth Park Hill. Sometimes on winter mornings we drank the Bloody Marys at home. Rapture: a fire burning hotly in the middle of the day, the open window letting in brilliant sunshine and cold air; that combination of opposites, heat and cold, that brought bliss. I would loll on the old brown leather sofa with my red peppery drink watching Jim down his and get on with painting. I loved sharing his space and I was in love with him and that desire and pleasure fed straight into my writing.

In 1990 I began writing *Daughters of the House* out of a sudden need to think about where I came from (parents and politics), about the Second World War's impact on civilians in occupied France, about collaboration. Jim was the muse whose love kept me going. Loving him, I became more confident about telling stories. Previously, I'd felt like a character in family stories (Mimi the crazy dreamer); now I could become the narrator, invent a subject who spoke. I still worked with apparently disconnected bits but now I could make them visibly join up. I still invented experimental forms but now I combined them with clearer storytelling. Understanding my reasons for distrusting omniscient narrators – God the Father; the Pope; my own father – who wedged me into their own fantasies, I could explore a woman's dodgy desire to control a story. Both Léonie and Thérèse, in *Daughters*, want omniscient control over the action, and have to tussle it out. The form of the novel enacts this: one narrator lists the contents of the house, trying to make it her own, while the other rigorously edits her life story, turning it into hagiography. Their versions clash. I couldn't have invented that form any sooner, before making sense of conflicts in my own life. At the same time I went on cherishing the multiple-narratives form I felt I'd invented in the *The Book of Mrs Noah* (of course other writers, such as Toni Morrison, whom I began to read in 1982, were doing it too), which I called plaiting, which told stories through interweaving down-to-earth voices rather than up-in-the-sky ones. Loving Jim felt inspiring and encouraging, made me want to make and make and make.

We rode everywhere on the motorbike, zigzagging around London exploring, zooming along empty backstreets on warm spring nights. Urban landscapes. Industrial landscapes. Always springing some new surprise. Sometimes we went out for fry-up breakfasts, black squashes of mushrooms on buttery toast and strong sweet black coffee, in Jim's favourite local greasy spoon, The Hercules Dining-Rooms, with its frosted-glass windows and door, chestnut-brown woodwork, black and white lino. We whizzed around Docklands, which seemed a soulless toytown, the old community carved up and destroyed, and we nipped around the Southwark backstreets, and we roamed back to Wapping and Limehouse and drank in The Grapes (known to Dickens), sitting on its little wooden balcony above the Thames, and talked about the artists who had been forced out.

The bike took us to shows. I discovered contemporary painting through accompanying Jim to openings and meeting lots of his friends and looking at their work. I learned about sculpture in the same way, and was similarly introduced to installation art, for example Richard Wilson's work at Matt's Gallery in the East End. On one occasion we admired Richard's reversed window, the light-space represented as a solid block thrusting in through the gallery wall, and then we drank beer in what Jim described as the 'heavy' black club opposite, mysterious rooms, papered in dark turquoise brocade, opening off each other, cocktails served at the 1950s bar with its high swivelling armchairs. People sashayed back and forth with huge spliffs, played Frank Sinatra and blues. The dance-floor was surrounded by leatherette banquettes and had a silver multifaceted ball hanging from the ceiling. The air was thick with blue hazes of cigarette smoke.

I liked riding pillion, especially at night, speeding through cool darkness, my arms wrapped around Jim, my cheek against his leather-jacketed back. Being swept along; carried away. A memory surfaced: myself as a small child being brought home, after a party, by a friend's father, on his motorbike, standing in front of him between his knees as he drove from the council estate to our house just along the road, my hands, inside his, clutching the handlebars, stars and blackness whizzing past, tremendous excitement inside me, the erotic containment of his arms. One evening, coming back across Blackfriars Bridge from a show somewhere in south London, Jim spotted some scaffolding at its side, parked the bike to take a look. He clambered over the balustrade of the bridge down on to the scaffolding, and I followed behind. We climbed down two rickety ladders to the water. Why? Because the scaffolding was there, teasing our curiosity, inviting us to climb down it. Because that way you got a different perspective, a new view of London our city, brave with lights. Because artists were always trying to invent new shapes, to put into the world marks and images that had not existed before. Because they needed to look at things differently. Because they knew they needed to play.

Jim taught me his version of London. He mapped his history on to the streets. He told me tales of coming up to town from East Dulwich as a boy in the 1960s, when after leaving school he worked briefly in Holborn as a typographer, on his 2-stroke Francis Barnett motorbike (nicknamed a Fanny B.) with his chum Len, both dressed up to the nines in post-Mod costumes of sharp trousers, Chelsea boots, bowlers and knitted dark blue silk ties, plus rolled umbrellas. No crash helmets compulsory in those days. Jim had an eye for outlandish outfits. He enjoyed the way Sylvia Ziranek, Richard Wilson's partner, liked dressing up in 1950s ballgowns for openings, pirouetting with red lips, white face, short blonde hair. He appreciated unconventional men, too. He described getting to know Quentin Crisp, who had modelled at Maidstone (the first time I met Quentin at the Chelsea Arts Club I thought he was a beautiful, elegant elderly woman) and then become a friend. Jim had his own very particular slant on life, which came partly from his working-class background: you had to be good to your own and you had to survive and you tried to give your children the good things you hadn't been able to have yourself. I learned his language, his phrases and expressions, his bits of rhyming slang, his jokes, his funny voices. I learned his names for things, inside and outside. All these sank into me and became part of my vocabulary, my repertoire. He pointed out an umbrella factory as we drove from Bethnal Green to Bermondsey: that's called More-Rain House. The Durex headquarters further along was called Rubber House.

Revisiting Peckham and Camberwell, we drove back into both our pasts and discovered they connected. We parked outside Kennedy's, at the bottom of Talfourd Road, my old street, to salute Jim's dad. We marvelled at how Len had lived in the flats bang opposite number 26, my old house. Jim showed me 205 Friern Road, in East Dulwich, where he had grown up. No bathroom; they'd put a tin bath in front of the fire. He pointed at the upstairs window: the room in which his father had lain, ill with cancer, when Jim was seventeen. That last night Jim had sat with him, listening to his rasping, rattling breaths, holding his hand, and then in the middle of the night his father had died.

Driving me around Camberwell and Peckham Jim gave them to me all over again. His aunts and uncles (ten on each side) had lived and worked all around here, from East Street market in Walworth, just down from Baldwin's the herbalist, where you bought and drank sarsaparilla, to the flower-stalls and newspaper-stalls of Brixton. With him I rediscovered the old landscapes I had known fifteen years earlier: the Rye, a huge swathe of misty green with great candled masses of chestnut trees; the little backstreets teeming with ancient ramshackle shops and wild gardens. The big mosaic of the Camberwell Beauty butterfly still flared, restored and preserved, on the former public wash-house wall, but many of the old factories and warehouses had come down, the wastelands converted to public lawns. The prefabs had been swept away. In their place: little green mounds; tiny parks. The old roughness all smoothed over. Loss marked by green presences. We put our geographies and histories together that day, combining with each other, mapping ourselves on to each other and on to London, tying ourselves together with stories and jokes, reminiscences and memories.

Our life had a very enjoyable playful, childish side. Apart from earning our livings, apart from Jim trying to be a good father to the boys, no need to be particularly grown-up. We could lark and frolic and invent daft games at the drop of a hat. How joyful that made me! Shared baths by candlelight. Singing and dancing and feasting and drinking. I loved setting up a big makeshift table on trestles for dinner parties in Jim's studio. Our friends liked coming to supper, and I ran up and down the stairs to and from the tiny kitchen above very happily. Even when drunkenly teetering in high heels, I could nip smartly up and down with bowls of pasta, trays of plates. The artists would stay until three in the morning, shouting, arguing and carousing, until I protested exhaustion and urged them out. *La vie de Bohème*: Holloway version. The downside of course existed too: it was easy to drink too much. Sometimes the artists lost their tempers too loudly, got into fights on pub pavements. Sometimes it could all feel too volatile. Sometimes Jim's untidiness, his clothes dropped all over the floor, enraged me. I wanted to control the space but couldn't. His mess dominated. I became the tidying-up housewife–mother, rather than the happy child making a lovely mess. Then I would have to get on the phone and complain loudly to women friends.

Where was I going to work? My work space continued to

shift about, as it always had. For a while, at the beginning, Sim very kindly let me use Polly's old study in Holland Park as my own. Jim would give me lifts over there on the motorbike. Nipping past the Zoo in Regent's Park we would delightedly spot the giraffes, their lofty necks rearing over the wall of their yard next to the road. Then, when I had properly moved in chez Jim, for a while I worked at a trestle-table we set up as my desk in the window of our little attic bedroom. This was fine as long as Jim was out of the house. Having completed his tenure at Essex, he was now running the gallery on the University of Sussex campus. He never disturbed me when he arrived home, but I couldn't write knowing he was on the floor below. Someone else's presence formed a boundary to my conscious-ness so that I couldn't completely let go of it; I remained trapped by the walls of ego. Jim, by contrast, had had to share studio space all through art school; he had learned to wall him-self off by turning on the radio.

Another version we tried was moving the bedroom down-stairs to the sitting-room and letting me use the attic as my sole studio. That did not work: Sam had moved rooms, and now had a bedroom just underneath us, a nicer room than the one he had had before. I had wanted to do something for Sam, so I had got in a carpenter (female of course, and gay to boot) to build him a platform bed so that he had a bedsit-cum-study. Unfortunately, when Jim and I tried sleeping in our former sitting-room, we were now too close to Sam, on top of each other, and Sam liked playing loud music late at night. This pre-vented Jim and me from sleeping. Rows ensued between father and son. Jim had a pretty passionate temper. When he and Sam got angry with each other I was reminded of two stags locking their antlers and fighting to mark their territory, neither pre-pared to give an inch. At the height of the row, either Jim or

Sam would rush out of the room. Finally Linda gave me permission to use Sam's former bedroom, in her territory, just above her kitchen, as a studio. (I painted the front half, near the window, silvery sage-green, and the back half apple-green. Why did I do that? I don't remember.) Kind as this was of Linda, as soon as she came home from work and I heard her moving about I felt I had to stop writing.

I supplemented my income by continuing to teach a weekly writing class at the City Lit. Among my students were Suzanne Moore, the journalist, and Esther Freud, the novelist. Of course their talent was their own, but I like to think I helped them believe in it. I grew fond of another student, Louise (whose surname I cannot remember), a fiercely intelligent Jewish woman. Over eighty, she was sharp and bright, flashing like a needle. At the end of one term she invited me to lunch with her in Swiss Cottage, at the restaurant where she used to go with her husband. Four months after his death, she told me, she went back alone, and the waiter held the door open after her and peered out into the street: where *is* he? Sigmund Freud (great-grandfather of Esther) used to eat here too, so the waiters had put up a photo of him on the wall. They had put up one of Jung too, but at a distance, so that the two couldn't see one another. Louise, tiny, erect, elegantly dressed in a black and white hound's-tooth suit with a black velvet collar, ordered duck for us. Half a duck each we were given, with red cabbage and apple and blackcurrant jelly. Louise put aside a large piece of her portion, telling me that the waiters would let her take it home. Indeed they did: they returned it to her wrapped in silver paper, sculpted into the shape of a swan. Louise got on to the bus with it and I waved her off; she sat upright and dignified, the silver swan on her lap. Then I bicycled home through Regent's Park and Camden in a swirl and whirl of yellow leaves.

I still loved bicycling, for example flying down Rosebery Avenue under the plane trees in sparkling autumn air – possessing my city by moving through it as fast as possible, the closest I could come to having wings.

In the late eighties I still held left-wing views, but, increasingly, since Thatcher's defeat of the left, put them on hold in the sense of being actively politically involved. My politics inspired the non-authoritarian way I tried to teach, trying to inspire students to get going, standing behind them, pushing and encouraging them to experiment and take risks, trying to help them achieve what they wanted to, rather than insisting I knew the right and wrong ways to do it.

Political change fed into writing. One night, sitting at a supper party in Sarah Maguire's flat in Notting Hill, we were all discussing the end of the Cold War: the recent fall of the Berlin Wall, the press and TV images of people embracing one another. In rushed Sarah's friend Neil, just back from Germany. Out of his pocket he produced a piece of the Wall. I broke off a chip and carried it home. Later I wrote a poem about it. Just before he died, I heard Malcolm Bradbury complaining that no English poet had written about the fall of the Berlin Wall. Well, I had, but even if he'd read it he wouldn't have recognised my poem as political, on his terms, because it combined the large historical event with a smaller one: my version, of suddenly becoming much closer to my twin sister and feeling certain old barriers between us fall away. Joy in the world and joy in the psyche: the one mapped on to the other. I hung on to the words of the poet Peter Redgrove, whom I had once heard say in a lecture: if we imagined the psyche as part of the universe, rather than seeing it as separate, then we wouldn't feel so 'wrong' writing about the psyche, feeling it self-indulgent to do so; we would simply be writing about an aspect of the universe. This affected my thinking about objectivity, how the imagination works, the unconscious transformation of lived experience, the perspective of narrators, and fed the essays on creativity I wrote from time to time. I wasn't romantic about the fall of the Berlin Wall. Like many others on the left I didn't think that capitalism would bring unadulterated happiness to the masses so ground down under the evil state-socialist heel. History has proved us right. Partly. Some of the time.

My political, feminist and psychoanalytical views also fed the writing of *Daughters of the House*. I needed to question the role of the historian. Who had the right to write or recount history? Could women of low social status, could small girls, be historians? Who decided whose version was true? I wrote the novel to find out. The desecration of graves in the Jewish cemetery at Carpentras in Provence also inspired me. I read an article in *Le Monde* that imaged fascism as a ghoul rising up from its tomb. French collective memories were beginning to stir. Just what had happened in Norman villages under the Occupation? Would an apparently holy priest be capable of betraying Jews to the Gestapo? I wanted to imagine some answers. Religious imagery necessarily tangled through the novel. I felt I had aroused the uncanny. I dreamed about the Virgin who would appear to one of my little protagonists: she had a powerful face, a big nose, and was dressed all in red. The following day I visited Amanda Faulkner's studio, in order to look at her new work. Amanda taught print-making at the Slade. She had asked me to write a catalogue piece for her forthcoming show. There on the wall was the exact image from my dream the night before of the red Virgin. The unconscious seems somehow to work outside past and present, which is why we can foretell events: we float outside time and see what's coming. Once, when Jim and I were driving through the rainy Mayennais countryside, late at night, I suddenly knew, at a sharp bend, that we were about to crash. Round the corner slithered a car, out of control, having skidded after being driven far too fast by its soldier driver. It rammed us.

Another example of this unconscious forecasting was that I knew that *Daughters of the House*, published in 1992, would be shortlisted for that year's Booker Prize. I just knew it, in a corner of my mind. The knowledge connected to an image of a woman in red. Since the thought of winning a prize seemed so disgracefully arrogant, I dismissed it as a simple wild wishful fantasy and forgot it. In late summer Jim and I went off to Normandy to visit Brigitte, my aunt, who now, after my grandfather's recent death, lived alone in the little family house. As usual, we travelled by car ferry. I had always loved these sea voyages, back and forth, which had structured childhood holidays. The heart of *Daughters of the House* is a description of translation as a metamorphosis occurring in the middle of the Channel, when languages, like monsters, change into each other far beneath the sea. On this occasion, chugging back on the ferry to England after our visit, Jim and I were sitting in the saloon, catching up with the English newspapers, bang in the very middle of the Channel, when Jim suddenly let out a whoop. He had just discovered that *Daughters* had been shortlisted for the Booker: a cartoon showed a group of cloth-capped punters in a bookies, each one solemnly reading a novel, and one of these was *Daughters*. We repaired to the bar and ordered two large gin and tonics.

The shortlisting changed my life. Not only did various hitherto toffee-nosed people now condescend to talk to me at literary parties but my novel sold well and I quickly paid off my advance. I had changed publishers after Methuen, who had published my three previous novels, had begun paring its literary fiction list and could no longer be really supportive. Spurning Picador's paltry offer of £1000, I had gone to Lennie Goodings of Little, Brown, who now ran Virago under the bigger firm's umbrella. Lennie was a good businesswoman, a survivor of the tumultuous recent changes in publishing. She made clear her support for my writing. Of course I was delighted and grateful. Lennie was very chic too, with fabulous legs. She owned the largest collection of little black 1940s frocks and jackets I had ever seen.

Dressing for the Booker dinner was a problem: I wasn't really an evening-dress type of person. I would have liked to be, but I was a coward. I remember seeing Liz Calder looking stunning in her long frock that left one shoulder bare, and wishing I had dared to try to look equally glamorous. I compromised and wore a French three-quarter-length slinky black tube I'd rushed out to buy at Liberty's. I was the only woman on the shortlist of six. Easier for the chaps: they just donned penguin suits. Jim wore Dad's evening togs and looked resplendent. We struggled together to tie his bow-tie. At the dinner at the Guildhall, Jim, taking on the role of minder, wouldn't let me drink any wine, telling me sternly that I would only get drunk and regret it afterwards. I felt his protectiveness and obeyed him. I didn't dare hope I would win but I longed to. During the month between the announcement of the shortlist and the Prize dinner my mind had slid around the dream of winning like a tongue exploring a sore tooth. I pretended to feel calm and cool but inside seethed with hope and doubt. Weeks of uncertainty ended: someone leaned over after the first course and whispered to me that I hadn't won, pointing to the TV cameras massing on the far side of the hall.

I felt shaky with disappointment, and also relieved. The Prize evening wears an aspect, for the writers concerned, of

Christians being thrown to lions, for the delectation of the TV audience, and at least the gladiatorial combat was over. I knocked back a few glasses of claret. After applauding the joint winners, Michael Ondaatje and Barrie Unsworth, I was tipsy enough, when chatting to David Lodge's wife, who had wandered up to say hello, to inform her that all her husband's novels dramatised the wish to commit adultery. Jim nipped my arm. Mrs Lodge said: really? That's very interesting. She wandered back towards her husband. I downed some more claret.

My unconscious did not inform me that I would win the W.H. Smith Literary Award in 1993. One morning Jim brought up the post as usual and scattered it on the quilt. I sat up in bed to scan the envelopes addressed to me. When I opened the letter informing me of the fact, I couldn't take it in for some time. Only another cliché will do: it was beyond my wildest dreams.

The award lunch was held in the foyer of the new British Library, next to St Pancras, which was still in the process of being built. We picked our way between bulldozers, manoeuvred by men in hard yellow hats, through the builders' yard, across rubble, to the reception area. Afterwards I felt able to boast that my novel had been the first book in the new British Library.

Sarah LeFanu came to the lunch with Chris. She reminded me recently that as part of my acceptance speech I mentioned my support for Salman Rushdie, forced into hiding as the result of the fatwa condemning his novel *The Satanic Verses*. I claimed that my experience, as a woman, of injustice and discrimination had made me able to connect to other writers' struggles against oppression. Sarah remembers that one journalist sourly commented afterwards that these radical sentiments did not stop me 'trousering' the cheque.

Indeed they did not. I had plans for that money. As the Library Scholar in the Department of Printed Books in the British Museum, I had dreamed of one day possessing my own house. Over the years this dream took firmer shape inside me, though I rarely mentioned it to anyone. I had always felt, without understanding why, that I was not allowed to want a home in the same way as other people did. Now I admitted to myself and friends I longed for a little French house. I wanted to acknowledge my French side, my identification with my French mother, my pleasure about being French and having had a French childhood as well as an English one. My mother and I had had, as I have described in previous chapters, a sometimes difficult and stormy relationship, full of pain, battling about our perceptions of each other and our versions of the past. Nonetheless, Mum had hung on in there, giving as good as she got, reading each novel as it was published and criticising it, beginning to talk to me in a way she hadn't felt able to do when I was young. The talks were often unsettling, disturbing, painful, but they drew us slowly closer.

Now, at last, those wounds of the past seemed to be healing. We reached an oasis. We felt able to express our love for each other. We forgave each other. A miracle in the desert: lightning struck the rock; it split, and sweetness and honey and milk poured forth. Now I could acknowledge how like Mum I was as well as how different. I could start to acknowledge my own strength, my own power. Part of that was harvested from feminism and the love of women friends, part from the fulfilment offered by writing and publishing novels and poetry, part from being happy with Jim (we'd got married in 1991). Mum now turned into my staunch defender. When a French relative bitterly criticised my little memoir 'Une Glossaire' (published in my short-story collection *During Mother's*

Absence) for mentioning family members by name, and threatened me with legal action for breach of privacy, Mum stuck up for me heroically, and finally brought about a reconciliation. I shall never forget that Mum saw me in trouble and defended me.

Marrying Jim at Finsbury Town Hall on Rosebery Avenue (then emerging under the elaborate glass porch on to the tree-shaded pavement with its backdrop of speeding red Routemasters) I chose to wear a 1940s black suit, a little black hat with an eye-skimming black veil, just as Mum had worn a black suit and veiled hat for her marriage to Dad during the war. This was a reparatory gesture and I think it pleased her. She helped me put up my hair for the occasion, twisting it into a French pleat, and helped me pin on my hat. Jim and I held a party afterwards at Yerbury Road. I lined the sides of the bare wooden stairs up to our flat with flower-heads and bay leaves, as I'd seen done in south-west France to mark the path from house to church. Linda, with welcoming generosity, opened up the downstairs and the garden to everyone, and set out the hand-carved wooden Noah's Ark the boys had played with as children.

The Yerbury Road house was our Ark: all of us in it together. Mum, family and friends brought food. Brigitte, my aunt and godmother, who came over specially from France (despite being ill with breast cancer) made dozens of tiny choux buns. James LeFanu's wife Juliet brought a black lacquer tray of canapés. Each guest brought a bottle of champagne, which we cooled in ice-filled dustbins. The artists stayed partying until three in the morning, when I shooed them out, and then Jim and I drove off to catch the ferry to France.

We journeyed to Italy and spent two weeks there pursuing paintings by Paolo della Francesca, cross-over images of Virgins and goddesses (*Our Lady of the Pomegranate* held the same fruit as Hera, Queen of Heaven), marble quarries used by Michelangelo, good food. In one mountain-top *albergo*, inland from Genoa, a three-storey stone house with a fine courtyard, a team of ladies, fired up by the novel concept of vegetarianism, wanting to please this handsome, sturdy, blue-eyed visitor who smiled at them so sweetly, eagerly turned out to provide Jim with delectable dishes at every meal: pastas and grilled vege-tables and soups. They were giving him their best gifts. Of course I feasted along with him but I think I wanted them to give me special gifts too. At any rate, I nicked, from our high bedroom, the relic perched next to the ashtray on the lofty overmantel: an envelope containing some dust of St Rita of Cascia, the patron saint of housewives. How apt that her relic was dust.

Connected to my passionate love for Jim, to the newfound clarity of knowing how much I loved Mum, came at last the dissolving of the Catholic-induced sexual guilt and sexual ter-rors of childhood and adolescence, which, I came to see, had shaped and afflicted my adult life even as they had also given me plenty to write about. Why bother writing about those Catholic conundra here? It could seem a merely personal matter, not to be mentioned in public. Worse: self-indulgent, narcissistic and trivial, as one journalist thought when she was interviewing me and asked about the impact of Catholicism on my life and I tried to explain to her. Get a life, the final para-graph of her article sneered. But Catholicism's effect on my being-in-the-world forms part of this story I am telling you here, and so I shall include it. I'm not the only woman dam-aged by Catholicism. My history is one tiny crumb among millions, but if I put it together with other people's histories then I can continue analysing how much over-rigid versions of religion can damage us, how dangerous fundamentalist religion can be, with its authoritarian emphasis on simple God-given truth, its denial of complex meanings expressed in art created by flawed human beings. That feels pertinent in these days of wars being excused as holy missions, as God's will for his people. Who is this God who wants to send all the young men to their deaths or to torture and imprisonment? Who shrugs at young women having their clitorises sawn off? At mass rapes? Catholicism radicalised me. All my novels demonstrate that.

So: Catholic guilt and terror. These had a lot to do with houses: houses of the past and houses of the future; and with houses' inhabitants.

It began with my father. Loving Jim, I began better to understand my love for Dad. In some ways they were similar: both working-class men who had had to strive for education. Dad, after being brutally sacked (at the age of fifty-five) by his firm for not having a degree, had pulled himself out of deep depression – he couldn't get another job – by starting to paint. He had no formal training and did not go to art classes; he just painted at home. Every time my sensible, ultra-realistic mother told him his paintings were not very good, I flinched and felt his pain. Dad also wrote a novel, which he wanted to get published. That was one thing I could do for him: get it read by an agent. I asked Caroline Dawnay (my agent at that time) to read it and she did. She sent him a kind and tactful letter of rejection. Mum was tough with Dad about his writing, too. I think my wish to give Jim all the support for his painting that I could expressed, on one level, a reparative wish towards Dad: if only I could have helped him become successful as an artist.

Jim and I remained committed to the family house in Yerbury Road, to our London life. At the same time, however, we began hunting for a French house to which we could retire periodically to paint and write. Thanks to the W.H. Smith Literary Award, we could now pursue our fantasy. First of all we wondered about buying the little 1920s redbrick cottage in Criquetot, in the Pays de Caux in Normandy, whither my French family had moved when the Second World War broke out and their house in the Le Havre docks was bombed. I had spent all my childhood summers in this house, and had continued visiting Brigitte there up to her death. But it would have cost too much (around £36,000, as I remember) and also the house, once on the very edge of the village, was now being swallowed up by new developments. I wanted to live deep in the countryside. We said no. Mum was sad. Her childhood home was sold to the son of her old friend Charles, the Mayor. So she retained a connection with the house, in that way, but would no longer be able to continue visiting it as of right.

The Criquetot house was most powerfully charged with memories. It vibrated with them. After Brigitte's funeral and burial, Jim and I spent a long weekend there, as a way of saying another farewell to the aunt/godmother I had so loved. We slept upstairs, in my parents' former bedroom. I couldn't face sleeping downstairs, in the room, formerly my grandparents', in which Brigitte had died and been laid out for three days. However beautiful the early autumn days were, filled with long walks down back lanes to the sea and along the beach, nonetheless, every night, when we returned to the house, as dusk came on, I became gripped by terror. Fingertips touched the back of my neck like cold cobwebs. Doors opened and slammed shut for no reason. At breakfast one morning the lid of the Marmite pot jumped up, flew sideways, landed on the cloth. At night in bed I shook with fear, as nameless horrors hovered just outside the door, skipped up and down the stairs. I couldn't speak of these fears: I felt afraid I'd gone crazy. Finally one night, before going to bed, I broke down in the sitting-room, clutched Jim, got him to pour me a gin and tonic, and began babbling. Jim listened. We talked for a long time.

Eventually, I worked out that the 'haunting' was probably a projection of old childhood fears and desires, re-evoked by all the emotion surrounding Brigitte's death, some of it unresolved, to do with earlier losses. Reading Ernest Jones's essay on ghouls and vampires a little later, I was comforted: he said the same thing. What came up for me, the ghoul that haunted me, I worked out, was the strong feelings I'd had in this house for my father. At puberty, aged ten, I was madly in love with him, flirted with him, competed with my mother for his attention. I didn't know this was normal, that little girls routinely fall in love with their dads. Catholicism taught that sex before marriage was wicked. Sexual feelings in a child of ten were therefore of course very wicked indeed, and sexual feelings for my own father were the wickedest of all. My father flirted back with me, and I think that both pleased and terrified me. I imagined I had seduced him and therefore fatally wounded my mother. I believed that what I most longed for had come to pass. This was a sin that definitely dared not speak its name.

I am sad, now, to think it took me so many years to understand that my love affair with my father took place metaphorically rather than actually; that it was a normal route into love and joy. I wasted so much time feeling guilty. On the other hand, I became able to see and accept, with deep pleasure, how much my father loved me once I had grown up and become myself.

Earlier, my father certainly was not able to help me. He didn't bother with us much when we were young and I wanted to matter to him. Sex was a way to do it. Perhaps I made up a story in which I was the centre of his attention. Perhaps, as I turned into an eager, adoring, flirtatious girl, my father was a bit too possessive, a bit too fond, a bit too responsive. He didn't know any better. He didn't know what a lively imagination I had, that I needed clearer boundaries. None of this could ever be mentioned or talked about with my parents, of course, not then and not now in the nineties. The guilt and fear had lodged deep inside me, unconsciously, unspoken, a sense of something badly wrong with me, a secret damage on the inside. Now I remembered how angrily I had reacted when my father gave me some sexy black underwear one Christmas. I was in love with Paula at the time, in a world far away from advertising clichés about provocative underwear. I had thought, then, that my anger sprang from my feminist views about not wanting to be objectified, but now I saw that my father's inappropriate gift had touched off a deep fear that he was claiming me as a sexual partner. Because I believed I was so wicked, I had felt exiled: the barbarian; the alien. I had not felt allowed to have a home of my own. Not just the neurotic compulsion to repeat a trauma, as the textbooks had it, but also an attempt to overcome it.

This father–daughter love with its ambivalent dream of incest was the stuff of Freud's case histories. Funny that I'd read them and not made any connection with my own life. Funny that Sandra-the-therapist had seemed (to me, anyway) completely unable to spot the problem and help me with it. Now that I was sexually happy I put it all together. No wonder my lesbian friends had seen me as just passing through; I saw now that lesbianism, for me, had been a good safe place in which to recover from fears around incest.

Doing up the house felt like wanting to make reparation towards the daughter I had been. Beginning a new life with Jim, having joyful sex with him, creating a house with him, told me I had forgiven myself, no longer felt wicked. The frightening secret damage inside me, a gnarled and twisted knot of badness and fear, dissolved, melted away. That Mother Superior in my head went into retirement.

I retain a rage against the Catholic Church to this day for the way that it twists children's minds, damages them. Celibate male priests, scared of their own feelings and desires, have created a theology that splits body from soul, despises the body, then denies and conceals the abuse of the body, the abuse of the soul. Male Catholic authorities, and the nuns they instruct in their anti-female, anti-body attitudes, really can fuck up their charges, as we know now from the revelations of sexual and physical abuse in orphanages and elsewhere, run so often by unwilling celibates.

My work attempts to heal that imposed and damaging body–soul split. I find the word soul no longer adequate, but nor is the word body without an understanding of the body's capacity to make meanings, to make art. To make soul. Anyway, the little French house, I discovered, would be the place in which that work would go on.

The search for a place in France took a couple of years. We ended up going south from Normandy into the Mayenne. We looked at many houses. None of them felt right. We went back to the *notaire* (the local lawyer who acted as estate agent). What other houses have you got for sale? He handed us another bunch of photocopied details. One description jumped out: a cheap house, small, two rooms plus kitchen. Sheds. Garden. It actually had an inside lavatory. Blimey. Next day we drove up a steeply curving lane. Both of us liked its twists and turns and looked eagerly to see what was round the corner. The little shoebox-shaped house at the top, I knew straight away, was the right one. Its view down over fields, hedgerows and mature trees was calmly beautiful. The big barn to one side would make a perfect studio for Jim. More prosaically, the house was not derelict, in need of major restoration, but had a sound roof and working plumbing and electricity, because it was currently inhabited.

We had just enough money, the W.H. Smith cheque for £10,000 plus my savings, to afford the house: £15,000 in total. We could move in straight away and the repairs, the painting and decorating, could happen around us. The mending went on inside me too. I dreamed my way through webs of images and re-wove them into story-nets. One concerned snakes. My neighbour, Mme Drouard, visiting, pointed out the snarl of grass-snakes in the disused bread-oven at the back of the kitchen fireplace, told me tales of how the snakes wriggled in through holes in the ceiling, how a huge grass-snake had once surprised the previous owner on the bidet and sent her scream-ing out into the garden with her knickers down. Snakes in the wrong place were scary. I dreamed of them, in great alarm. Dreams of a father's penis in the wrong place were scary too. Eventually, I put the whole story of my past together, knotted it firmly, held it in my hands, then put it away. My love for my father shone clear. We got workmen in to mend the holes in the bedroom ceiling. We banished the snakes back to their proper place, in the garden.

I got the studio fixed up for Jim as a priority: a concrete floor put down, a pair of glass doors and a window to fill in the open front. I didn't mind that I hadn't yet got a studio of my own: I had a whole house. In the first two winters I worked on my new novel, *Flesh and Blood*, in a curtained-off section of our bedroom, liking my soft, collapsible wall. Then Jim converted the little pigsty in the wild depths of the garden for me, as a summer studio. He made me a window and put on a roof. I hung a lace curtain across the doorway and nailed up a silver ex-voto of a heart. Inside this little shelter in the scorching heat, running with sweat, I wrote my next novel *Impossible Saints*. Finally we converted the ruined *grenier* (grain-store) upstairs in the house, putting in a floor, a staircase, and a new ceiling, and at last I had a studio of my own in which to write.

That's where I have been sitting to write this book. My room is big, walled with packed bookshelves, and crossed at shoulder-height by the great roof-beams that hold the house together and up. The pointed ceiling gives the room a chapel effect. A small square window, high up, lets in a square of gold dawn light which patches itself on to the opposite wall. My collection of statues of the Virgin (my extra virgins) strides along the massive beams. I've nailed up my collection of silver ex-votos of hearts and legs and ears and stomachs and backs. Jim painted the hardboard floor for me: grey. Along the central beam, painted in invisible gold lettering, runs the legend 'For love is as strong as death'. Do I believe that? Sometimes. I suppose that's why it's written on the beam in invisible letters.

The first book I wrote in the house, *Flesh and Blood*, partly began as an experiment in collage, in samplers. I was asking myself, how should I write and how should I live? I had a freedom (thanks to Lennie's generous advance prompted by the Booker shortlisting) I had never known before. I needed to imagine possible lives and writings, to try them out by inventing them. My mind criss-crossed the Channel, zigzagged between men and women, the present and the past.

One piece of inspiration came from a troubled young woman, very afraid and speechless, whom I had met years before by chance at a reading given by Sara Maitland, whose protégée she was. Her body language in the street made her a convincingly slouching boy, and inside, safe in a bar, a sullen girl. She metamorphosed seamlessly from one to the other then back again. I thought I had met two different people, not one. Meeting the 'girl' by the ticket desk, I looked around, puzzled, and said to Sara: where's that boy who was outside with you just now?

So what was the difference between men and women? Once again I wanted to explore it. Once again, even though Jim shouted Please Mimi No More Nuns, I wanted to put in a convent (an erotic one this time), and I wanted to put in a fairy story about a girl's fear of incestuous love. Gradually, I realised that the book would re-dramatise then mend a split relationship between a mother and her daughter. Their love was broken in two and so the book had to be too. Accordingly, the narrative keeps breaking off, breaking down, and changing, metamorphosing. The novel begins in the present and works back into history, then into the time before history. It is composed of a series of stories. You get half of each one, as the narratives are compelled to jump backwards and begin again, just as, when you're wounded in a relationship, you jump backwards. At the centre of the book, in an imaginary space outside time, a beginning time, only expressible in a sort of poetry, a turnaround happens. The reader can now start to move forwards, reading back towards the present, reading the other half of each story. So reading the novel joins up the stories; like doing up a zip. The story broken in two gets mended. At the end of the novel, its beginning is explained, and a possible future suggested.

I still love *Flesh and Blood* because I invented that particular experimental shape. Other, younger writers, have since reused its form and not given me credit for it. That makes me angry. I think you should acknowledge your sources. I also think: well, at least that new form has passed into the culture.

The novel was a gift to my mother, an offering, as all my

novels are, even if they are also inspired by particular muses. She and I tried to mend our broken house and also went on fighting from time to time. I go on building paper houses. Scrunching them up then putting them into my pocket. I go on walking the London streets, feeling them flow through and around me like streams of words. I can't do without the city. I repeat the pattern of my childhood, zigzagging between England and France, between town and country. I open the front door of my little French house and sit down on the threshold, my back to the door-frame, my feet on the step, and enjoy feeling half inside and half outside. When I write, the outside comes inside, and then the inside goes back outside again, as new forms of language now existing materially in the world (Marion Milner has written about this).

I loll and daydream as I look out from my house towards the horizon, the next bit of writing.

My house, when I bought it, represented to me the maternal body; a myth of a daughter and mother reunited. Paradise lost but then regained. Then lost again. Now I know I've got to be born from it. I've got to leave it. I don't know what will happen next. I go away from it and come back; go away and come back. Writers are part-time hermits. We need lots of time alone and then we need to get out and party. So we have to invent the lives that suit us. Not easy. I love living alone in France, know-ing that the house is mine and that I can arrange and decorate it as I choose, move the furniture and pictures around at whim without having to consult anyone else. I love being able to structure my own time, work at my own rhythm. I love friends coming for weekends. I love it when they depart and leave me alone again. Too much aloneness for too long does feel tricky. Sometimes in France I do get lonely. That's part of the set-up and has to be accepted and lived through.

Conventional marriage, like conventional family life, did not suit me. I didn't manage to invent an unconventional marriage that would last for ever, either. Jim and I didn't have a conventional happy ending. We separated after seventeen years together and got divorced. After a period of indescribable pain and sorrow we have re-created a good loving friendship. We care about and try to help each other. The marriage, ending, metamorphosed into something else; a different kind of love. Move on! the self-help gurus tell us. But I take my past with me. History matters. The continuity remains: the relationship continues to evolve and change, while our artists' bond stays as strong as ever. I still love and see Jim's boys, and Linda too. I have become a grandmother. Too much of a mouthful to say ex-stepmother-cum-grandmother. Leo's son calls me Mimi. There are other very important children in my life. They know I love them, but they are not the subject of this book.

Love goes on. The love of friends. Friendship my oxygen. I've said that often and it's true. Writing goes on too: I keep on building my paper house; my chrysalis.

Also by Michèle Roberts

DAUGHTERS OF THE HOUSE

Winner of the WHSmith Award
Shortlisted for the Man Booker Prize

Secrets and lies linger in the very walls of the solid old Normandy
house where Thérèse and Léonie, French and English cousins,
grow up after the war. Intrigued by the guilty silences of the adults
and the broken shrine they find in the woods, the girls weave their
own fantasies, unwittingly revealing the village's buried shame, a
shame that will haunt them both for the rest of their lives.

'Remarkable and beautifully written'
Independent on Sunday

'A brave and richly imagined novel,
full of thrilling set pieces'
Guardian

'Subtle and persuasive'
Cosmopolitan

THE MISTRESSCLASS

Above the bed in Adam and Catherine's bedroom is a painting of a female nude; 'her face was deliberately blurred, screwed-up in ecstasy. Her intensity leapt out at you like a shout or a punch.' What would it be like to sleep under such a picture? Especially when it was painted by your father – your recently dead father. That's what Catherine's sister Vinny wonders. She doesn't wonder who the woman is though.

Set in contemporary London and provincial France, *The Mistressclass* is a wonderful novel about the repercussions of past impulses; Adam's dead father haunts his son; Vinny haunts her sister; and haunting the whole novel is Charlotte Brontë and her passionate search for creative fulfilment.

'Michèle Roberts is one of those writers descended perhaps as much from Monet and Debussy as Virginia Woolf or Keats . . . To read a book by her is to savour colour, sound, taste, texture and touch as never before'
The Times

THE LOOKING GLASS

Geneviève is a teller and a collector of stories. In the orphanage, she whispers her tales at night. In her place as maid to Madame Patin in the café next to the sea, she becomes the breathless audience for her mistress's alarming folk stories, beginning with the one about the mermaid – the beauty who is also a monster – who must be killed.

Geneviève happily falls into the ways of Madame Patin until her own comeliness and cunning ripen to siren beauty. To avoid the mermaid's fate she must take flight.

She goes to another word-spinner – a poet who holds close the hearts of all his women. Kind the poet may be, but he too is a collector of stories, and when you speak your story, 'when you smooth and flatten and straighten the story out, make it exist word by word in speech, you lose that heavenly possession'. You give away more than words.

You can order other Virago titles through our website:
www.virago.co.uk or by using the order form below

☐	Daughters of the House	Michèle Roberts	£6.99
☐	The Mistressclass	Michèle Roberts	£7.99
☐	The Looking Glass	Michèle Roberts	£6.99
☐	Reader, I married him	Michèle Roberts	£6.99
☐	Playing Sardines	Michèle Roberts	£6.99

The prices shown above are correct at time of going to press. However, the publishers reserve the right to increase prices on covers from those previously advertised, without further notice.

——————————— 🍎 ———————————

Please allow for postage and packing: Free UK delivery.
Europe: add 25% of retail price; Rest of World: 45% of retail price.

To order any of the above or any other Abacus titles, please call our credit card orderline or fill in this coupon and send/fax it to:

Virago, PO Box 121, Kettering, Northants NN14 4ZQ
Fax: 01832 733076   Tel: 01832 737526
Email: aspenhouse@FSBDial.co.uk

☐ I enclose a UK bank cheque made payable to Abacus for £ . . . .
☐ Please charge £ . . . . . . to my Visa/Delta/Maestro

Expiry Date [| | |]   Maestro Issue No. [|]

NAME (BLOCK LETTERS please) . . . .

ADDRESS . . . .

. . . .

. . . .

Postcode . . . . Telephone . . . .

Signature . . . .

Please allow 28 days for delivery within the UK. Offer subject to price and availability.